Great Stage of Fools

Great Stage of Fools

A Guide to Six Shakespeare Plays

∼

Peter J. Leithart

CASCADE Books • Eugene, Oregon

GREAT STAGE OF FOOLS
A Guide to Six Shakespeare Plays

Copyright © 2021 Peter J. Leithart. All rights reserved. Except for brief quotations in critical publications or reviews, no part of this book may be reproduced in any manner without prior written permission from the publisher. Write: Permissions, Wipf and Stock Publishers, 199 W. 8th Ave., Suite 3, Eugene, OR 97401.

Cascade Books
An Imprint of Wipf and Stock Publishers
199 W. 8th Ave., Suite 3
Eugene, OR 97401

www.wipfandstock.com

PAPERBACK ISBN: 978-1-5326-3852-7
HARDCOVER ISBN: 978-1-5326-3853-4
EBOOK ISBN: 978-1-5326-3854-1

Cataloguing-in-Publication data:

Names: Leithart, Peter J., author.

Title: Great stage of fools : a guide to six Shakespeare plays / Peter J. Leithart.

Description: Eugene, OR: Cascade Books, 2021 | Includes bibliographical references.

Identifiers: ISBN 978-1-5326-3852-7 (paperback) | ISBN 978-1-5326-3853-4 (hardcover) | ISBN 978-1-5326-3854-1 (ebook)

Subjects: LCSH: Shakespeare, William, 1564-1616—Criticism and interpretation. | Shakespeare, William, 1564-1616—Political and social views.

Classification: PR2976 .L40 2021 (print) | PR2976 (ebook)

Unless otherwise noted, Scripture quotations are taken from the
New American Standard Bible® (NASB),

Copyright © 1960, 1962, 1963, 1968, 1971, 1972, 1973, 1975, 1977, 1995 by
The Lockman Foundation

Used by permission. www.Lockman.org

To my next grandchild,
who has not yet smelled the air
in this great stage of fools.

Table of Contents

Acknowledgments ix

Shakespeare the Christian? xi

1. Cannibal Mother: *Coriolanus* 1

2. Smiling Villain: *Richard III* 28

3. Crawling Toward the Grave: *King Lear* 63

4. The Course of True Love: *A Midsummer Night's Dream* 94

5. Tempests Are Kind: *Twelfth Night* 129

6. Mercy Seasons Justice: *The Merchant of Venice* 160

Bibliography 197

Acknowledgments

NEARLY A QUARTER CENTURY has passed since I published my first book on Shakespeare, *Brightest Heaven of Invention* (Canon Press, 1996). During the intervening years, during which the study guides collected here took form, I have lectured and written on Shakespeare in more venues than I can remember. I've taught electives at New Saint Andrews College, written chapters or sections of chapters of books and essays online and in print, delivered a paper at the American Political Science Association, lectured in Ukraine and probably in St. Petersburg and London. I am poor in gratitude because I am poor in memory. Poor as it is, my gratitude is genuine. Few things delight me more than writing and talking about Shakespeare, and I am always thankful for the opportunity.

My gratitude does have one very direct object: Rev. John Barach, who carefully read through the manuscript, saved me from a lot of sloppiness, prepared the manuscript for typesetting, and raised many intriguing questions that I have no time to address. This is a far, far better book as a result of John's work.

This book is dedicated to my forthcoming grandchild, my thirteenth, who will be the fourth child of my son Sheffield and his wife Laura and who will join a merry band—Ellie, Col, and Warren. Merry band notwithstanding, I expect he or she will do what Lear says all babies do: "When we are born, we cry that we are come / To this great stage of fools." I trust that the next Leithart will find much joy in the midst of tears, and will know Wisdom in this world of folly, a Wisdom that like Lear's, like Saint Paul's, bears a strong resemblance to folly.

Shakespeare the Christian?

THIS STUDY GUIDE TO six Shakespeare plays is openly, unapologetically theological. I highlight biblical imagery and Christian themes in each of the plays.

Of course I would. I'm a theologian, trained to find theology under every rock and behind every bush. But is there any reason to think *Shakespeare* knew any theology or intended his plays to be understood from a religious angle? In short, was Shakespeare a Christian?

We don't know exactly when Shakespeare was born, but we do know he was baptized on April 26, 1564. *Baptized*, but was he a *Christian*?

The answer partly depends on what we think happens when someone is baptized. Many Christians believe that baptism marks the beginning of life as a Christian. I am one of those Christians. My short answer is, Will Shakespeare was a Christian because he was christened.

Some will think that an evasion. When people ask "Was Shakespeare a Christian?" they usually have something more specific in mind. Was he a *true* disciple? Did he actually believe? Did his faith, whatever it was, come out in his poetry? In the anachronistic jargon of modern evangelicalism, they want to know if he had a personal relationship with Jesus.

To that question, we have no certain answer. Shakespeare left no personal papers, no spiritual diary, no *Confessions*, no *Journal*. Many in his time *did* write spiritual journals. As far as we know, Shakespeare did not. Without such records, we have no window into his soul or his head.

What we have are plays and poems, but there Shakespeare is typically a ventriloquist, speaking different voices. We can't conclude that Shakespeare was a nihilist who believed that life "is a tale / Told by an idiot, full of sound and fury, / Signifying nothing" just because Macbeth says it (*Macbeth* 5.5.26–28). It's *Gloucester's* opinion that "As flies to wanton boys, are we to th' gods; / They kill us for their sport" (*King Lear* 4.1.37–38). We have to do a good bit of sifting before we conclude that

Shakespeare agreed. We have better reason to think he believed "all the world's a stage," but before we draw too hasty a conclusion we should remember those words come from Jaques in *As You Like It* (2.7.138). When we hear John of Gaunt wax nationalistic about "This blessed plot, this earth, this realm, this England, / This nurse, this teeming womb of royal kings" (*Richard II* 2.1.50–51), we should be alert, because the play's action is likely to ironize such enthusiasms.

We're not *completely* at a loss. We know, for instance, quite a lot about the aims and intentions of Elizabethan and Jacobean playwrights. Recent Shakespeare scholars have recognized that the theater, like everything else in early modern England, was infused with religion. Debora Shuger writes, "If it is not plausible to read Shakespeare's plays as Christian allegories, neither is it likely that the popular drama of a religiously saturated culture could, by a secular miracle, have extricated itself from the theocentric orientation informing the discourses of politics, gender, social order and history."[1]

In his 2002 *Shakespeare's Tribe*, Jeffrey Knapp argues that scholars like Shuger don't go far enough. While they stress "the centrality of religion to the study of Renaissance drama," they still assume that "Renaissance playwrights [are] 'Christian' only cognitively or subliminally, rather than purposively and devotionally." Even recent revisionist scholars don't reckon with "the possibility that Renaissance plays may have been intended and received as contributions to the cause of true religion," nor have they considered the possibility that "Shakespeare and his contemporaries were capable of envisaging their profession itself—their acting and playwriting—as a kind of ministry."[2]

Knapp claims that "English theology and ecclesiology shaped the drama at a fundamental level." Theology was one of the factors determining the "conceptualization of the player and the playwright as professions, and of the theater as an institution." Those theologically informed concepts "disposed theater people toward the enacting of certain confirmatory plots, themes, and characters on stage; and thus religion had a crucial say in the creation of plays, in their content, and, by extension, in their presumed social effects." In short, "religion had a more direct role in the production of plays than as the deep structure of dramatized ideology; it provided the rationale and even motives for acting and

---

1. Shuger, "Subversive Fathers," 46.
2. Knapp, *Shakespeare's Tribe*, 9.

playwrighting."³ Not accidentally and unwittingly, but deliberately and carefully, playwrights and stage managers made the stage an alternative pulpit.

We don't need to speak in generalities, because Shakespeare's plays *do* reveal some things about their author, and from the plays we can infer conclusions about Shakespeare's knowledge of Christian faith and, with great caution, his commitment to those beliefs. They may be opaque, but we can see through them, as through a glass darkly. When I look at the plays, what I think I see is a playwright with a poetic imagination molded by the Christian Bible and Prayer Book liturgy.

Shakespeare's work is a prime exhibit of what E. M. W. Tillyard called, controversially, the "Elizabethan World Picture."⁴ Tillyard pointed out that educated Elizabethans pictured reality as a hierarchical "chain of being" made up of many analogous chains. There is a hierarchy in the heavens among the planets and stars, one in the animal kingdom, in marriage, in political society. Each region of creation has its own structure, but the structures resemble one another. The lion is the king of the beasts, the king the lion among men, Jupiter king among the planets.

Whatever the merits of Tillyard's thesis in detail, his work illuminates Elizabethan poetry. When Shakespeare compares rulers to suns or mighty beasts, it's not a random metaphor or a reflection of the individual talent of the poet. His imagery is part of a system, a "sacramental" vision, that encompasses all reality.

Living in a dangerous world, Elizabethans placed high value on maintaining order. "Take away ordre," wrote Thomas Elyot in *The Boke named The Governour*, and the only thing that remains is "chaos," a "confused mixture" where everything is in "perpetuall conflicte."⁵ When one hierarchy is overturned—when mice-men topple the lion-king—society and the natural world are both thrown into chaos. Everything has a "degree," as Ulysses puts it in a famous speech in *Troilus and Cressida* (1.3), and the world remains harmonious only so long as everything stays in its assigned place. When degree is "shaked" or taken away, when the string of hierarchy is "untuned," then "discord follows." When Macbeth kills King Duncan and steals his throne, nature rebels. One character sees "A falcon, tow'ring in her pride of place, / . . . by a mousing owl hawked at

---

3. Knapp, *Shakespeare's Tribe*, 9–10.
4. Tillyard, *Elizabethan World Picture*.
5. Elyot, *Boke Named the Governour*, I.1.

and killed" (*Macbeth* 2.4.12–13). Nature is turned upside down at Julius Caesar's assassination. Disorder in the human realm is replicated in the natural realm.

The Elizabethan World Picture has roots in ancient philosophy, but it draws heavily from the Bible. It's a theocentric vision of reality. God is at the peak of the great pyramid of being, and the highest beings in each of the chains—king, sun, lion—are the highest beings because they most resemble the King of all, the Lion of Judah who shines brighter than the sun.

It would be possible to pile up dozens of examples of Shakespeare's use of this classical-biblical world picture, but I will limit myself to one, the garden scene from *Richard II*. The play dramatizes Henry Bollingbroke's overthrow of King Richard II. In Act 3, Richard is under threat but still on the throne. As scene 4 opens, the Queen is walking with two of her attendants in the Duke of York's garden, and they step into the shadows of the trees when they see gardeners coming. The Queen expects them to "talk of state," since that's what's on everyone's mind. The conversation she overhears seems to be an interlude:

> GARDENER
> Go bind thou up young dangling apricots,
> Which, like unruly children, make their sire
> Stoop with oppression of their prodigal weight.
> Give some supportance to the bending twigs.
> Go thou and, like an executioner,
> Cut off the heads of too-fast-growing sprays
> That look too lofty in our commonwealth.
> All must be even in our government.
> You thus employed, I will go root away
> The noisome weeds which without profit suck
> The soil's fertility from wholesome flowers. (3.4.29–39)

The servant quickly turns the conversation to politics: Why should the gardeners "keep law and form and due proportion" when the "sea-walled garden" that is England "is full of weeds, her fairest flowers choked up, / Her fruit trees all unpruned, her hedges ruined"? Why worry about gardening when the whole land is "swarming with caterpillars" (3.4.40–47)?

Of course, the Gardener was *already* talking about politics. Like a good Elizabethan, he thinks that care of the natural world resembles a king's rule in the garden political. Pruning is like removing the heads of "sprays" who grow too lofty. Weeding is like clearing out profitless freeloaders from the land, who suck up the land's fertility but produce no fruit. A garden is a kind of commonwealth, a gardener a kind of king. And vice versa: A wise king cares for his realm like a gardener for his garden, cutting the ambitious down to size, rooting out parasites, supporting the stooping branches that bear the land's fruits.

In response to the Servant, the Gardener makes his political assessment explicit:

> O, what pity is it
> That he [Richard] had not so trimmed and dressed his land
> As we this garden! We at time of year
> Do wound the bark, the skin of our fruit trees,
> Lest, being overproud in sap and blood,
> With too much riches it confound itself.
> Had he done so to great and growing men,
> They might have lived to bear, and he to taste
> Their fruits of duty. Superfluous branches
> We lop away, that bearing boughs may live.
> Had he done so, himself had borne the crown,
> Which waste of idle hours hath quite thrown down. (3.4.56–67)

Richard has been an inattentive gardener, and both he and England are about to be overrun with weeds and wild beasts. The Gardener tells the servant that the king is about to be "deposed" (3.4.68).

The Queen can't bear any more, "pressed to death" by what she hears and by her silence (3.4.72). She springs out and rebukes the Gardener, and her speech raises the discussion of political horticulture into a theological register:

> Thou old Adam's likeness, set to dress this garden,
> How dares thy harsh rude tongue sound this unpleasing news?
> What Eve, what serpent, hath suggested thee
> To make a second fall of cursed man?
> Why dost thou say King Richard is deposed? (3.4.73–77)

At the risk of spoiling the music of the poetry, we can extract the imaginative logic underlying the scene: The king is a gardener, and Adam was the first gardener; England is an Edenic garden, with Richard the Adam appointed to tend it; but Richard has failed to protect his garden from a serpentine usurper. He is a fallen Adam, and his failure to maintain degree and social harmony plunges England into a cursed political chaos that, in Shakespeare's telling, stretches intermittently from Richard's fall to Henry Tudor's defeat of Richard III at Bosworth Field nearly a century later. Only then does England once again become what John of Gaunt says it is, "this other Eden, demi-paradise" (2.1.42).

This is a poetic politics and a political poetics deeply rooted in Scripture. It is, I think, written by an informed Christian poet. In the end, though, the question I started with is a distraction. We don't need to know what Shakespeare really thought in his heart of hearts to determine that the *plays* assume and present a Christian vision of reality. We don't need to know if we'll meet Will in the new creation to discover that the plays are infused with Scripture. The plays and poems stand on their own, among the great edifices of Christian artistry, whatever Shakespeare's personal beliefs might have been. And for that reason, we should read and watch not merely for entertainment but for edification.

How To Use This Book

This book isn't an academic contribution to Shakespeare studies, but a study guide for general readers. When I started, I intended to write for high school students. I'm not sure I was able to realize my intentions. I may have overshot the target. Time, and readers, will tell.

Each chapter examines a different play. I have included three tragedies, *Coriolanus*, *Richard III*, and *King Lear*. If you like to tally up subgenres, I've covered a Roman and an English history play, as well as a "straight" tragedy. The volume also includes three comedies, *A Midsummer Night's Dream*, *Twelfth Night*, and *The Merchant of Venice*.

The arrangement is neither chronological nor thematic, but it makes intuitive sense to me. It would be best to follow the order of the chapters, since I introduce concepts along the way that I reuse in later chapters. But it's not strictly necessary. At one crucial point, the arrangement of the book has a polemical intent. Many works on or collections of Shakespeare place the tragedies last, on the implicit assumption that tragedy is a "higher" form of drama than comedy. For reasons I explain in chapter 4, I disagree, and so my book starts with tragedy and ends with comedy.

The study guide in each chapter assumes at least a general familiarity with the play. I suggest that students watch a film or stage version of a play before diving in to detailed study. You need to know the characters and story so you can make your way through the intricacies of plot and poetry. There are fairly recent, fairly good, fairly accessible productions of each of the six plays. Each chapter is divided into four or five sections. Each section ends with "Review Questions" that are answered in the text and a handful of "Thought Questions" that require students to study sections of the play I haven't discussed or to embark on some small research projects.

For the most part, I say very little about textual history, sources, or performance history. Students should consult a standard edition of Shakespeare's works for such background information. Some years ago, I picked up *The Complete Pelican Shakespeare*, edited by Stephen Orgel and A. R. Braunmuller, and I've been using it ever since. Quoted texts, as well as line numbers, are taken from that edition.

1

Cannibal Mother
Coriolanus[1]

WHAT IS TRAGEDY? You might think it's an easy question to answer. Crack open the nearest copy of Aristotle's *Poetics*, and there you have it.

It's *not* so easy. *Whom* are you asking? What Chaucer meant by tragedy is not what Aristotle meant, and in the modern age Hegel and Nietzsche proposed entirely different theories of tragedy. To make things complicated, in his classic study of Shakespearean tragedy, A. C. Bradley reads Shakespeare through the lenses of Hegel, who lived centuries after Shakespeare.[2]

Let's refine the question: What is *Shakespearean* tragedy? To get a clear angle, it's helpful to review Aristotle's theory, and to do that we have to reach back to Plato. Plato famously argues in the *Republic* (Book 10) that poetry, which includes drama as well as lyric and epic, "has a terrifying capacity for deforming even good people. Only a very few escape." Apart from "hymns to the gods and eulogies of virtuous men," he "flatly refused to admit any representational poetry" into his ideal city.

Plato has both metaphysical and moral objections to poetry. On the metaphysical side, Plato believes only the forms are fully real; sensible things—things you see, touch, hear, taste, and touch—are mere images of intelligible reality. Poets who write about this world create representations

---

1. This chapter draws on two of my earlier discussions on Coriolanus: Leithart, "City of In-Gratia" and Leithart, *Gratitude*, 115–20.
2. Bradley, *Shakespearean Tragedy*.

of things that aren't really real to begin with. Because they're two removes from Truth, artists can't help but lie. On the ethical side, Plato says poets represent forms of behavior that ought not to be encouraged in a virtuous city and arouse passions of lust and anger that "should be left to wither" (*Republic*, Book X).[3]

Plato may have been one of the targets of Aristotle's *Poetics*. We don't know for sure. Whether he does it intentionally or not, Aristotle's theory answers both sides of the Platonic suspicion of poetry. In contrast to Plato, Aristotle argues that all art is "mimetic," an attempt to imitate something in the world. Plato believes the same, but the two philosophers mean something quite different by "imitation." Plato thinks of artistic imitation as a mirror held up to reality that should directly reflect what is real. Since it cannot mirror reality, it lies. Aristotle knows artists can't fully copy reality but insists that even a partial image can reveal something true.

Aristotle's response to the ethical objection is evident in his definition of tragedy as "an action that is serious, complete, and of a certain magnitude; in language embellished with each kind of artistic ornament . . . in the form of action, not of narrative; through pity and fear effecting the proper purgation of these emotions." The last clause highlights the moral effect of drama and provides Aristotle's answer to Plato's ethical objection (*Poetics*, 1.6).[4]

Aristotle's theory has sometimes been interpreted as moralistic. Tragedy, it is said, tells of a generally decent fellow in a high position who falls because of some "tragic flaw" (*hamartia*). Usually, the tragic flaw is "hubris" or pride. Guilty of pride, the hero receives his just deserts in the end. The bloody finale brings "poetic justice" down on the head of the fallen hero. Watching this spectacle, the passions of the audience are "purged" (*katharsis*), uplifted and purified. Members of the audience go home better people for having watched the morality tale.

This interpretation of Aristotle is largely a product of French and English commentators from the early modern period. They misunderstand Aristotle very badly. It's true that Aristotle believes the best tragic hero is a man in a high position, but he does *not* say that the hero falls because of an immoral act. In fact, he explicitly denies it: Anyone who acts immorally *should* suffer for it. There's nothing tragic about justice.

3. This translation is found in Badiou, *Plato's* Republic.

4. Translation by S. H. Butcher, available at http://classics.mit.edu/Aristotle/poetics.1.1.html.

The main aim of tragedy is to have a cathartic effect on the audience, and poetic justice doesn't produce any catharsis. The fall of a wicked man "would, doubtless, satisfy the moral sense, but it would inspire neither pity nor fear," since "pity is aroused by unmerited misfortune, fear by the misfortune of a man like ourselves" (*Poetics*, 2.13).

The moral interpretation of Aristotle depends on a Christian understanding of *hamartia*, the word used by New Testament writers for "sin." In Aristotle, the word doesn't mean "sin." It refers instead to errors of judgment or mistakes that lead to catastrophe. Even when he uses the word in an ethical context, Aristotle intends something close to the original meaning: The "mean" of virtue is a target between two extremes, and the unvirtuous man fails because he "misses the mark" (*hamartano*).

When applying Aristotle's theory, it's vain to search for a moral flaw in Oedipus. Oedipus makes a series of (mostly innocent) blunders that lead to his downfall. These blunders are his *hamartiai*. For Aristotle, tragedy *doesn't* illustrate the Pauline claim that "the wages of *hamartia* is death." Oedipus is led to tragedy because he cares enough for the people of Thebes to search out the cause of the plague and to search it out relentlessly, even as it becomes clearer and clearer that *he* is the virus who must be expelled. His end is tragic because he exercises characteristic strengths, *not* because he deserves to end badly. The case is even clearer with Euripides, whom Aristotle believes is the most tragic of poets. Medea slaughters her own sons and gruesomely poisons her rival and her rival's father. In the end, she escapes to Athens, where she has already made sure she will receive a welcome. She doesn't get her just deserts *at all*.

We don't know whether or not Shakespeare was familiar with the *Poetics*. But his tragedies work on very different principles from Aristotle's. Shakespeare's protagonists have the same social and political stature that Aristotle's theory requires. They're men in high position—princes, kings, generals. They have to be high so they can make a big crash when they fall. But in Shakespeare the cause of tragedy isn't a blunder but an immoral act, often a deliberate one. Shakespeare never uses *hamartia*, but if he did, his use would be closer to the apostle Paul than to Aristotle.

Macbeth begins his spiral to insanity when he listens to the infernal prophecy of the weird sisters, dreams of wearing the crown of Scotland, and kills King Duncan in cold blood. He wades so far into a river of blood that he can't turn back, and finally he drowns. Othello is as much sinned against as sinning. His self-defensive closing speech is not altogether false:

"one that loved not wisely, but too well" (5.2.344). Yet he drinks deeply and almost delightedly of the poison the tempter Iago pours into his ear. Othello opens himself to Iago's devilry, and it *is* devilry. One scholar found over sixty references to the devil or hell in the play.[5] Othello's mind is so mastered by Iago he finally regards the once-angelic Desdemona as a devil: To him, she is not fair but "black," a demonic whore (3.3.387). Desdemona's servant, Emelia, gets it right, when she rages at Othello: "Thou dost belie her, and *thou* art a devil" (5.2.134). Satanic Iago has made Othello over into his image, filling his victim with murderous jealousy. And that jealousy drives Othello to kill and then take his own life.

It would be perverse to suggest that Shakespeare's tragedies are simplistic depictions of "poetic justice." One of the greatest of Shakespeare critics, Samuel Johnson, said his greatest flaw was the opposite: Shakespeare "makes no just distribution of good or evil."[6] Johnson is right about the fact, and ticking off the names of the (semi) innocents slaughtered in *Hamlet* alone is enough to prove it: Ophelia, Polonius, Rosencrantz, and Guildenstern. Desdemona and Cordelia are *completely* innocent but no less dead for that.

Whether or not this is a defect is another question. Shakespeare isn't interested in presenting a world where all threads are neatly tied off. He's more interested in depicting the real world of human experience, a world where actions have unintended consequences and where passionate strife engulfs innocent bystanders. Still, his tragedies show a kind of justice at work. It doesn't work with mathematical precision, but the plots of villains fall on their own heads. Claudius is killed by the rapier he poisoned. Macbeth is overcome by Macduff. Iago is exposed and sent to the torturers. Edmund, Oswalt, and the two wicked sisters are dead at the end of *King Lear*. Shakespeare's dramas are dramas of sin, and for that reason they're also dramas of judgment.

These Christian principles of Shakespearean tragedy hold, even when Shakespeare sets his plays in the world of ancient Rome.

Rome in the Elizabethan Mind

Rome loomed much larger for Elizabethans than it does for us. It loomed much larger than Greece. We tend to look back to Greece as the primary

---

5. Bethell, "Shakespeare's Imagery," 35.
6. Johnson, "Preface to Shakespeare," 1.

pagan source for Western civilization, but that perspective took hold in the nineteenth century when Greek studies were revived by German thinkers as an alternative to Christianity.[7] Elizabethans, by contrast, viewed Rome as the great pagan alternative to Christendom, evidenced by the large number of Roman plays produced in the England of the late sixteenth and early seventeenth centuries.

Early modern Europeans studied Roman history and literature as a source for reflection and argument, for moral and political wisdom, but there was no single perspective. Debates concerning contemporary political and moral issues often appealed to Roman history. University students sometimes used an incident of Roman history as the focal point of a *disputatio*. Luther's associate Melanchthon, for instance, suggested that students debate the justice of tyrannicide by debating the ins and outs of the assassination of Julius Caesar.

Shakespeare wrote a number of works set in ancient Greece (*Troilus and Cressida*; *Timon of Athens*; *A Midsummer Night's Dream*; *Venus and Adonis*), but for the most part these are set in a mythological Greece, not a historical Greece, about which Shakespeare probably knew very little. (According to Ben Jonson, Shakespeare had "small Latin and less Greek.") Shakespeare's Roman plays, however, are historically rooted, and Romanness, with its associated politics, values, and character, plays an important role in these plays.

For Elizabethans, Rome was not merely a power of the distant past. The Eastern "Roman" empire fell in 1453, a little more than a century before Shakespeare's birth, and Papal Rome's dominance of English Christianity ended only with the reign of Henry VIII. The defeat of the Spanish Armada in 1588 was seen as a victory over *Rome*, as was the foiling of Guy Fawkes's plot to blow up Parliament in 1605. Shakespeare was aware of the debates between Catholic and Protestant, and often combined ancient and contemporary history in his plays about Rome. In *Julius Caesar*, for instance, Decius says Romans will dip cloths in Caesar's blood for "relics," and *Titus Andronicus* includes anachronistic references to monasteries, "popish tricks," and martyrdom.

Shakespeare has another contemporary setting in mind in his Roman plays: the court of King James I. James styled himself a "new Augustus" and said he united and pacified Britain, as Augustus had done in ancient Rome. James's court was notoriously dissolute, with excessive

---

7. See Gress, *From Plato to NATO*.

banquets and sex scandals, reminiscent of the Rome of *Antony and Cleopatra*.

Shakespeare's four Roman plays have a number of features in common. All are set in ancient Rome, and all were staged in Roman costume with Roman sets. Blood, mutilation, violence, and mayhem are important features of these plays. *Titus Andronicus* is far and away the most gruesome. There is a dismemberment and sacrifice; Aaron kills his baby's nurse; Lavinia's tongue is cut out and her arms cut off after she's raped; Titus cuts off his own arm; he slits the throats of Tamora's sons, cooks them into a meatloaf, and serves it to Tamora; the play ends with a barrage of stabbings. Most of the violence takes place on stage. Suicide is common in the Roman plays. Brutus and Cassius, Antony, and Portia all commit suicide, and Coriolanus submits to death at the hands of the Volscians. In most of the plays, Roman violence turns on Rome or other Romans. Shakespeare's Romans are self-conscious, theatrical, and historically aware characters, who jump at any chance to deliver a rhetorically intricate speech.

Shakespeare is as interested in the political and cultural history of Rome as he is in English history. Shakespeare's primary Roman plays (*Coriolanus, Julius Caesar, Antony and Cleopatra*) aren't merely psychological studies of prominent Romans, nor merely tragedies for the title characters. Together, the plays form a trilogy laying out the tragedy of the Roman Republic.[8] They form Shakespeare's primary contribution to Elizabethan and later debates about Rome.

Rome is a different place in each of the three plays. *Coriolanus* begins with famine, and no one is ever shown eating or drinking. Coriolanus's mother Volumnia refuses a dinner invitation with the revealing comment, "Anger's my meat. I sup upon myself" (4.2.50). In *Antony and Cleopatra*, by contrast, banqueting seems nonstop (1.2.13–17; 2.7; 4.2.9–10). Coriolanus isn't a romantic hero, and his play includes a speech in favor of chastity (5.3.64–67). *Antony and Cleopatra* is voluptuous, dramatizing one of the great erotic stories of Roman history. We might attribute this to the exotic influence of the erotic East, of Egypt, but the Romans of *Antony and Cleopatra* are as Egyptian as any of the Egyptians.

The atmosphere of Rome changes because of the massive political shift that occurs over the course of the trilogy. Coriolanus lives in the old Republican Rome, devoted to civic gods, a warrior's warrior, exhibiting

---

8. Cantor, *Shakespeare's Roman Trilogy*, 83. The next several pages summarize Cantor's analysis of how the three major Roman plays form a tragic unit.

the martial virtues that made Rome great. Julius Caesar, of course, lives and dies at the hinge between Republic and Empire. Cassius and Brutus conspire against him to preserve old Rome, but instead unleash the spirit of Caesarism that forges a new Rome. *Antony and Cleopatra* is set only a few years after Caesar's death, but already Rome has become an empire, which will soon be ruled by a single emperor, Octavius (Augustus).

Shakespeare links this political shift with deep changes in Roman psychology, religion, and thought, as Romans adjust to the collapse of the Republican system. Philosophy, for instance, doesn't come up at all in *Coriolanus*. Coriolanus would think philosophers too feminine for Rome. Philosophy is everywhere in *Julius Caesar*. According to Casca, Cicero's speeches are all "Greek to me" (1.2.284), a funny line that signals growing Greek influence in Rome and a widening gap between Greek-speaking elites and Latin-speaking commoners. Cassius is a self-conscious Epicurean and Brutus a Stoic. Their philosophies offer little help, since both Epicureanism and Stoicism are apolitical philosophies that cannot guide the characters through the titanic struggles of the age.

Religion too is transformed. Like a good old Roman, Coriolanus expects Rome's gods to support Rome, so long as Romans honor the gods. For him, religion is an aspect of political and military life. Julius Caesar, by contrast, consults with soothsayers and is warned by a seer not to go to the Senate on the fateful Ides of March. Much of *Antony and Cleopatra* takes place in Egypt, where Romans have been introduced to new gods and new religious possibilities.

Under the Republic, a man of courage and cunning could make his mark. The Republic rewarded political ambition, and many shared power. Once the Republic yielded to empire, there was room for only *one* ambitious man, the emperor. Emperors regarded every other powerful man as a potential rival. Soldiers who prove too successful come under suspicion. In *Antony and Cleopatra*, the general Vendentius admits he didn't press his advantage in a battle because he was worried about arousing Octavius's envy. Empire changes the very nature of politics. Rome no longer makes decisions through public debate in the Senate. Emperors do all the deciding. Distanced from the people and even from their own underlings, emperors rely on public image to exercise power. They manipulate spectacles and transform politics into theater.

In the Republic, there's no distinction between private and public. Coriolanus is married and has a son, but his family is utterly devoted to the service of Rome. Once the emperor blocks the way to political success, the empire throws Romans back onto their own private desires. Besides, the growth of the empire expands "lifestyle choices." Antony discovers what Coriolanus saw when he was exiled from Rome: "there is a world elsewhere" (3.3.136). Peace paradoxically weakens the Romans' attachment to the common good. With no threats from outside, Romans indulge their private whims.

Coriolanus is confident his fate is in his own hands, and no ghosts or omens intervene to dissuade him. In *Julius Caesar*, men are wafted about by forces outside their control, and the sense of powerlessness becomes stronger in *Antony and Cleopatra*. Brutus is already defeatist; he kills himself at the moment of the conspirators' victory. Antony occasionally acts like a traditional hero, as when he issues a challenge to man-to-man combat with Octavius. Octavius laughs him off. Political power no longer depends on individual daring or strength, but on the ability to manage large armies from a distance. In Antony, this erosion of personal agency collapses into a sickly longing for death.

Why did the Republic fall? Machiavelli said the Republic was victim of its own success. The larger its territory became, the longer its military excursions; lengthy campaigns enabled generals to form strong bonds with soldiers, the kind that Caesar eventually exploited to seize control of the capital.[9]

Shakespeare, by contrast, emphasizes the role of Rome's citizens. Represented by the tribunes in the time of Coriolanus, the plebs provide a counter-weight to patrician power and a brake on the power of possible dictator. Citizens play a significant role in *Coriolanus*. They're responsible for a number of the key turning points of the plot. When the curtain parts for Act 1, a hangry mob is massed on stage, read to lynch Caius Martius (Coriolanus) for robbing them of bread (1.1). Citizens discuss Coriolanus's bid for consulship (2.3) and cast their voices or votes for or against him (2.3). Representatives of the plebs conspire to exile Coriolanus from Rome (3.3).

Plebs, so prominent in *Coriolanus*, disappear over the course of the next two plays. Patricians no longer know any commoners by name. Even their soldiers are cogs in a military machine. Power gets concentrated in the hands of a single patrician, the emperor. But the plebs aren't mere victims. They sell out. Antony is able to buy their loyalty by promising to distribute Caesar's fortune to the commons. Brutus wants to restore

---

9. Cantor, *Shakespeare's Roman Trilogy*, 30.

the Republic, but when the people hear him, they acclaim: "Let him be Caesar" (*Julius Caesar* 3.2.50). Rome collapses because the people refuse to take responsibility for Rome. In Paul Cantor's words, the plebs "voted themselves out of history."[10]

Coriolanus offers a subtle portrait of the Republic. It's a political drama and has often been exploited, though in opposite directions. A production at Drury Lane in 1789 idealized the patrician characters and represented the plebs as clowns and dolts. Nazis produced the play during the 1930s to expose the evils of democracy and to celebrate Hitler as a conqueror greater than the Roman Martius. *Coriolanus* was so popular with Nazis that the Allies banned it after World War II. Other productions highlight the distasteful pride of Coriolanus and present the tribunes as champions of democracy. During the 1930s, Eastern European productions turned the plebs and tribunes into heroes and condemned Martius as a tyrant. Bertold Brecht's unfinished adaptation thoroughly reinvented the story. Instead of being fearful and demoralized by Martius's attack on Rome, the tribunes organize the plebs into a defense force so fearsome that Martius withdraws of his own accord.

Each of these political interpretations has a basis in the text. Few viewers or readers warm to Coriolanus, and it is not difficult to turn the play into a critique of aristocratic elitism. "What's the matter, you dissentious rogues, / That, rubbing the poor itch of your opinion, / Make yourselves scabs?" are Coriolanus's first words and set the tone for his other speeches to the plebs (1.1.162–64). He condemns the people as cowardly hares with souls of geese; at his banishment, he dismisses them as a "common cry of curs" (3.3.121); he often complains of their body odor and bad breath. His politics are profoundly anti-democratic. He wonders at the "double worship" of Rome's famously mixed political system, where "gentry, title, wisdom / Cannot conclude but by the yea and no / Of general ignorance" (3.1.143–45). From the beginning, he so despises the commoners and common soldiers that he threatens to treat them as Volscians and attack them: "I'll leave the foe / And make my wars on you!" (1.4.39–40). If Shakespeare had a neon "Foreshadowing!" sign, he would have placed one here, because that's exactly where the play is headed.

On the other hand, it's difficult not to feel the force of Coriolanus's opinions. Isn't it better for the wise and informed to make political

---

10. Cantor, *Shakespeare's Roman Trilogy*, 34.

decisions, rather than to subject them to the veto power of the ignorant and apathetic? Further, Shakespeare does *not* make the people of Rome very attractive. They truly don't know what's good for them. The tribunes manipulate the plebs and are as dictatorial and contemptuous of the people in their own way as Coriolanus is. The people of Rome gleefully banish their Hector, not stopping for a moment to ask what it will cost them.

Left and right, democrats and elitists, seem to have equal claim to the play, which suggests that Shakespeare's political interest lies elsewhere. Neither the elitist nor the democratic interpretation gets to the political heart of the play, which raises a more fundamental question about politics, the relation of gratitude and political life. *Coriolanus* identifies the tragic flaw of Republican Rome, the flaw that will lead to its collapse. The Republic falls because it's monstrously ungrateful. Rome is a cannibal mother who devours her own children.

Review Questions

1. How does Aristotle answer Plato's objections to poetry?
2. How is Aristotle's theory of tragedy different from Shakespeare's?
3. How are Shakespeare's plays tragedies of sin and judgment?
4. Discuss what Elizabethans thought of Rome. How was ancient Roman history relevant to Shakespeare's contemporaries?
5. What are the common elements of Shakespeare's Roman plays?
6. Explain the political, religious, and philosophical differences among *Coriolanus, Julius Caesar,* and *Antony and Cleopatra*.
7. What is the role of the Roman people in *Coriolanus*?
8. Does *Coriolanus* support authority or freedom, the upper or lower classes?

Thought Questions

1. Paul Cantor compares Shakespeare's analysis of Rome to Friedrich Nietzsche's. Nietzsche claimed Christianity destroyed ancient

heroic morals, which worked from a duality of "good" versus "bad," by introducing a duality of "good" versus "evil." For ancient heroes, whatever advanced their honor was "good" and whatever inhibited honor was "bad." Christians, however, regarded the assertiveness of glory-seeking heroes as "evil," a form of pride. In Cantor's view, Shakespeare is more perceptive, since he uncovers a profound moral shift *within* pagan Rome, before Christianity arrives. Discuss.

2. What Roman plays did Ben Jonson write? What are they about?

3. Read Machiavelli, *Discourses on Livy*, Book 1, discourse 3. Why did Rome establish the institution of the tribunes?

Mutiny of the Members, Act 1

So far as we can determine, no one prior to Shakespeare ever turned the story of Coriolanus into a drama. For us, Coriolanus is a small figure in the Roman world, a much lesser character than Julius Caesar, Brutus, Cassius, Octavius, Antony, or Cleopatra. We know how Shakespeare came across the story. Thomas North's English translation of Plutarch's *Roman Lives* was available in Elizabethan England, but, unlike Plutarch's *Moralia*, it was not hugely popular. We can tell both from *Coriolanus* and Shakespeare's other Roman plays that he knew Plutarch's *Lives*, but the fact that he wrote a play based on a relatively obscure character from a relatively unknown book gives us an insight into Shakespeare's "method." He wouldn't have had an Oxford Classics edition of Plutarch in a handy paperback; in Shakespeare's day, the book was published in large folio volumes. Shakespeare probably worked on his play while studying a copy in some nobleman's library.

Coriolanus's given name is Caius Martius, which indicates he is a devotee of the war god, Mars. He was Rome's greatest warrior in the time of the early Republic (fifth century BC), whose greatest exploit was the single-handed (according to Shakespeare) conquest of the Volscian city of Corioli (or Corioles), after which he was given the honorific title, "Coriolanus."

Coriolanus's father died when he was young and he was raised by his mother, Volumnia. Plutarch says Coriolanus did everything for the pleasure of his mother, and Shakespeare plays up this aspect of Coriolanus's character by focusing on Volumnia. She's a martial, thoroughly

Roman mother, who presses her son into war and praises him for his deeds of honor (1.3.1–25). She celebrates the fact that "Before him / He carries noise, and behind him he leaves tears. / Death, that dark spirit, in's nervy arm doth lie; / Which, being advanced, declines, and then men die" (2.1.154–57). When he returns from battle, she shows an excessive interest in his twenty-seven battle wounds (2.1.143–52). She encourages Coriolanus's wife Virgilia to take more joy in her husband's honor than in "the embracements of his bed where he would show most love" (1.3.4–5).[11] Allegorically, Volumnia symbolizes Rome herself, the "nursemaid" of Coriolanus and all the Romans. She is, as one Senator later says, "our patroness, the life of Rome" (5.5.1).

Early on, Shakespeare introduces the rivalry between Martius and the Volscian commander, Aufidius. Martius has bested Aufidius many times in single combat and looks for opportunities to fight him again (1.8.1–15). He finds and fights Aufidius on the battlefield and later searches him out in Antium after he is banished from Rome. Aufidius is equally obsessed with Coriolanus. After being defeated in one battle, he vows that nothing—"nor sleep nor sanctuary, / Being naked, sick, nor fane nor capitol"—will limit his hatred for Martius (1.10.19–27).

Uncannily contemporary, *Coriolanus* is replete with the stuff of day-to-day politics: Handlers, plots, propaganda, demagoguery, street riots, restive mobs, corrupt electioneering, and spin. The political drama unfolds against the backdrop of the parable of the stomach, which the patrician Menenius tells to the assembled plebs in the first scene.

> There was a time when all the body's members
> Rebelled against the belly, thus accused it:
> That only like a gulf it did remain
> I' th' midst o' th' body, idle and unactive,
> Still cupboarding the viand, never bearing
> Like labor with the rest, where th' other instruments
> Did see and hear, devise, instruct, walk, feel,
> And mutually participate, did minister
> Unto the appetite and affection common
> Of the whole body. (1.1.94–103)

Deliberately and gravely, and "with a kind of smile," the stomach explains he receives food first only to send nutrition through the veins that keep the rest of the body healthy:

---

11. Volumnia isn't the only character to praise war more highly than sex: Martius does (1.6.29–32), as does Aufidius when Coriolanus joins the Volscians (4.5.117–22).

"True is it, my incorporate friends," quoth he,
"That I receive the general food at first,
Which you do live upon; and fit it is,
Because I am the storehouse and the shop
Of the whole body. But, if you do remember,
I send it through the rivers of your blood,
Even to the court, the heart, to th' seat o' th' brain;
And, through the cranks and offices of man,
The strongest nerves and small inferior veins
From me receive that natural competency
Whereby they live . . .
   Though all at once cannot
See what I do deliver out to each,
Yet I can make my audit up that all
From me do back receive the flour of all,
And leave me but the bran." (1.1.128–44)

Menenius's parable is a picture of a "mutually participate" civic body, where each member is bound together by mutual benefit and assistance. "The senators of Rome are this good belly," he says (1.1.146), and they "digest" everything needed for the good of the city. Instead of complaining against the patricians, the plebs ought to recognize that their lives depend on the stomach of the Senate. Menenius's parable initially seems to serve as an ideal by which the real Rome is measured, though ultimately we shall see it has a more disturbing message. Wise though it is, we suspect his parable is self-serving. After all, Menenius is a patrician, and his parable supports the superior position of the patricians.

Shakespeare's Roman plays are all overshadowed by an ideal of unified political order. In each case, Rome fails to live up to its ideal. Rome is always double Rome, though the doubling differs from play to play. In *Julius Caesar*, Rome is divided between Pompey's remaining allies and the plebs who celebrate Caesar (1.1). Then it divides again, between Caesar and the conspirators, then again among the conspirators themselves. In *Coriolanus*, the division is part of the system, reflected in the distinction between the Senate and the tribunate, who represent the plebs. The imagery of the play makes it clear enough Rome isn't a unified body. The play is littered with references to body parts (cf., e.g., 3.1.294).[12] From one perspective, the play is a straightforward dramatization of Menenius's

---

12. Zvi Jagendorf provides a helpful catalogue: "legs, arms, tongues, scabs, scratches, wounds, mouths, teeth, voices, bellies, and toes" ("*Coriolanus*: Body Politic and Private Parts," 458).

fable: It depicts the failure of the limbs to be thankful for the stomach's labors. The people are guilty of forgetful ingratitude for the service of her benefactor and protector(s).

Coriolanus isn't known for its gorgeous poetry. It has no encomium to music like Act 5 of *Merchant of Venice*, no transcendentally tragic lyricism as in *Lear*, *Macbeth*, *Hamlet*, or *Othello*, none of the melancholy pathos of Prospero's "Our revels now are ended" (*The Tempest* 4.1.148). But if it's invective you're looking for, or vituperation, well, *Coriolanus* is your go-to play.

Nearly every time Coriolanus opens his mouth, creative insults, sharp rebukes, and high-minded disgust come pouring out. Menenius has just calmed the rabble clamoring for Coriolanus's death when Coriolanus makes his first entrance. After a quick "Thanks" to Menenius, he launches in against the people:

> What's the matter, you dissentious rogues,
> That, rubbing the poor itch of your opinion,
> Make yourselves scabs? (1.1.162–64)

In three lines, he undoes everything Menenius achieved.

Coriolanus calls his fellow Romans "geese," "hares," "fragments." When they refuse to follow his charge into the Volscian city of Corioli, he threatens to change sides and attack his own men, foreshadowing his eventual exile from and siege of Rome. When he's sentenced to exile, he replies with a speech of breathtaking intensity:

> You common cry of curs, whose breath I hate
> As reek o' th' rotten fens, whose loves I prize
> As the dead carcasses of unburied men
> That do corrupt my air, I banish you! . . .
>   Have the power still
> To banish your defenders, till at length
> Your ignorance—which finds not till it feels,
> Making but reservation of yourselves;
> Still your own foes—deliver you
> As most abated captives to some nation
> That won you without blows! Despising,
> For you, the city, thus I turn my back.
> There is a world elsewhere. (3.3.121–36)

Banished from the city that made him, Coriolanus seeks another world. Banished by Rome, he banishes Rome.

Coriolanus isn't just letting off steam. Behind the vitriol is a keen military and political intelligence. He exposes the tension at the heart of Rome. He dismisses the city's commitment to "mixed" government as a form of "double worship" that requires leaders who possess title and wisdom to wait on the "yea and no / Of general ignorance" (3.1.141, 144–45). Why, he asks, should experienced men of the world take their cues from commoners whose intellectual scope is limited to fluctuations in the price of grain? It's a good question.

Coriolanius's verbal venom expresses his sense of his own value to the city. He initially refuses to go through the usual rituals of political campaigning, which require him to re-tune his warlike voice "into a pipe / Small as an eunuch, or the virgin voice / That babies lulls asleep." He won't bend his "armed knees" to beg for votes. To beg for approval from the plebs, he would have to deny his own status, and he refuses to "surcease to honor mine own truth" or teach his mind "a most inherent baseness" (3.2.111–23).

Here is his tragic dilemma: To protect and serve Rome, Coriolanus must be true to himself. But his insistence on self-consistency and maintaining his honor puts him at odds with the city that demands his services. He can't be himself without clashing with Rome; Rome can't survive unless he has the liberty to be himself. It's an ancient-modern dilemma, going back at least to Aeschylus: Can a hero (Achilles, or Mr. Incredible) settle down in a quiet suburb or a desk job at an insurance company? Can a city afford to let him?

Act 1 focuses on public events that shake Roman political and social life. Scene 1 begins with a mob; Menenius appears and tells his parable; Martius appears and berates the people; finally, senators arrive to tell Martius he's needed to resist the threat from the Volscians. The scene ends with the tribunes Sicinius and Brutus hatching a plot against Martius. The scene turns full circle:

    A. Mob threatens to kill Martius
      B. Menenius's parable
        C. Martius's appearance
      B'. Senators ask Martius for help
    A'. Tribunes plot Martius's downfall

Act 2 switches to the city of Corioli, where Aufidius is holding a strategic planning session with his advisors. The last part of the Act (scenes 4–10) depicts Martius's heroic victory at Corioli.

Tucked among these scenes of politics and war is a domestic scene (1.3), which introduces us to Martius's mother Volumnia, his wife Virgilia, and Virgilia's friend Valeria. In tone, the scene is a quiet interlude between the loud riots on the streets of Rome and the clash and clamor of war. But Shakespeare doesn't include the scene merely to vary the pace of the play.

He has historical reasons for introducing Volumnia so early in the play. As noted above, she was a major influence on her son. Having lost his father early in life, Coriolanus feels an unusual sense of filial loyalty toward his mother, Volumnia. According to Plutarch, Coriolanus was so attached to his mother he continued to live with her even after marrying Virgilia: "He took a wife, also, at [Volumnia's] request and wish, and continued, even after he had children, to live still with his mother, without parting families."[13]

Shakespeare plays up the oddity of their relationship. Despite his manly manliness, Coriolanus has never cut himself away from his mother's apron strings and lives only for her looks. When she threatens to withdraw that praise, he crumbles and gives himself to the Volscians. Coriolanus has a young man's awkwardness in verbal conflict; though unparalleled on the battlefield, he is easily manipulated and bested in debate in the fully adult world of Roman politics. His rivalry with Aufidius looks like nothing more than an adolescent rivalry, more than slightly charged with homoerotic interest. In the end, Aufidius provokes Coriolanus with the *coup de grace*—he calls him a "boy of tears."

Just as importantly, the domestic scene reveals where Martius got his martial demeanor. Volumnia chides Virgilia for worrying about Martius going off to war:

> If my son were my husband, I should freelier rejoice in that absence wherein he won honor than in the embracements of his bed where he would show most love. When yet he was but tender-bodied and the only son of my womb, when youth with comeliness plucked all gaze his way, when for a day of kings' entreaties a mother should not sell him an hour from her beholding, I, considering how honor would become such a person—that it was no better than picturelike to hang by th' wall, if renown made it not stir—was pleased to let him seek danger where he was like to find fame. To a cruel war I sent him, from whence he returned, his brows bound with oak. I tell

---

13. Plutarch, *Cor.* 3.3–4.

thee, daughter, I sprang not more in joy at first hearing he was a man-child than now in first seeing he had proved himself a man. (1.3.2–17)

What if he had died? Virgilia protests. Volumnia replies, "Had I a dozen sons . . . I had rather had eleven die nobly for their country than one voluptuously surfeit out of action" (1.3.22–25). Volumnia passes her militancy to another generation. Valeria recounts how she watched Martius's son catch a butterfly then "set his teeth and tear it! Oh, I warrant, how he mammocked it!" (1.3.57–65). Volumnia embodies the spirit of mother Rome, a mother who infuses her passionate love of the city into her son, a mother who is willing and even eager to see her sons die in Rome's service. Her devotion to Rome will come back to hurt her.

Review Questions

1. Where did Shakespeare learn about Coriolanus?
2. Where does Coriolanus get his name? What is his given name?
3. Discuss the relationship between Coriolanus and his mother Volumnia.
4. Who is Aufidius? What is his relationship with Coriolanus?
5. What is Menenius's parable of the stomach about? Why does he tell it to the people?
6. Discuss the language of *Coriolanus*.
7. Why does Coriolanus think popular rule is a mistake?
8. Describe the character of Volumnia.

Thought Questions

1. Describe the different views of Coriolanus expressed by the citizens in the first scene (1.1.1–48).
2. What is Aufidius's strategy in attacking Rome (1.2)?. How does this foreshadow later developments in the play?

3. What did Coriolanus's son do to a butterfly (1.3.57–65)? How do the other women react to the story? How does this connect to later references to "butterflies" (4.6.90–96; 5.4.11–14)?

4. Compare the various uses of the word "proud" in the opening scene (1.1.32, 37, 167–68). Who charges whom with pride?

Hero to Outcast, Acts 2–3

The last half of Act 1 is concerned with Martius's one-man battle at the Volscian city of Corioli. As one of his soldiers says, "He is himself alone, / To answer all the city" (1.4.51–52). Cominius, his commander, tells the story in more detail:

> He stopped the fliers,
> And by his rare example made the coward
> Turn terror into sport. As weeds before
> A vessel under sail, so men obeyed
> And fell below his stem. His sword, death's stamp,
> Where it did mark, it took. From face to foot
> He was a thing of blood, whose every motion
> Was timed with dying cries. Alone he entered
> The mortal gate of th' city, which he painted
> With shunless destiny; aidless came off,
> And with a sudden reinforcement struck
> Corioli like a planet. Now all's his. (2.2.103–14)

Instead of retreating before a Volscian onslaught, he dashes through the gates and has to fight his way out. His soldiers think he's dead, until he appears, bloodied but victorious. When that battle is over, Martius insists on joining another Roman regiment so he can fight with Aufidius man to man. This is the day that makes his reputation, giving him a new name: Coriolanus, a name that proclaims his conquest of Corioli.

Following his victory, Coriolanus stands for consul. In this, he follows in the footsteps of many great Romans, who used military success as a springboard to political power. The link between war and politics is quite direct for Coriolanus, since he is asked to show off his war scars to win votes from the common people. Acts 2–3 depict the honors Coriolanus receives for his victory and his tumultuous campaign to become consul:

    A. Coriolanus returns to Rome in triumph, 2.1
        B. Senate approves Coriolanus for consul, 2.2.
            C. Citizens discuss election;
                tribunes turn crowd against Coriolanus, 2.3
    A'. Tribunes provoke an outburst, 3.1
        B'. Volumnia and Senators convince Coriolanus to stand, 3.2
            C'. Coriolanus is banished, 3.3

    Under the Republic, the consul was the highest magistrate. Two consuls were elected to one-year terms, a kind of co-presidency that ensured no one could gain too much power. To become consul, Coriolanus has to gain the voices of both the Senate and the people. The former he easily secures, but to gain the support of the people he must don the robes of a pleb and campaign for their support. He makes three attempts. Though Coriolanus is reluctant from the first, he initially softens his soldierly rhetoric to win the grateful support of the commoners. After Coriolanus leaves, the tribunes remind the people of Coriolanus's contempt for them and stir the mob up to oppose his bid for consul (2.3). Back to square one, Coriolanus attempts to win over the people again, but the tribunes again thwart him by provoking an anti-democratic outburst. I have alluded to it above, but it is worth quoting a larger section:

> This double worship,
> Where one part does disdain with cause, the other
> Insult without all reason; where gentry, title, wisdom,
> Cannot conclude but by the yea and no
> Of general ignorance—it must omit
> Real necessities, and give way the while
> To unstable slightness. Purpose so barred, it follows
> Nothing is done to purpose. (3.1.141–48)

    Rome's "double worship" makes it politically double-minded: Patricians rule, but even they have to bow to popular will. The tribunes spin Coriolanus's outburst as an attack on the foundations of Roman order. Sicinius and Brutus convince the people that Coriolanus is conspiring to take away their ancestral liberties (2.3.213–17; 3.1.193–95).

    Once again, Coriolanus is back to the beginning. His patrician allies remove Coriolanus from the fray before he can do more damage and convince him to change his tone. Volumnia confesses, "I would dissemble with my nature where / My fortunes and my friends at stake required / I should do so in honor" (3.2.62–64). Menenius thinks Coriolanus is "too noble for the world," unable to flatter or modulate his tone to gain approval (3.1.254-55). Coriolanus thinks he will betray himself if he follows Volumnia's advice to "perform a part." Coriolanus sees it as unmanly harlotry, an offense against "mine own truth":

> Away, my disposition, and possess me
> Some harlot's spirit! My throat of war be turned,
> Which quired with my drum, into a pipe
> Small as an eunuch, or the virgin voice
> That babies lulls asleep! The smiles of knaves
> Tent in my cheeks, and schoolboys' tears take up
> The glasses of my sight! A beggar's tongue
> Make motion through my lips, and my armed knees,
> Who bowed but in my stirrup, bend like his
> That hath received an alms! I will not do't,
> Lest I surcease to honor mine own truth
> And by my body's action teach my mind
> A most inherent baseness. (3.2.111–23)

Volumnia tells him to do what he likes but reminds him she is big-hearted as her son: "Thy valiantness was mine, thou suck'st it from me, / But owe thy pride thyself" (3.2.129–30). Volumnia's rebuke convinces Coriolanus: "Mother, I am going to the marketplace, / Chide me no more" (3.2.131–32). It's another foreshadowing. Coriolanus will not be able to withstand his mother's appeals later, when his very life is at stake.

His effort fails in any case. Sicinius and Brutus know how to push his buttons. They accuse him of conspiracy to seize "power tyrannical." He is a "traitor to the people" (3.3.63–66). This time round, Coriolanus doesn't even try to contain himself. Coriolanus reminds the people of his service to Rome and confesses, "I do love / My country's good with a respect more tender, / More holy and profound, than mine own life, / My dear wife's estimate, her womb's increase, / And treasure of my loins" (3.3.111–15). But the tribunes interrupt his speech, until he erupts in a titanic rage: "I banish you!" (3.3.124).

So much is on the surface of Acts 2–3. Beneath the surface, Shakespeare is examining the politics of gratitude and ingratitude. At the beginning of Act 2, scene 2, an officer tells a fellow officer that Coriolanus's military accomplishments "deserved worthily of his country" and says that "for [the plebs'] tongues to be silent and not confess so much were a kind of ingrateful injury." They owe their voices/votes to Martius for his past services. In the following scene, the "Third Citizen" offers a similar opinion: "if he tell us his noble deeds, we must also tell him our noble acceptance of them. Ingratitude is monstrous; and for the multitude to be ingrateful were to make a monster of the multitude; of the which we being members, should bring ourselves to be monstrous members" (2.3.8–12). A "monster" is unnatural. A literal monster doesn't share the nature of his parents, and a metaphorical monster renounces the common nature he shares with others.

As we shall see again in our study of *King Lear*, "nature" is sometimes linked to the word "kind": Those who refuse to receive or return kindness prove that they are of a different kind or genus. The unkind are monsters in human shape, not men. Thus, besides obvious words for gratitude, "kindness" and "unkindness" are often synonyms of "gratitude" and "ingratitude."[14] When the multitude fails to acknowledge Martius's contributions to Rome's prosperity and safety, Rome becomes "unkind." When the tribunes describe Coriolanus as a disease, infection, poison, and gangrene that must be excised from the body of Rome, Coriolanus charges that the officers' fears have come true: Rome is a monster, a "Hydra" for whom the tribunes serve as "horn and noise o' th' monster's" (3.1.92, 94). Unkindness/ingratitude has turned the plebs at least into a thing unnatural, not of humankind. If the citizens are freaks, so is Rome. For, "What is the city but the people?" (3.1.198). The city denies the nature she shares with her civic "father" and becomes just what the Third Citizen fears: A monster.

Monstrous ingratitude turns cannibalistic, and so it is for Coriolanus (see 2.1.1–12). After the tribunes' plot traps Martius, Menenius prays that Rome will not be transformed into a cannibal mother: "Now the good gods forbid / That our renowned Rome, whose gratitude / Towards her deserved children is enrolled / In Jove's own book, like an unnatural dam / Should now eat up her own!" (3.1.288–92). It's too late. Rome expels her leading son, but it will soon devour him.

In Coriolanus's mind, Rome's ingratitude dissolves his bonds to Rome so completely that nothing obliges him to serve the city that gave him birth. Rather than endure contempt, injury, and exile, he plots revenge, and, at the urging of the Volscian commander Aufidius, determines to pour war "into the bowels of ungrateful Rome" (4.5.133–34). Ultimately, the patricians join the plebs in forgetful ingratitude (4.6.122–25), and Coriolanus despises them more deeply than the plebs, rejecting both his commander, Cominius, and his surrogate father, Menenius, who appeal

---

14. Dunn, *Concept of Ingratitude*, 13, 86–91.

to him to abandon his assault on Rome. Rome forgets the benefits they owe to Martius's heroism, expresses hatred rather than thanks, and does not support him in grateful repayment for his contributions to Rome. The more their ingratitude matures, the more monstrous Rome becomes.

Rome is ungrateful to Coriolanus. Coriolanus is ungrateful to Rome.[15] Curiously, Martius's first word in the play is "Thanks" (1.1.162), yet he immediately begins to chide the plebs assembled in the public square as "dissentious rogues" who have nothing better to do than to rub "the poor itch of your opinion" so as to produce "scabs" (1.1.162–64). His expression of gratitude is immediately undermined by harsh attacks on the people.

Besides, Coriolanus refuses to *receive* benefits. As Terry Eagleton puts it, Coriolanus "envisions no reciprocity: he sees this mutual relationship of plebeians and patricians as circular, destructive, self-defeating." He's another Achilles, seeking "self-creation without reference to society" and rejecting any need for others to verify his status.[16] When his general Cominius commends his action at Corioli, Coriolanus complains he cannot bear to be praised. This might seem to be an act of commendable humility, evidence that Martius is neither proud nor ambitious, but Cominius sees cruelty and ingratitude lurking beneath: "Too modest are you, / More cruel to your good report than grateful / To us that give you truly" (1.9.52–54).

Here is another variation of his tragic dilemma: Coriolanus's status as hero depends on his reputation, which depends on the approval of his fellow Romans. Yet he strives to rise *above* his fellows. Martius attempts to struggle free of the dilemma by refusing the plaudits of his commanding officer, but he knows he depends on them for his fame. And he resents his dependence.

Review Questions

1. How does Coriolanus conquer the Volscian city of Corioli?
2. Describe the structure of Acts 2–3.

15. This is the way Seneca read the story of Coriolanus, and there is reason to think that Shakespeare was familiar with Seneca's treatise: "Coriolanus was ungrateful, and became dutiful late, and after repenting of his crime; he did indeed lay down his arms, but only in the midst of his unnatural warfare" (*Ben.* 5.16).

16. Eagleton, *Shakespeare and Society*, 104.

3. How many times does Coriolanus attempt to win the "voices" of the people? Why does he fail?
4. What does Volumnia advise Coriolanus to do? Why is he reluctant to do it?
5. How is gratitude linked to Shakespeare's use of the words "kind" and "natural"?
6. How is Rome ungrateful to Coriolanus? How is Coriolanus ungrateful to Rome?

Thought questions

1. Discuss the conversation between Menenius and Brutus (2.1.27–39) in the light of Coriolanus's boast that he conquered Corioli "alone."
2. Summarize Cominius's speech in praise of Coriolanus (2.2.82–122). To whom does he compare Coriolanus?
3. What does Coriolanus agree to court the commoners (2.3.111–30)?
4. Read Thomas Aquinas's discussion of gratitude and ingratitude in *Summa theologiae* II–II, questions 106–7. How does Thomas define gratitude and ingratitude? How does *Coriolanus* exemplify these features of gratitude and ingratitude?

Cannibal Rome, Acts 4–5

After his banishment, Coriolanus searches out his old rival, Aufidius, to offer his services. He wants to attack and conquer Rome for the Volscians. Coriolanus's Volscian forces win several battles and besiege Rome. It looks as if Coriolanus has found himself a new city. Perhaps "there is a world elsewhere."

In reality, Coriolanus remains a loner. When the plebs refuse to pay the respect they owe him, he thinks, the contract between them becomes null and void. He acts as if he doesn't need to do any more favors for the Romans because they have refused to accept his favors. As a result, he's a man without a city. Alone he conquers. Alone he is banished.

At a number of points in the play, Coriolanus is described as a monster, specifically, a dragon: "Believe't not lightly—though I go alone, / Like to a lonely dragon that his fen / Makes feared and talked of more than seen, your son / Will or exceed the common or be caught / With cautelous baits and practice" (4.1.29–33). Aufidius says, "he bears all things fairly, / And shows good husbandry for the Volscian state, / Fights dragonlike, and does achieve as soon / As draw his sword" (4.7.21–24).

Everything he is depends on Roman society. He inherited his position, status, title, and even his martial spirit from his parents. When he leaves Rome, he leaves behind everything that makes him who he is. He becomes, in Cominius's words, "a kind of nothing, titleless" (5.1.13), who leads men as if they were "boys pursuing summer butterflies / Or butchers killing flies" (4.6.93–96). Menenius tells Sicinius "there is a difference between a grub and a butterfly; yet your butterfly was a grub. This Martius is grown from man to dragon. He has wings; he's more than a creeping thing" (5.4.11–14).

Rome's ingratitude made her cannibalistic, and Coriolanus responds with a similarly monstrous appetite to consume Rome. Marjorie Garber puts the matter well: "More than almost any other Shakespearean hero, he aims at a status that is less like that of a man and more like that of a dragon, a god, or a machine—someone or something, in other words, that does not feel. . . . That to be human is to suffer, and that to be aloof from suffering is to turn one's back on humanity, and to be merely a thing, a tin god."[17]

Try as he might, Coriolanus cannot remain isolated forever. He is *not* a god, and he will come crashing to earth. His return to Rome, and to humanity, takes place in three stages, as three delegations from Rome visit the Volscian camp to convince Coriolanus to break his siege:

1. Cominius, Coriolanus's military superior.

2. Menenius, Coriolanus's personal mentor.

3. His family: Volumnia, Virgilia, Valeria, and Coriolanus's son.

The triple structure parallels Coriolanus's three attempts to win the voices of the common people.

The male, politically-oriented delegations are unsuccessful. Instead of welcoming Coriolanus back to Rome, they reinforce his inhuman isolation. Coriolanus's inhumanity comes to a climax in his internal soliloquies as he waits for Volumnia's arrival in the Volscian camp. He intends

---

17. Garber, *Shakespeare After All*, 786, 791.

to resist the instinct to honor his mother and city. He will renounce all filial and marital attachments:

> But out, affection!
> All bond and privilege of nature, break!
> Let it be virtuous to be obstinate.
> What is that curt'sy worth, or those doves' eyes,
> Which can make gods forsworn? I melt, and am not
> Of stronger earth than others. My mother bows,
> As if Olympus to a molehill should
> In supplication nod; and my young boy
> Hath an aspect of intercession which
> Great nature cries "Deny not." Let the Volsces
> Plow Rome and harrow Italy! I'll never
> Be such a gosling to obey instinct, but stand
> As if a man were author of himself
> And knew no other kin. (5.3.24–37)

This is his dream: To be godlike, self-authored, without obligation to city or family. Renouncing kin, he becomes unkind.

Coriolanus's relationship with his mother is a key to the resolution of the story. Volumnia personifies Rome.[18] To tread on Rome is to tread on the womb that gave him birth (5.3.120–25). She pulls these strings in her appeal to Coriolanus and uses the tried-and-true methods of motherly manipulations: "Thou hast never in thy life / Showed thy dear mother any courtesy" (5.3.160–61), this to a man who is twisted around her little finger. Her final zinger hits the target: "This fellow had a Volscian to his mother; / His wife is in Corioles, and his child / Like him by chance" (5.3.178–80). Coriolanus has spent the last Act trying to become a Volscian, but now he realizes what it means: If he's a Volscian, then his mother isn't Roman, his mother Volumnia isn't his mother. He can withstand any loss, become a nothing, titleless, a dragon without maker or kin. But he *cannot* survive the prospect of losing his mother. He agrees to break the siege. The "unnatural scene" turns back to nature. By acting kindly toward his mother, Coriolanus returns to humankind.

Volumnia's triumph over her son is a political as well as a personal and familial victory. When Coriolanus recognizes the obligations he owes Volumnia, he simultaneously recognizes his obligations to Rome. Time, history, heritage, mother, Mother-city reassert their claims, and

---

18. So Menenius: "This Volumnia / Is worth of consuls, senators, patricians, / A city full; of tribunes, such as you, / A sea and land full" (5.4.53–55).

Coriolanus's experiment in (un)natural individualism and freedom collapses. Coriolanus's *aim* is to become "no more a Roman than Aufidius is a Volscian."[19] He tries to renounce Romanness when it conflicts with his own truth. His capitulation to Volumnia shows that he cannot achieve it. He comes crashing back to earth, to his family, to Rome. He re-humanizes.

The parable of Menenius is "the Pauline doctrine that we are all members one of another," and "*Coriolanus* is a poetic demonstration of this truth, and its hero, with all his virtues, made, by his own confession, the capital mistake of trying to live 'As if a man were author of himself / And knew no other kin.'" Being an individual is "not enough to be one's self," and Coriolanus's melting before his mother, wife, and son, means that "for the first time he lets his various 'parts' become members one of another and becomes himself something like the complete man he never was on the battlefield for all his valor. The dragon reverts to the butterfly."[20] But like the butterfly, he's "mammocked."

While his mother returns to the city in a triumphal procession like those Martius once enjoyed, Martius returns to Aufidius. Aufidius is waiting for him—lying in wait, to be precise. Nearly as soon as he arrives in Antium, Coriolanus becomes as much a rival to Aufidius as an ally. Aufidius complains to his lieutenant that his men "fly to th' Roman" (4.7.1) and looks forward to revenge: "When, Caius, Rome is thine, / Thou art poor'st of all; then shortly art thou mine" (4.7.56–57). When Coriolanus withdraws from Rome and concludes a peace between Volscians and Romans, Aufidius's hostility comes into the open. He gets his wish: Nothing, not even a military alliance, stands in the way of his hatred. Like the tribunes, he accuses Coriolanus of treason (5.6.83–87; note the repetition of "traitor . . . traitor . . . traitor"). When Coriolanus calls on his patron god, Mars, to hear Aufidius's false charge, Aufidius forbids him to name the god and calls him "boy of tears" (5.6.100). He is indeed, a boy still attached to his mother, a boy whose decisions can be swayed by "drops of salt" (5.6.92).

Aufidius has prepared the scene and has the thugs to pull it off. In death as in life, Coriolanus is alone, surrounded by Volscians. "Alone I did it," he can boast; alone I win, alone I leave, alone I die. But this final isolation isn't self-isolation. By responding to his mother's appeals, he

19. Eagleton, *Shakespeare and Society*, 112.
20. Goddard, *Meaning of Shakespeare*, 2.233–34.

ceased to be nothing, ceased to be a dragon. He became again what he always was—a Roman, a soldier, a son of Volumnia. But this return to Rome means his death, because Rome, like Volumnia, is eager for her sons to die for the city.

Coriolanus affirms the goodness of the bonds of family, city, and people. Coriolanus's discovery that he is intractably Roman after all comes too late. The play shows that these bonds, good as they are, can suffocate. Coriolanus saves Rome by giving himself to be devoured by the city, that cannibal mother, that smiling stomach of a city, who smiles *gravely.*

Review Questions

1. Where does Coriolanus *go* after he's banished from Rome?
2. What does Coriolanus *do* after he's banished from Rome?
3. What happens to Coriolanus when he's isolated from Rome? How does the play use animal imagery to describe this?
4. What three delegations are sent to Coriolanus?
5. How does Coriolanus try to protect himself from his mother's appeal? How does Volumnia persuade him?
6. What happens to Coriolanus after he agrees to break the siege?

Thought Questions

1. What is Coriolanus's attitude as he leaves Rome (4.1)? How does he comfort his wife?
2. How does Coriolanus weed "a root of ancient envy" from the heart of Aufidius (4.5.69–139)?
3. How does the 2011 film version of *Coriolanus* reinforce Coriolanus's influence over the Volscian soldiers? See 4.7.
4. Compare Act 5, scene 5 with Coriolanus's triumph in 2.2. How are they similar? How different?

2

Smiling Villain

Richard III

SHAKESPEARE WROTE TWO TETRALOGIES (four-play sequences) about English history. One includes *Richard II*, two parts of *Henry IV*, and *Henry V* and covers English history in the time of the Hundred Years' War, a dynastic war between England and France for control of the French crown. Richard II (1377–99) is overthrown by Henry Bolingbroke, who becomes Henry IV (1399–1413) and is succeeded by his son, Prince Hal, who becomes Henry V (1413–22).

The other tetralogy covers the reigns of Henry V's son, *Henry VI* (in three parts), and *Richard III*. King Henry VI reigned from 1422 to 1461, was dethroned, and returned to reign for about two hundred days between October 1470 and April 1471. Richard Gloucester was deeply involved in English politics throughout his life and reigned as Richard III during his last years, from 1483 to 1485. This tetralogy dramatizes the Wars of the Roses, civil wars between the house of Lancaster and the house of York, who fought for the crown of England.[1]

To get our bearings in this complex history, we need to start with the Hundred Years' War (1337–1453). In the mid-fourteenth century, King Edward III of England claimed the French crown and invaded France to seize it. He won renowned victories at Crecy (1346) and Poitiers (1356), but his conquest was short-lived. His son, Edward the Black Prince, died

---

1. To complicate matters, Shakespeare wrote *Henry VI* and *Richard III* before the other tetralogy, the reverse of chronological order.

fighting in France the year before his father died. Without a clear successor to Edward III, England couldn't hold its territories in France, while in England various factions vied for the English crown.

Richard II, son of the Black Prince, succeeded his grandfather, Edward III, at the age of ten. For the first years of his reign, his relatives controlled him. As he came to maturity, he tried to free himself from his family and allied himself with favorites who gained power at court. The conflict between Richard's family and Richard's friends eventually led to the exile of Henry Bolingbroke, one of Richard's powerful relatives. (Henry's exile takes place at the beginning of Shakespeare's *Richard II*.) Two years later, John of Gaunt, Henry Bolingbroke's father, died, and King Richard seized his property. Henry responded by invading England on the pretext of regaining control of his ancestral lands. In fact, he wanted to become king. In Shakespeare's *Richard II*, Henry overthrows Richard and has him murdered in Pontefract Castle.

As king, Henry IV was occupied with a battle against the powerful Mortimer and Percy families, who had supported him in his effort to dethrone Richard but later turned against him. Shakespeare's *1 Henry IV* ends with the battle of Shrewsbury, where Henry IV kills Henry Percy (Hotspur) to quash the Percy rebellion.

By the time Henry V came to the throne, his power was relatively secure and he could renew the English claim to the French crown. Shakespeare's *Henry V* compresses events that took place over a number of years: The wars in *Henry V* are those of Henry's first French campaign (1415), but the play ends with Henry's engagement to the French queen Catherine (spelled Katharine in the play), which actually took place in 1420 as part of the Treaty of Troyes.

Henry V had the same destiny as Edward III. He died prematurely, leaving a young son, Henry VI (1422–61/1470–71), on the throne of England and France. Though a pious and good man, Henry VI couldn't control England's nobles or retain France. England lost its French territories, thanks to the heroics of Joan of Arc, and England slid into civil war between two branches of Edward III's family, the houses of Lancaster and York. This series of civil wars is known as the Wars of the Roses because each side used a rose as a family symbol: Lancaster was represented by the red rose, York by the white.

The Wars of the Roses were a bewildering period of English history.[2] Henry VI's reign was split in two parts. Edward of York, son of Richard II, defeated Henry VI at Towton (1461), in the bloodiest battle ever fought on English soil. Henry didn't even show up to the battle. It was Palm Sunday, and the king spent the day in prayer. After his defeat, Henry was imprisoned in the Tower of London for the better part of a decade.

The victorious Yorkist leader was crowned Edward IV (1461–70). The early part of his reign was unsettled because of the machinations of the Earl of Warwick, known as the "Kingmaker." Warwick helped Edward gain the throne and planned to arrange a marriage to a French princess, thus uniting the two countries under a single royal family. Instead, Edward secretly married Elizabeth Woodville, a woman from the middle rank of English nobility. Elizabeth's relatives began to occupy a powerful position at the court. Her brother, Earl Rivers, and her son by a previous marriage, known as Lord Grey, are characters in Shakespeare's *Richard III*. Another of Elizabeth's brothers, Anthony Woodville, is mentioned.

After Edward's marriage, Warwick saw his influence waning. So he switched his support to Queen Margaret, Henry VI's energetic, unforgiving, vengeful French wife. Warwick conspired with Margaret and her son, Edward the Prince of Wales, to restore Henry VI to the throne. Warwick had his own interests in view: Prince Edward was married to Anne Neville, Warwick's daughter. Warwick invaded from France while King Edward was suppressing an uprising in the north of England. Realizing he couldn't defend himself, Edward fled to Holland. Henry VI emerged from the Tower and reassumed the throne.

The restoration lasted only seven months. Edward returned to England, joined by his brothers, Richard Gloucester (Richard III) and George, the Duke of Clarence, both of whom had defected to Warwick for a time. At the battle of Barnet (April 1471), Warwick was killed and Henry VI was defeated and returned to the Tower. Margaret continued her doomed effort for another month, until King Edward defeated the Lancastrian forces at Tewkesbury (May 1471). Prince Edward was killed and Margaret captured. Richard did not kill Edward, as Shakespeare claims. Henry VI died in the Tower shortly after. No one knows whether Henry died by natural causes or by assassination. Shakespeare, like many, places the blame on Richard Gloucester. Queen Margaret was sent back

---

2. I base this overview on Thomas Costain's popular history, *The Last Plantagenets*, and Peter Saccio's indispensable *Shakespeare's English Kings*.

to France, where she remained for the rest of her life. (For thematic reasons, Shakespeare brings her back to England for his play.)

During the second phase of Edward's reign, his brother Clarence plotted to undermine the upstart Woodvilles, the family of Edward's Queen Elizabeth. Clarence was eventually executed for his troubles. Perhaps he was drowned in a vat of malmsey wine, as Shakespeare describes, but Shakespeare is wrong to hold Richard responsible for his death. During the trial, King Edward himself was the chief witness against Clarence.

When Edward died, one of his two sons, Edward and Richard, should have taken the throne. Young Edward was crowned as Edward V, but since he was still a boy, his uncle Richard Gloucester became Lord Protector, the caretaker for the young king. Shortly after Edward V's accession to the throne, he and his brother were declared to be bastards, and therefore unfit to rule England. Richard of Gloucester succeeded Edward, crowned as Richard III in 1483. The boys were sent to the Tower and disappeared forever, their fate one of the great mysteries of English history.

The civil wars finally ended when Henry Richmond, who had Lancastrian and Yorkist ancestors, defeated King Richard III at Bosworth Field (1485). Henry became Henry VII (1485–1509) and inaugurated the Tudor dynasty that included Henry VIII, Edward VI, Mary I, and Elizabeth I. *Richard III* depicts Richard's brief reign and ends with Richard's death and Richmond's coronation.

Shakespeare wrote *Richard III* in the late 1590s, during the reign of Elizabeth I, the granddaughter of Henry VII, the Richmond of *Richard III*. The play was a turning point in Shakespeare's career, the first of his great tragic plays. It's an immature play in many ways. Some of the scenes are bloated, the dialogue repetitive, some characters cartoonish. Still, Richard was the first of Shakespeare's great villains and has become a proverbial murderous tyrant.

Shakespeare always takes liberties with historical facts, but in *Richard III* the gap between drama and history is wider than usual. Contrary to Shakespeare's portrayal, Richard was probably not a hunchback or physically deformed in any way. He did not seduce Lady Anne in the presence of her father-in-law's corpse (see 1.2). He did not have his brother Clarence murdered, but instead pled with King Edward to spare him. Richard was hostile to Edward's Queen Elizabeth and her family (see 1.3), but not to Edward himself. It is possible Richard had Edward IV's sons murdered in the Tower. It certainly benefited him.

Shakespeare didn't invent the legend of the monstrous Richard. He discovered it in the *Chronicles* of Raphael Holinshed, who drew from Sir Thomas More's *History of King Richard III* (1557), both of whom made Richard look bad so the Tudors would look good. Shakespeare did *popularize* the villainous portrayal of Richard, and Shakespeare's depiction has been popularly accepted as historically accurate, despite repeated attempts by historians to defend Richard's reputation.[3] The pen may be mightier than the sword, but poets, it appears, wield mightier pens than historians.

Though Shakespeare distorts historical details, the two tetralogies trace a real historical shift in English life, from a political order based on religious beliefs and respect for holy things (*Richard II*) to a "Machiavellian" order of manipulation, spin, murder, and cunning plots (*Richard III*). Richard II is a skillful melodramatist who exploits his victim status to fight back against his enemies and to advance his own ends.[4] But his conception of kingship is rooted in theology and ritual and an understanding of sacred things.

> Not all the water in the rough rude sea
> Can wash the balm off from an anointed king.
> The breath of worldly men cannot depose
> The deputy elected by the Lord.
> For every man that Bolingbroke hath pressed
> To lift shrewd steel against our golden crown,
> God for his Richard hath in heavenly pay
> A glorious angel. Then, if angels fight,
> Weak men must fall; for heaven still guards the right
> (*Richard II*, 3.2.54–62).

Like King Saul, Richard believes he's protected because he is the "Lord's anointed."

Henry IV takes Richard's crown, and that raises a monumental political dilemma: What is the basis of Henry's authority? Henry isn't the only man with a genealogical claim to the throne; why should *he* rule, rather than one of his cousins? He can't do what Richard did; that is, he cannot appeal to the balm of anointing. If anointing is the basis for political authority, Henry would have to give his crown back to Richard.

---

3. Richard's defenders have their own "Richard III Society," complete with a website: http://www.r3.org.

4. Ben Wishaw brings this out brilliantly in his performance as Richard II in the Hollow Crown production of *Richard II*.

Henry's son, King Henry V, knows how tenuous his power is. In his famous meditation on ceremony before the battle of Agincourt, he asks what makes a king a king. He doesn't have an easy time answering.

> O, be sick, great greatness,
> And bid thy ceremony give thee cure!
> Think'st thou the fiery fever will go out
> With titles blown from adulation?
> Will it give place to flexure and low bending?
> Canst thou, when thou command'st the beggar's knee,
> Command the health of it? No, thou proud dream,
> That play'st so subtly with a king's repose.
> I am a king that find thee; and I know
> 'Tis not the balm, the scepter, and the ball,
> The sword, the mace, the crown imperial,
> The intertissued robe of gold and pearl,
> The farced title running 'fore the king,
> The throne he sits on, nor the tide of pomp
> That beats upon the high shore of this world—
> No, not all these, thrice-gorgeous ceremony,
> Not all these, laid in bed majestical,
> Can sleep so soundly as the wretched slave. (*Henry V*, 4.1.243–60)

Over time, Richard's belief in sacred oil is replaced by other conceptions of royal power. Just before his death, Henry IV gives his son advice about how to secure his power against ambitious nobles: Distract them by going off to war in France. In Henry IV's own words, "Busy giddy minds / With foreign quarrels" (*2 Henry IV* 4.5.213–14).[5] Since he can't awe his rivals with the balm of anointing, Henry V has to distract them. If you can't unite them behind you, Henry IV says, at least unite them against a common enemy. And the French are as convenient as any.

With Richard III, we reach a further stage in the degeneration of politics: The king becomes a Machiavellian. Machiavelli (1469–1627) was an Italian political thinker who advised princes how to gain and maintain political power in a world of secular politics, a political world without God or the sacred. According to Machiavelli, politics is an amoral grappling for mastery, and a prince must be vicious to get and retain power. A Machiavellian ruler manipulates his courtiers and his people to advance

---

5. Busying giddy minds is still a widely used political tactic. When a president's popularity is slipping at home, he stokes up patriotic spirit by bombing distant targets, usually in the Middle East.

his own political interests. The end—political power—justifies any means, including lies, betrayals, and murders.

We don't know if Shakespeare read Machiavelli, but the Italian thinker's work was in the air of Elizabethan England. In any case, Richard Gloucester, who becomes Richard III, is a self-conscious disciple of Machiavelli. Long before he becomes king, Richard starts plotting to seize the crown himself. He's playing the long game, and he confides his ambitions to the audience:

> And yet I know not how to get the crown,
> For many lives stand between me and home.
> And I—like one lost in a thorny wood,
> That rends the thorns and is rent with the thorns,
> Seeking a way and straying from the way,
> Not knowing how to find the open air,
> But toiling desperately to find it out—
> Torment myself to catch the English crown.
> And from that torment I will free myself,
> Or hew my way out with a bloody ax.
> Why, I can smile, and murder whiles I smile,
> And cry "Content!" to that which grieves my heart,
> And wet my cheeks with artificial tears,
> And frame my face to all occasions.
> I'll drown more sailors than the mermaid shall;
> I'll slay more gazers than the basilisk;
> I'll play the orator as well as Nestor,
> Deceive more slyly than Ulysses could,
> And, like a Sinon, take another Troy.
> I can add colors to the chameleon,
> Change shapes with Proteus for advantages,
> And set the murderous Machiavel to school.
> Can I do this, and cannot get a crown?
> Tut, were it farther off, I'll pluck it down (*3 Henry VI*, 3.2.172–95).

Richard thinks he can teach the "Machiavel" a thing or two, partly because he conceives himself as something more than a mere politician. He imagines he's one of the classical heroes—a Homeric Nestor or Ulysses who can take a city greater than Troy.[6] He can achieve his ambitions because of his flexibility. Richard is Proteus, the shape-shifting god of rivers; he's a chameleon who will change colors to suit his surroundings. Richard tells us how he's going to treat other characters, but his speech is

---

6. Leggatt, *Shakespeare's Political Drama*, 49.

also a caution to us who read or see the play. Richard seems to confide in us, but he cannot be trusted. We know he can't be trusted because he tells us so! He's apt to change colors when we're not paying attention.[7]

Next to Hamlet, Richard III is the largest role in Shakespeare. He has far more lines than anyone else in the play, and he controls much of the action like a stage manager. Dominant as he is, however, Richard is surrounded by a large number of other characters. It's difficult to keep track of them all, especially since several have the same name. Edward IV is the king, he has a son named Edward, and Edward is also the name of Henry VI's son. Queen Elizabeth has a daughter named Elizabeth. I have introduced many of these characters above, but it's worth pausing to get a handle on the *dramatis personae* of the play.

The characters may be grouped by family connection or by alliance. First, there is the royal family itself. At the beginning of the play, Edward IV is king, with Elizabeth his queen. They have two young sons, Edward and Richard. King Edward's two brothers, Richard Duke of Gloucester and George Duke of Clarence, are important members of the court. The king's mother, the widow of Richard Duke of York, known as the "Duchess of York," is still alive. Apart from Elizabeth herself, the most important member of her family is the Earl of Rivers.

Another group of characters comes from a previous generation of the royal family. They are Lancastrians living after the triumph of the house of York. Queen Margaret, the widow of Henry VI, is a ghostly reminder of the unfinished business of the past. Her daughter-in-law, Lady Anne, was married to Henry VI's son Edward and marries Richard of Gloucester early in the play. This group of characters includes the ghosts of Henry VI and Prince Edward who haunt Richard in Act 5.

Finally, there are characters linked by political alliance rather than blood. "Richmond," the future Henry VII, leads a company of noblemen. Among the nobles allied at one time or another with Richard of Gloucester are Hastings, Lord Stanley, the Earl of Derby (known as "Derby" in the play), Buckingham, and Norfolk. Richard also has a gang of henchmen at hand to do his dirty business. James Tyrrel is the most important of these.

I imagine some of you have skipped the last few pages. I understand. There are a lot of names and dates, and it's all very confusing. But you need to pay attention, because all this history climaxes in *Richard III*. To us, these wars and rumors of wars are ancient history. For the characters,

---

7. Garber, *Shakespeare After All*, 133.

they happened the day before yesterday, and for Shakespeare's audience they were in the recent past. Besides, in Shakespeare's world yesterday is never entirely dead. We need to know what happened because the characters of *Richard III* are thoroughly, sometimes literally, haunted by the past.

Review Questions

1. What is a tetralogy? How many tetralogies did Shakespeare write about English history? What plays are included?
2. Summarize the history dramatized in Shakespeare's English history plays.
3. How does *Richard III* fit into this history?
4. How is Shakespeare's Richard III different from the historical Richard III? Why did Shakespeare make the changes he did?
5. What is Richard II's "sacred" understanding of kingship?
6. Why can't Henry IV and Henry V continue Richard II's earlier politics? What do they put in its place?
7. Describe Richard III's "Machiavellian" politics.
8. What are the different groups of characters in *Richard III*?

Thought Questions

1. Construct a family tree of English kings between Edward III and Richard III.
2. Write a short paper on the deaths of the two princes in the Tower. What do you think happened?
3. Read a portion of Thomas More's *History of King Richard the Third* (available online). How is it similar to Shakespeare's play?
4. Read a summary of the theory of the "king's two bodies." What does that theory teach about political power? How is the theory related to the beliefs of Richard II?

5. Think about political life today. Does it still have religious or sacred elements? How?
6. Write a short paper on Machiavelli. What were his most important books? What were his key political principles?

Smiling Villain, Act 1

Richard III enacts Richard Gloucester's relentless pursuit of the English crown. As we saw above, he's been plotting to seize the crown for some time, but a lot of people, most of them relatives, stand in his way. This play describes how, one by one, sometimes in clusters, Richard eliminates his rivals.

He's plotting as soon as the play begins, and before the end of the first Act, Richard has eliminated one rival and is ready to strike at others as soon as Edward IV is out of the way. The structure of the opening scene graphically displays the centrality of Richard's plots:

> A. Richard's monologue, 1.1.1–41
>   B. Dialogue with his brother Clarence, 1.1.42–83
>   C. Conversation with Brakenbury and Clarence, 1.1.84–116
>   B'. Dialogue with Hastings, 1.1.117–44
> A'. Richard's monologue, 1.1.145–62

Richard opens with a soliloquy describing what he's planning, and scene 1 ends with another soliloquy, where he unveils another plot. Richard's plans enclose and control everything that happens on stage.

It's unusual for Shakespeare to put his title character on stage in the opening scene. Other thanes talk about Macbeth before he appears, and Gloucester and Kent discuss King Lear before his entrance. *Hamlet* opens with frightened guards on the battlements of the castle of Elsinore. Richard III, however, is on stage in the opening scene and has the stage to himself. That allows him to introduce himself before any other characters assess him.

We may think we know Richard better than we know other characters. After all, he's being so open. But we should be cautious. We may not like to admit it, but other people often know us better than we do. Besides, even though he's speaking only to us, the theater audience, Richard never stops planning and plotting; he never stops using rhetoric to persuade his audience. He tries to win us over with his honesty about his villainy.

From this opening speech, we expect Richard to be a bad guy who is very good at being bad and very good at pretending to be good. He wants to make us enjoy watching him being bad, and he succeeds. But he's not straight with the audience, any more than he is with other characters.

Richard's soliloquy describes the change in England's political mood as a change of seasons:[8]

> Now is the winter of our discontent
> Made glorious summer by this sun of York;
> And all the clouds that lowered upon our house
> In the deep bosom of the ocean buried.
> Now are our brows bound with victorious wreaths,
> Our bruised arms hung up for monuments,
> Our stern alarums changed to merry meetings,
> Our dreadful marches to delightful measures.
> Grim-visaged war hath smoothed his wrinkled front,
> And now, instead of mounting barded steeds
> To fright the souls of fearful adversaries,
> He capers nimbly in a lady's chamber
> To the lascivious pleasing of a lute (1.1.1–13).

War has given way to peace. The military trumpet has been replaced by the lute, men have stabled their horses, and war himself "capers nimbly in a lady's chamber." There's a time for war, and there's a time for love. Like Claudius's speech at the beginning of *Hamlet*, Richard's monologue expresses the feeling of relieved endurance, the proud sense of being "bruised but unbowed" that comes at the end of a long, successful battle.

The first line is one of the most memorable, best-known lines in the play. Richard contrasts the wartime "winter of our discontent" with the "glorious summer" of Edward's victory and reign. But the first line feels as if it stands alone, and we wonder whether England still shivers in midwinter; we wonder whether some, Richard especially, think *now* is the time of "discontent."

We don't have to wonder long. Richard tells us he doesn't plan to give up war, even in peacetime:

---

8. In the 1995 film version staring Ian McKellen, Richard delivers the first part of the speech at a party celebrating King Edward's victory over Henry VI. The first ten lines or so fit such a setting, but before the speech ends, Richard is unveiling his plots. That must be taken as a soliloquy. McKellen speaks the latter part of the speech standing at a urinal and then looking at himself in a mirror.

> But I, that am not shaped for sportive tricks,
> Nor made to court an amorous looking glass,
> I, that am rudely stamped, and want love's majesty
> To strut before a wanton ambling nymph,
> I, that am curtailed of this fair proportion,
> Cheated of feature by dissembling Nature,
> Deformed, unfinished, sent before my time
> Into this breathing world, scarce half made up,
> And that so lamely and unfashionable
> That dogs bark at me as I halt by them—
> Why, I, in this weak piping time of peace,
> Have no delight to pass away the time,
> Unless to spy my shadow in the sun
> And descant on mine own deformity.
> And therefore, since I cannot prove a lover,
> To entertain these fair well-spoken days,
> I am determined to prove a villain
> And hate the idle pleasures of these days. (1.1.14–31)

Shakespeare's Richard is a twisted hunchback with a withered arm and bad teeth, the product of a premature birth that sent him "unfinished" into the world, "scarce half made up." His appearance is so appalling that "dogs bark at me as I halt by them." He's a victim from birth, "cheated . . . by dissembling Nature." Since he's "not shaped for sportive tricks" or made to be a lover or a lute-player, his only option is to revel in his deformity. Since he cannot be a lover, he'll be a villain. If he cannot fight on the battlefield, he'll hide land mines around Edward's court and wait for the explosions.

What motivates Richard? Sigmund Freud, the founder of psychoanalysis, thought Richard was making up for childhood pain: "Richard is an enormous magnification of something we find in ourselves as well. We all think we have reason to reproach Nature and our destiny for congenital and infantile disadvantages; we all demand reparation for early wounds."[9] Freud takes Richard too much at face value. Richard *claims* to be taking revenge for the abuse he received from Nature, but he's really using his "congenital disadvantages" for his own advantage. He doesn't really pity himself; rather, "self-pity is only a tool, a guise, and a ploy."[10] He's a professional victim, using his deformities to worm his way to power.

---

9. Freud, "Some Character-Types," 155.
10. Garber, *Shakespeare After All*, 138.

But there's a deeper level to his villainy: Richard is an *artist* of evil, motivated by his sheer delight in seeing a job well—that is, evilly—done. He no longer does evil for some other purpose. He isn't like a miser who hoards money so he can buy more things. He's like a miser who hoards for hoarding's sake. Modern artists believe in "art for art's sake." Richard is a Rembrandt, a Mozart, a Michelangelo of crime. He believes in crime for crime's sake.[11]

He's already initiated one of his elegant peacetime plots, against his brother, Clarence:

> Plots have I laid, inductions dangerous,
> By drunken prophecies, libels, and dreams,
> To set my brother Clarence and the king
> In deadly hate the one against the other;
> And if King Edward be as true and just
> As I am subtle, false, and treacherous,
> This day should Clarence closely be mewed up,
> About a prophecy, which says that G
> Of Edward's heirs the murderer shall be. (1.1.32–40)

Clarence might become king if Edward dies. To preempt that possibility, Richard spreads rumors about Clarence's disloyalty to his brother the king.

In trapping Clarence, Richard exploits the king's and the court's gullibility about signs, portents, and prophecies. As Clarence says, the king "hearkens after prophecies and dreams" and listens to a "wizard" (1.1.54, 56). So Richard spreads a rumor that "G of Edward's heirs" plots to kill Edward. Clarence's first name is George, and suspicion falls on him. The prophecy is doubly ironic. As Richard of Gloucester, Richard should come under as much suspicion as "*George*." More importantly, this is the first of many prophecies in the play. At this point, Richard is certain he can manipulate prophecies and manage curses without becoming cursed himself. Over the course of the play, it becomes clear that the Machiavel doesn't have as much control as he thinks. Prophecies and curses will come back to haunt him.

Richard is a chameleon, an enemy one moment and a close confidant the next. He touches off rumors to defeat his rivals, and then he cozies up to them as if he were an ally and defender. Even though he starts the rumor about Clarence, he pretends to reassure Clarence. If the

---

11. Moulton, "From *Shakespeare as a Dramatic Artist*," 163–68.

problem is Clarence's name, Richard says, the King can change his name. Perhaps Edward is sending Clarence to "be new-christened in the Tower" (1.1.50), to be baptized with a name that doesn't start with "G." Before he takes leave of Clarence, Richard promises to put in a word with the king (1.1.114–15). We know his true colors: "Simple plain Clarence, I do love thee so / That I will shortly send thy soul to heaven" (1.1.118–19). He will put in a word with the king, but it will be a poisonous one.

The plot against Clarence has another layer. Richard blames Edward's queen, Elizabeth, and her family for Clarence's trouble. England suffers because, since war ended, "men are ruled by women" (1.1.62). Plotting against the Woodvilles is a side-plot to his plot against Clarence: "I do the wrong, and first begin to brawl. / The secret mischiefs that I set abroach / I lay unto the grievous charge of others" (1.3.324–26). Richard is like a football receiver who bumps into a safety but makes it look as if he's been fouled.[12]

If Richard's plots are successful, he'll damage several rivals at once. As Hastings reports, King Edward is already "sickly, weak, and melancholy" (1.1.136). God, Richard thinks, will take care of him (1.1.151). With Clarence and Edward out of the way, Richard will have a more spacious world "to bustle in" (1.1.152). If he can weaken the Woodvilles in the process, they'll be unable to resist him once he becomes king. Artist that he is, Richard likes the elegant efficiency of plunking several birds with one stone.

At the end of the first scene, Richard is again on stage *solus*, describing his plan to woo Anne, widow of Edward the Prince, whom Richard himself killed (1.1.153–60). Richard has practical political reasons to marry Anne. She will link him, a Yorkist, to Henry VI's Lancastrian line. But he also seems to relish the challenge of trying to overcome her hatred.

Like scene 1, scene 2 begins with a soliloquy, this one from Lady Anne, who weeps into the wounds of her father-in-law's corpse and curses his murderer, Richard.

> Lo, in these windows that let forth thy life
> I pour the helpless balm of my poor eyes.
> O, cursed be the hand that made these holes.
> Cursed the heart that had the heart to do it.
> Cursed the blood that let this blood from hence.
> More direful hap betide that hated wretch

---

12. NBA fans will recognize the tactic. Richard is the James Harden of medieval British politics.

> That makes us wretched by the death of thee
> Than I can wish to wolves—to spiders, toads,
> Or any creeping venomed thing that lives.
> If ever he have child, abortive be it,
> Prodigious, and untimely brought to light,
> Whose ugly and unnatural aspect
> May fright the hopeful mother at the view,
> And that be heir to his unhappiness.
> If ever he have wife, let her he made
> More miserable by the death of him
> Than I am made by my young lord and thee. (1.2.12–28)

Richard complains to Clarence about women ruling England. His words are truer than he realizes. Though militarily and often politically powerless, the women of *Richard III* have contact with supernatural powers that will prove stronger than anything Richard can muster.

The wooing scene is bizarre in every way. Richard approaches Anne while she's with Henry VI's dead body. She greets him as a "foul devil" (1.2.50), whose evil power makes Henry's wounds bleed afresh (1.2.55–56). Richard is a poisonous toad (1.2.147–48) and a hedgehog (1.2.102). Richard denies killing Anne's husband Edward (1.2.91), then admits it (1.2.181). Yet, by the end of the scene, she leaves him in hope and bids him farewell (1.2.223–24). How does he change her mind?

The scene isn't entirely convincing, no matter how well played. But we should take a moment to consider Anne's position. She is daughter of Warwick, a defeated plotter. She was married to Edward, prince of a deflated house. Her father-in-law, King Henry VI, is dead. No one is left to protect her, and, as a Lancastrian princess, she might easily come under suspicion. Distasteful as she finds Richard, his offer of marriage gives her security within the house of the victor. She doesn't fall in love with Richard over the course of the scene, but it's natural for her to conclude Richard's offer is the best she can hope for in a terrible situation.

We can also track Richard's tactics. His inconsistent answers unsettle and destabilize a woman who is already beside herself with grief. When he denies he killed Edward, a glimmer of doubt flashes through Anne's mind, and Richard takes advantage of the opening. He asks Anne if the one who caused Edward's death is as blameworthy as the executioner (1.2.114–19). We expect him to blame King Edward, who was Richard's commander when he killed the prince (cf. 1.2.92). Instead he points the finger at Anne as the "causer": "Your beauty was the cause of that effect— /

Your beauty, that did haunt me in my sleep / To undertake the death of all the world, / So I might live one hour in your sweet bosom" (1.2.121–24). Would a real woman believe this blatantly insincere flattery? Probably not, and Anne isn't immediately moved either. She threatens to tear her beauty to shreds with her fingernails (1.2.125–26). Still, Richard's flattery seems to change the atmosphere of the scene. She softens.

Richard makes a show of remorse. He's not a man of tears. He didn't cry when he received news of his own father's death, but when he sees Anne's sorrow and rage at the murder, when he stands in the glow of her beauty, "My manly eyes did scorn an humble tear" (1.2.164). He offers Anne a knife so she can carry out her vengeance directly. When she refuses, Richard offers to kill himself at her command. She refuses to order his death: "Though I wish thy death, / I will not be thy executioner" (1.2.184–85). Anne no longer sees a devil, a hedgehog, or a toad, but a man wracked with guilt. "Shall I live in hope?" Richard asks, meaning both hope for forgiveness and hope for Anne's love. "All men, I hope, live so" is Anne's ambiguous reply. She makes no promises, but he has won her pity. His promise to "wet [Edward's] grave with my repentant tears" brings her joy (1.2.215, 219–20). Richard proves to be good even at a role that he claims he is ill-suited to play—the role of lover (see 1.1.28).

The wooing scene exemplifies Richard's joy in the artistry of evil. Why else would he approach Anne so soon after her husband's and father-in-law's deaths? The best answer comes at the end of the scene, when Richard steps back to admire his handiwork:

> Was ever woman in this humor wooed?
> Was ever woman in this humor won?
> I'll have her, but I will not keep her long.
> What, I, that killed her husband and his father,
> To take her in her heart's extremest hate,
> With curses in her mouth, tears in her eyes,
> The bleeding witness of her hatred by,
> Having God, her conscience, and these bars against me,
> And I no friends to back my suit withal
> But the plain devil and dissembling looks?
> And yet to win her, all the world to nothing!
> Ha! (1.2.227–38)

No villain has been brash enough to attempt such a thing before: That's enough for Richard to give it a go.

The wooing scene illustrates another key element of Richard's character, his ability to impose his will through the force of fascination. Richard's villainy captivates because it seems all-powerful. He can twist the smallest occurrence to his advantage. Obstacles get swallowed up into his plots. Instead of exhausting him, each new plot opens up new opportunities and unleashes new energies. He's utterly unfazed by the immorality of his actions. Most of us hesitate to do evil, but Richard storms ahead without a second thought. Richard's evil seems boundless. Nothing stops him, and his villainy comes to seem irresistible to everyone around him.[13]

Yet, high above his cunning plots is a deeper cunning and a larger plot, the cunning plot of divine vengeance. Richard is destined for destruction. There is a power in the world that Richard cannot stage manage. That power is represented by the women characters, who function like a chorus in a Greek tragedy, commenting on the action and predicting the future. Sometimes they are like the Fates, mythological characters who spin, weave, and cut the life-thread of mortals.

The most dramatic revelation of God's justice and vengeance comes from Queen Margaret, the widow of Henry VI, who pronounces curses against Queen Elizabeth and Richard (1.3.191–24) that lay out the progress of the whole play. As a representative of the older, departing generation, Margaret's role is similar to that of the ghost of King Hamlet, a reminder of past crimes that will be punished. Margaret is a prophetess, as a number of the characters recognize (3.3.14–18; 5.1.25–27), and her premonitions are buttressed by omens, dreams, and portents.[14]

As Marjorie Garber points out, "The cadences of Margaret's language deliberately recall the biblical rhythms of *lex talionis*, the law of retaliation," which demands an "eye for an eye, and a tooth for a tooth." When Margaret says, "Edward thy son, that now is Prince of Wales, / For Edward our son, that was Prince of Wales" (1.3.199–200), she "emphasizes the degree of similarity and repetition involved in this conflict between Lancaster and York" (cf. 4.4.40–41, 44–45).[15] Richard may attempt to escape the consequences of his actions, may attempt to cover his tracks with yet another murder or yet another plot. But something

---

13. Moulton, "From *Shakespeare as a Dramatic Artist*," 167–69.

14. Other characters see the future too. Clarence dreams of drowning after Richard knocks him from a ship. Stanley dreams that a boar—Richard's sign—will attack. Often, omens are ignored, with predictable consequences.

15. Garber, *Shakespeare After All*, 148–49.

beyond Richard's power controls the course of events. Call it Fortune. Call it Justice. Call it God. It's the "more" Richard fails to reckon with.

The threat of divine justice comes to the fore again in Act 1, scene 4, when two murderers, commissioned by Richard, kill Clarence in the Tower. Clarence dreams of being drowned by his brother Richard (1.4.9–33) and is haunted by the ghosts of those he betrayed and killed (1.4.43–63). He fears that God will "be avenged on my misdeeds" (1.4.70).

Clarence isn't the only character in the scene to tremble at God's vengeance. Even before they get to Clarence, Richard's hit men have reservations about the plan. They decide not to stab him in his sleep, lest he wake on Judgment Day and accuse them of cowardice (1.4.101–6). The phrase "Judgment Day" breeds "a kind of remorse" in the Second Murderer. It's one thing to kill a man. It's another thing "to be damned for killing him" (1.4.108, 111). When his companion reminds him that he's being well paid for the job, his conscience disappears into "the Duke of Gloucester's purse" (1.4.128–29). Consciences can be bought.

Their consciences are awakened again as soon as Clarence starts talking to them. Richard warned them about his brother's gift of speech: He "may move your hearts to pity if you mark him" (1.3.349). Though they assure Richard they'll use their hands more than their tongues, they end up in a debate with Clarence. Clarence reminds them that "the great King of kings / Hath in the table of his law commanded / That thou shalt do no murder" (1.4.195–97), and warns them that God will avenge him. Clarence issues an altar call:

> Have you that holy feeling in your souls
> To counsel me to make my peace with God,
> And are you yet to your own souls so blind
> That you will war with God by murd'ring me? . . .
> Relent, and save your souls (1.4.250–56).

To fight off the pity they feel, they stab Clarence and dump him into a vat of wine. Immediately, the Second Murderer feels guilty: "A bloody deed, and desperately dispatched. / How fain, like Pilate, would I wash my hands / Of this most grievous murder" (1.4.271–73). He should have paid closer attention in Sunday school. Pilate's efforts were futile. The blood has stuck to Pilate for millennia, and the blood of Clarence will be a witness against Richard and his thugs. Not all the water in the green sea can wash off the stain.

Review Questions

1. Describe the structure of Act 1, scene 1.
2. What is Richard's opening soliloquy about? What has happened in England? How does Richard plan to exploit the situation?
3. Who is Clarence? What has Richard done to him?
4. How much does Richard actually reveal to the audience?
5. What kind of man is Richard? Why does Richard do what he does?
6. Who is Anne? What is her relationship to Richard? How does he persuade her to marry him?
7. How does Richard function as a "stage manager"? Is he successful at it?
8. Who is Margaret? What does she say to the other characters?
9. What happens to the two murderers sent to kill Clarence?

Thought Questions

1. Queen Margaret calls Richard a "bottled spider" (1.3.242). How does that fit with other animal imagery in the play? How is Richard like a spider? How like a *bottled* spider?
2. Margaret lurks in the shadows before pronouncing her curses in scene 3. Why? How does her position on the stage fit with her thematic role in the play?
3. What does Richard think of his allies—Derby, Hastings, Buckingham (1.3.328–31)?
4. Summarize the discussion of conscience between the two murderers in 1.4.126–45.

Disorder, Acts 2–3

The problem with gaining power through murder is: Once you kill, you can't stop. Macbeth wants the world to end as soon as he murders King Duncan, but the world doesn't cooperate. Eventually, Macbeth realizes he's waded into a river of blood so far it's easier to keep going than to turn back. Richard kills more cunningly, by indirection and secretive instructions rather than by his own hand. But his life follows the same logic as Macbeth's. Clarence is dead. Edward is dying. But if the king dies, one of his sons becomes king after him, and Queen Elizabeth will also stand in Richard's way. There's *always* another obstacle, another rival, another victim, always somebody else who needs to be killed. Richard has to keep tearing through the thorns, until they shred Richard to tatters.

Act 2 begins in hope. Edward knows he's dying and wants to leave behind a peaceful, harmonious England. He's aware of the tensions in his court—between Elizabeth and other nobles, between the nobles who fought on opposite sides of the civil war. He gathers everyone to form a "united league" (2.1.2). It works. Everyone is reconciled. Hastings swears perfect love for Rivers, and Rivers declares he loves Hastings "with my heart" (2.1.17). Elizabeth promises to forget "our former hatred" (2.1.24), while Buckingham promises to cherish Elizabeth and her children, on pain of divine punishment.

When Richard makes his appearance, he greets everyone with shows of affection: "I do not know that Englishman alive / With whom my soul is any jot at odds / More than the infant that is born tonight," adding, to the audience, "I thank God for my humility" (2.1.70–73). We know he's entered this love feast only to disrupt it. When Elizabeth tries to crown the day of reconciliation by asking Edward to receive Clarence back into his good graces (2.1.74–77), Richard drops the bomb: "Who knows not that the gentle duke is dead?" (2.1.80). Of course, *no one* knows Clarence is dead, and the news breaks up the group and sends Edward into a tailspin of shocked remorse. He chides the nobles for not reminding him of Clarence's long and faithful service, ending with: "O God, I fear thy justice will take hold / On me and you, and mine and yours, for this" (2.1.132–33). The sins of the past are being visited on the present.

Richard is always ready to capitalize on a disaster. Never waste a crisis. He's created chaos at the court, perhaps sending Edward to the grave. But he covers his bases. When everyone else has left the stage, he confides in Buckingham: "Marked you not / How that the guilty kindred of the queen / Looked pale when they did hear of Clarence' death?" (2.1.135–37). Of course they look pale; the king's brother is dead. But Richard wants Buckingham to suspect the Woodvilles are behind Clarence's murder. One stone—the news of Clarence's death—kills two birds, Edward and Elizabeth.

For the next few Acts, Buckingham will be at Richard's side as a principal co-conspirator. Richard begins the play *solus*, and throughout the opening scenes he confides only in us, the audience. Yet somehow, sometime, while he is out of view offstage, he forms alliances. We who read or view the play should be suspicious. He pretends to confide *in us*, pretends to be completely open and frank. Meanwhile, he whispers in the shadows behind *our* backs! We only *think* we're confidants.[16] But the same is true of his co-conspirators. They never know his plans, and some suspect he's plotting against them as he plotted against Clarence, the king and queen, and everyone else.

The main character of *Richard III* is a man. He's been a soldier, and a highly successful one. He knows how to get his way in the rough world of politics. He's a public man, who knows how to sway a crowd with a speech, how to manipulate rumors to his own advantage, how to create and exploit public images. Early in the play, though, he complains to Clarence that England is ruled by women. Richard isn't literally correct, but, as we've noted, women do play a prominent role in the play. They have little public power. They never speak to crowds. But their private prayers, curses, and prophecies have more to do with the outcome of the play than Richard's scheming.

Children are important to the play as well. In Act 2, scene 2, the Duchess of York, the mother of King Edward, Richard, and Clarence, speaks with her grandchildren, Clarence's son and daughter. They know their father is dead, but their grandmother refuses to confirm. Richard's lies have reached into the family circle. Clarence's son tells the Duchess, "my good uncle Gloucester / Told me the king, provoked to it by the queen, / Devised impeachments to imprison him" (2.2.20–22). The boy is a prodigy in English law. But the point is that Richard manipulates children to set up a pattern of alliances and hostilities that suits him.

In the midst of the scene, Queen Elizabeth announces her husband, the king, is dead. The Duchess of York immediately recognizes how vulnerable she and England are. Her sons, Edward and Clarence, were her "two crutches." Since they have been taken, Richard will be in charge of Edward's sons, making him the most powerful man in England. Richard's mother knows her son is monstrous, and she weeps for the world. In the repetitive, ritualized laments that follow, we hear an echo of Margaret's eye-for-eye curse:

---

16. Leggatt, *Political Drama*, 37.

> Alas, I am the mother of these griefs;
> Their woes are parceled, mine is general.
> She for an Edward weeps, and so do I;
> I for a Clarence weep, so doth not she;
> These babes for a Clarence weep, and so do I;
> I for an Edward weep, so do not they (2.2.80–85).

She thinks of herself as "mother" of these griefs because she bears them all. She is mother of these griefs also because she's mother of the causer of griefs, her fiendish son Richard.

In Shakespeare, the reign of a villain upsets natural and social order. Three citizens discuss the political situation after Edward's death. "Woe to that land that's governed by a child," says one, echoing Isaiah (2.3.11; cf. Isa 3:4, 12). England has been in this situation before, during the minority of Henry VI. At that time, though, the land "was famously enriched / With politic grave counsel" (2.3.19–20). Now Richard of Gloucester cares for the princes, and the citizens recognize he poses a danger to the royal family and the land. One citizen links the political confusion with the confusion of the natural world:

> When clouds are seen, wise men put on their cloaks;
> When great leaves fall, then winter is at hand;
> When the sun sets, who doth not look for night?
> Untimely storms makes men expect a dearth (2.3.32–35).

The "winter of our discontent" *hasn't* given way to glorious summer. The commoners see signs of rain, winter, darkness, and "untimely storms" that are portents of famine. Everyone distrusts "days of change," just as one expects a "boist'rous storm" when the water swells (2.3.44). "All will be well," one philosophic citizen assures his friends (2.3.31). The Third Citizen hopes he's right, but qualifies it: "All may be well, but if God sort it so, / 'Tis more than we deserve or I expect" (2.3.36–37).

King Edward is dead. Long live King Edward! Edward needs a successor, and Richard leads the noblemen who plan the coronation of the elder of Edward's sons, who will be crowned Edward V. Richard's ally Buckingham suggests "some little train" meet Edward and escort him to London. He reasons that a large entourage will open up "the new-healed wound of malice" and spark another civil war (2.2.124–26). The real reason is to leave the prince vulnerable to diversion or arrest.

Before Richard follows through on his plan to remove Edward's sons, he closes the noose on Elizabeth's family. Richard has planted rumors and accusations throughout the nobility, accusing the Woodvilles of treachery against Clarence and of turning King Edward against his own family. While the Duchess of York and Queen Elizabeth wait for the Prince's ascent to the throne, they receive word that Elizabeth's relatives have been arrested (2.4.42–43). Elizabeth sees the handwriting on the wall and quickly escapes with her son, the young Duke of York, to find sanctuary, church protection from arrest. "I see the ruin of my house," she cries. The tigerish Richard is attacking the "gentle hind": "Welcome destruction, blood, and massacre. / I see as in a map the end of all" (2.4.53–54). Act 1 ended with the death of Clarence. Act 2 also ends in the nearly certain death of Elizabeth's family. Richard keeps wading into his river of blood.

Act 3 unspools two of Richard's plots. On the one hand, he plots to rid himself of his last rivals, the princely sons of Edward and Elizabeth. On the other hand, his plot against Elizabeth's family comes to its climax. Through this pincer movement, Richard closes in on the prize, the crown. At the same time, there's another, contrary movement: The closer Richard gets to his goal, the smaller his circle of advisors becomes. As his plots unfold successfully, fissures appear among his allies, and he begins to eliminate former friends.

When Prince Edward arrives in London, the young prince is wary of the small size of the welcome party: "I want more uncles here to welcome me" (3.1.6). Richard tells him his other uncles are false friends. Edward is too young and innocent, Richard says, to recognize the poison hearts behind the "sugared words" of his relatives. It is an ironic warning, because Richard is serving up sugar-coated poison by saying those very words. Edward already suspects Richard: "God keep me from false friends—but they were none" (3.1.16). But Edward is powerless. He has no real allies, no one to resist Richard.

Edward's one lifeline is his brother, the Duke of York, who has escaped to find sanctuary with his mother. Richard quickly cuts off that path of flight. Buckingham convinces Cardinal Bourchier to seize the boy from his mother (3.1.37–58). The right of sanctuary was one of the oldest and most protected privileges of the medieval world. No king or ruler was allowed to seize someone who had come under the church's protection. By violating this right, Richard and his allies prove themselves to be tyrants. They recognize no limits to their power. By this abuse of power, Richard is able to get both princes to London and houses them in the Tower until the coronation.

Like their Uncle Clarence, the two princes are eventually murdered in the Tower, but Richard needs a pretext for taking the throne. He works out a two-pronged strategy. On the one hand, he sends Buckingham to spread the rumor that King Edward lived a life of "hateful luxury / And bestial appetite in change of lust, / Which stretched unto their servants, daughters, wives, / Even where his raging eye or savage heart, / Without control, lusted to make a prey" (3.5.80–84). King Edward fathered the two princes by a French woman, not by his wife. Since the princes are illegitimate, they cannot inherit the crown. Buckingham disseminates the rumor, but it falls flat. When he calls on the people to cry out, "God save Richard, England's royal king!" no one answers. He plants a few people in the crowd to answer, and uses their shouts to celebrate the "general applause and cheerful shout" that proved their "love to Richard" (3.7.1–41). It just enough of a response to pretend Richard has popular support.

Richard's favorite pose is that of a simple, straightforward, honest, childishly innocent man, too soft to handle the challenges of politics (1.3.142). He uses his rhetoric to pretend he's not using rhetoric. He disguises himself as a man incapable of wearing disguises. Marjorie Garber recognizes the biblical themes in the background:

> When Buckingham urges him to go after the young Princes and separate them from the Queen's relations, Richard replies, "I, as a child/ Will go by thy direction." His is a malign parody of the biblical injunction "and a little child shall lead them" (Isaiah 11:6), as well as of the instruction of Jesus: "Suffer the little children to come unto me, and forbid them not: for of such is the kingdom of God." But Richard is not Christ but Antichrist.[17]

Richard *pretends* to be an innocent child. He *is* a Herod, a child-killer.

Richard creates a public image of Edward as a lecher who fathered bastards. The other prong of Richard's strategy is to present a contrasting public image of himself. Buckingham gathers citizens to meet with Richard, but Richard refuses to greet them, on the excuse that he's too busy praying. Buckingham hammers home the contrast:

> Ah ha, my lord, this prince is not an Edward.
> He is not lolling on a lewd love bed,
> But on his knees at meditation;
> Not dallying with a brace of courtesans,
> But meditating with two deep divines;

---

17. Garber, *Shakespeare After All*, 140.

> Not sleeping, to engross his idle body,
> But praying, to enrich his watchful soul. (3.7.71–77)

England, Buckingham concludes, needs such a virtuous prince.

When Richard emerges from his "prayers," he stands before the people holding a prayer book, flanked by two priests. Buckingham tells Richard the people want him to become king, but Richard refuses: "Your love deserves my thanks, but my desert / Unmeritable shuns your high request" (3.7.154–55). Even if the path to the throne were open, his "poverty of spirit" would stand in the way. He professes to be "unfit for state and majesty" (3.7.205). His show of humility only confirms Buckingham's earlier characterization: He is just the virtuous king England needs. Buckingham turns away: "Zounds, I'll entreat no more" (3.7.219). But Richard calls him back: "I am not made of stones, / But penetrable to your kind entreaties, / Albeit against my conscience and my soul" (3.7.224–26). It's a well-honed play. By appearing to be piously humble, Richard finally achieves his ambition: He becomes king of England.

Richard has manipulated things to perfection. He has tarnished the reputations of his brothers and nephews, so they're disqualified from kingship. He has put on a show of humility and piety, and so won over the citizens. He has stage-managed everything. The question is, can he keep it up? Or is there something more at work in this world than plots, lies, and rumors? Is the Machiavel right that politics is about nothing more than power?

As we've noticed, there are signs Richard can't succeed in the long run. While he plots against the princes, Richard advances another plot, against Hastings, his one-time ally. Buckingham and Catesby have become Richard's closest co-conspirators, and he sends them to discover whether or not Hastings will support Richard's bid to be king. Catesby laments the state of the "reeling world," and adds: "I believe [it] will never stand upright / Till Richard wear the garland of the realm" (3.2.38–40). Hastings forcefully dismisses the idea: "I'll have this crown of mine cut from my shoulders / Before I'll see the crown so foul misplaced" (3.2.43–44). Later, at a conference to plan the coronation ceremony, Richard charges Elizabeth with sorcery. She turned his arm into "a blasted sapling, withered up" (3.4.67–72). When Hastings reasonably responds with "If they have done this deed," Richard interrupts: "If? . . . / Talk'st thou to me of ifs?" (3.4.74–75). He accuses Hastings of protecting the "damned strumpet" Elizabeth, and threatens to execute Hastings for treason. Hastings's vow comes to ironic fulfillment: As Richard makes his way to the throne, his crown (head) is removed from his shoulders (3.5.22–23).

Richard plunges on, but his tragic dilemma arises in a different form. Once he eliminates his enemies, he begins to distrust his friends. For a fiend, *everyone* is a rival, and Richard won't feel entirely secure until everyone is dead. And when everyone is dead, what's the point of being king?

Review Questions

1. What is King Edward trying to accomplish in the first scene of Act 2? How does Richard undo Edward's efforts?
2. Who is Lord Buckingham? What is his relationship to Richard?
3. Explain the role of women and children in *Richard III*.
4. How are the women's experiences similar?
5. Who are the Woodvilles? How does Richard eliminate them from the court?
6. How does Richard eliminate his nephews as rivals to the throne? What rumor does Richard spread about his brother King Edward and his nephews, the princes?
7. What does Richard do to Hastings? Why?
8. How does Richard manipulate his image to make himself look pious?

Thought Questions

1. The recent Hollow Crown production of *Richard III* leaves out Richard's claim that the princes are illegitimate. Why would the producers do that? What effect does that have on the play?
2. During the conference where he accuses Hastings of treason, Richard asks the Bishop of Ely to fetch some of his famous strawberries (3.4.31–33). Why?
3. What does Hastings say about Richard just before Richard accuses him of treason (3.4.51–53)? How is Hastings's statement ironic?

Summer, Acts 4–5

God's justice looms over *Richard III*, but that justice isn't a distant threat. Throughout the play, characters pay for past sins,[18] and most *recognize* they're paying for past sins. Clarence swears loyalty to the Lancastrians but betrays them to join the victorious Yorks. The Murderers remind him he's guilty of "false foreswearing and . . . murder too: / Thou didst receive the sacrament to fight / In quarrel of the house of Lancaster" (1.4.202–4). They chide him for warning them about "God's dreadful law" when he himself "broke it in such dear degree" (1.4.209–10). Richard's plot against Clarence is unjust, but Richard is an unwitting agent of divine justice.

King Edward dies in remorse for Clarence's death: "O God, I fear thy justice will take hold / On me and you, and mine and yours, for this" (2.2.132–33). Hastings is another victim of Richard's schemes, but like Clarence and the King he suffers for his own sins. He leads the anti-Woodville faction at court and takes pleasure in watching Queen Elizabeth's family disintegrate. The Woodvilles are responsible for Hastings's imprisonment (1.1.121–43), and he delights in sweet revenge: "I shall laugh at this a twelvemonth hence, / That they which brought me in my master's hate, / I live to look upon their tragedy" (3.2.57–59).

These are not disconnected, isolated instances of God's judgment; they form a chain of destruction that moves the turning wheel of justice. King Edward pronounces the death sentence on Clarence (though he tries to reverse it), and Elizabeth's family is the beneficiary. Once the king dies, the queen's family is exposed to their many enemies, without the king's protection. The queen's downfall is Hastings's highest moment, but the wheel of fate turns again and he is crushed beneath.

Were Richard paying close attention, he would be fearful for his own future. But he's too confident in his own powers to hesitate. Readers and viewers, however, recognize symptoms of a breakdown. At the beginning of the play, Richard is poetic and witty, but once he becomes king his jokes are tired and strained, and he becomes less poetic. His imagination has been focused too long on his plots and inductions, and it begins to shrivel. He thinks he plays the role of Vice (3.1.82–83). Morality plays in the Middle Ages often included an allegorical character known as "Vice," a semi-comic villain, often the devil's assistant, who takes delight in causing disorder just because he likes disorder. Richard has the

---

18. The following paragraphs are indebted to Moulton, "From *Shakespeare as a Dramatic Artist*," 174–84.

same childlike delight in chaos. But other characters understand Richard more accurately. They don't see Richard as the devil's assistant, but as the devil himself, a "fiend," a "devil," and a "hellhound."

Richard's plots become less and less effective. While Richard was stunningly successful in wooing Lady Anne, his later attempt to arrange a marriage to Princess Elizabeth, daughter of Edward IV, fails. Richard's plots stall. Shakespeare's tragic characters don't fall off a cliff. Richard is typical. His fall is stretched out over two Acts, and goes throughout distinct stages. Once it gets underway, it is inexorable.

One of the crucial turning points is Richard's decision to remove the last threat to his reign—the two princes in the Tower. Throughout the play, he has been able to get his allies to do his bidding without difficulty. He gives Buckingham and Catesby hints and winks, and they improvise. With this final plot, Richard cannot get Buckingham to see the point:

> KING RICHARD
> Ah, Buckingham, now do I play the touch,
> To try if thou be current gold indeed.
> Young Edward lives. Think now what I would speak.
> BUCKINGHAM
> Say on, my loving Lord.
> KING RICHARD
> Why, Buckingham, I say I would be king.
> BUCKINGHAM
> Why, so you are, my thrice-renowned liege.
> KING RICHARD
> Ha! Am I king? 'Tis so. But Edward lives.
> BUCKINGHAM
> True, noble prince.
> KING RICHARD
> O bitter consequence,
> That Edward still should live "true noble prince."
> Cousin, thou wast not won't to be so dull. (4.2.8–17)

Finally, Richard is forced to state his intentions directly: "I wish the bastards dead" (4.2.18).

Even when he receives a direct request, Buckingham doesn't immediately agree to carry out the king's pleasure. Buckingham has been Richard's closest confidant, willing to carry out Richard's plots. "Your grace may do your pleasure" (4.2.21), he tells Richard; in effect, "If you want it done, do it yourself." Then Buckingham asks to pause before answering. As Garber says, "The play is not proceeding as King Richard intends, and

Buckingham refuses to take direction."[19] When Buckingham returns, he doesn't want to talk about the princes in the Tower. He wants Richard to make good on his promise to give Buckingham an earldom as a reward for eliminating Hastings (cf. 3.1.193–96). Richard dismisses the request: "I am not in the giving vein today" (4.2.114). We aren't surprised to learn later that Buckingham, once Richard's closest ally, has fled to raise an army against Richard (4.2.117–20; 4.3.50).

Richard loses control of his noble allies, and he turns to a page boy for advice about where to find a murderer. The page points Richard to Sir James Tyrrel, who is only too happy to kill Richard's "two enemies" (4.2.28–41). Garber points out the double irony of this situation: "a child advises a king, and aids in the assassination of children."[20] Here is a king in decline, served only by page boys and thugs. Something larger has shifted too. Richard's other victims deserved to be punished for their sins. When Buckingham is captured and executed on All Souls' Day, he recognizes the divine symmetry, since he dies on the same day when he betrayed King Edward: "This, this All Souls' Day to my fearful soul / Is the determined respite of my wrongs. / That high All-Seer which I dallied with / Hath turned my feigned prayer on my head" (5.1.18–22). But the princes are innocent, and their murder is, as even the thuggish Tyrrel recognizes, a "tyrannous and bloody act" of "ruthless butchery" (4.3.1, 5). Tyrrel has no conscience, yet he recognizes it as "the most arch deed of piteous massacre / That ever yet this land was guilty of" (4.3.2–3). Even the henchmen he hires, Dighton and Forrest, "melted with tenderness and mild compassion" when they found the boys sleeping together in the Tower, a prayer book between them on the bed (4.3.4–14). Here is *truly* a king in decline: He's become such a thug that even his thugs recoil from his butchery.

Richard's conscience is pricked by the queens who confront him on the road to remind him of God's relentless vengeance. Initially, Margaret watches from hiding, while Elizabeth and the duchess lament the death of the princes. When Margaret steps forward, she declaims the symmetry of their experience of grief, echoing the earlier speech of the duchess:

> Tell over your woes again by viewing mine.
> I had an Edward, till a Richard killed him;
> I had a husband, till a Richard killed him:

---

19. Garber, *Shakespeare After All*, 146.
20. Garber, *Shakespeare After All*, 153.

> Thou hadst an Edward, till a Richard killed him;
> Thou hadst a Richard, till a Richard killed him.
> DUCHESS OF YORK
> I had a Richard too, and thou didst kill him;
> I had a Rutland too, thou holp'st to kill him.
> QUEEN MARGARET
> Thou hadst a Clarence too, and Richard killed him. (4.4.39–46)

Margaret places the blame firmly on Richard, the "hellhound" that came from the duchess's womb to worry England's lambs (4.4.48). Margaret is "hungry for revenge" (4.4.61) and sees it unfolding before her eyes. She tells the duchess:

> Thy Edward he is dead, that killed my Edward;
> Thy other Edward dead, to quit my Edward;
> Young York he is but boot, because both they
> Matched not the high perfection of my loss.
> Thy Clarence he is dead that stabbed my Edward,
> And the beholders of this frantic play,
> Th' adulterate Hastings, Rivers, Vaughan, Grey,
> Untimely smothered in their dusky graves. (4.4.63–70)

Richard worries as long as the princes live. The women are more frightened that Richard lives. One thing remains to tie up the loose ends. Richard, "hell's black intelligencer," is still king, but his end is "at hand, at hand." Earth is gaping, the fires of hell are heating up, while devils roar and saints pray "to have him suddenly conveyed from hence" (4.4.71–76).

Margaret exits, but Elizabeth and the duchess remain on stage when Richard appears with his entourage. They confront him with his sins: Where are Clarence, and Rivers, and Hastings? Richard is too busy to listen, but his mother denounces him anyway for everything from his "tetchy and wayward . . . infancy" to his "proud, subtle, sly, and bloody" adulthood (4.4.166–75). "Either thou wilt die by God's just ordinance," she concludes, "Or I with grief and extreme age shall perish / And never more behold thy face again." She sends her son into battle with her bitterest curse (4.4.185–90).

When night falls, ghosts haunt Richard's sleep. On the night before the decisive battle of Bosworth Field, his victims parade before him: Prince Edward, son of Henry VI; Henry VI; Clarence; members of the Woodville family; Hastings; the princes; his wife Anne; Buckingham. Each delivers a message both to Richard and to his rival, Henry Tudor (Richmond). To Richard, Hastings has a simple message:

> Bloody and guilty, guiltily awake
> And in a bloody battle end thy days.
> Think on Lord Hastings. Despair and die! (5.3.147–49)

Blood will have blood. Eye for eye, tooth for tooth, bloody life ends in bloody death. Each of Richard's victims also pronounces blessings to Richmond:

> Quiet, untroubled soul, awake, awake!
> Arm, fight, and conquer, for fair England's sake. (5.3.150–51)

Another telling sign of Richard's disorder is the collapse of language, the failure of Richard's rhetorical strategies. He becomes forgetful and confused. He storms at Catesby for not delivering a message, forgetting that he hasn't told Catesby what message to deliver. Events pick up speed, until even the agile Richard is unable to keep up with the surge of bad news (4.4.498–527). As he awakes from his nightmare, he babbles nonsensically:

> Give me another horse! Bind up my wounds!
> Have mercy, Jesu—Soft! I did but dream.
> O coward conscience, how dost thou afflict me.
> The lights burn blue. It is now dead midnight.
> Cold fearful drops stand on my trembling flesh.
> What do I fear? Myself? There's none else by.
> Richard loves Richard; that is, I and I.
> Is there a murderer here? No. Yes, I am.
> Then fly. What, from myself? Great reason why—
> Lest I revenge. What, myself upon myself?
> Alack, I love myself. Wherefore? for any good
> That I myself have done unto myself?
> O, no, alas, I rather hate myself
> For hateful deeds committed by myself.
> I am a villain. Yet I lie: I am not. (5.3.178–92)

This is a brilliant moment in the play. At one level, this is the jabbering of a man waking from a nightmare. Richard's language is slipping because his mind is chaotic, heading toward madness. But in Shakespeare madness is never without its method, and Richard's desperate speech is revealing. No murderer attacks him; no murderer is present—except Richard himself. There's no one to flee from—except Richard, but how can Richard flee Richard? Sunk into blood and villainy, lacking supporters, he's reduced to self-love: Richard loves Richard, a godlike isolation underscored by his repeated uses of the biblical name for God, "I am." His isolation has not brought unity or peace to his soul. It splits him in two, into the murderer he wants to escape and the fearful child cowering under the covers.

Early in the play, Richard manipulated prophecies and omens for his own purposes. His conscience was well-armed against any intrusion; he felt no guilt. But even Richard has to *sleep*, and during sleep his guard comes down and his unconscious guilt emerges, like Queen Margaret, from the shadows. Sleep can be refreshing. It "knits up the raveled sleave of care" and is "great nature's second course, / Chief nourisher in life's feast," as Macbeth puts it (2.2.40–43). But sleep is also a moment of weakness, and a devil like Richard cannot afford moments of weakness.

Richmond's entry into the play is one of the clearest signals that God is catching up with Richard. The duchess of York is the first to mention his name, when she urges Dorset to escape from Richard to find refuge with Richmond. When Stanley tells Richard that Dorset has fled to Richmond, Richard reminisces about Henry VI's prophecy that "Richmond should be king, / When Richmond was a little peevish boy" (4.2.93–95). Richard wonders why he didn't kill Richmond right then, to secure his future crown. He remembers a bard's prediction:

> Richmond! When last I was at Exeter,
> The mayor in courtesy showed me the castle,
> And called it Rouge-mount, at which name I started,
> Because a bard of Ireland told me once
> I should not live long after I saw Richmond. (4.2.101–5)

Richard has played the role of Nemesis to many in the play. He meets his own Nemesis in Richmond.

Shakespeare's tragedies rarely end on a note of pure tragedy. Most offer a glimmer of a better world rising from the carnage. In *Richard III*, Richmond is the harbinger of a new age. Richard begins the play announcing that the "winter of our discontent" has given way to "summer." But his own actions ensure the season of death continues. *Richmond*, not Edward or Richard, is the Sun King who brings glorious summer. At the beginning of Act 5, Richmond, the future Henry VII, appears in the play in person. He encourages his followers, who have suffered under Richard's murderous tyranny, with promises of new life:

> Fellows in arms, and my most loving friends,
> Bruised underneath the yoke of tyranny,

> Thus far into the bowels of the land
> Have we marched on without impediment;
> And here receive we from our father Stanley
> Lines of fair comfort and encouragement.
> The wretched, bloody, and usurping boar,
> That spoiled your summer fields and fruitful vines,
> Swills your warm blood like wash, and makes his trough
> In your emboweled bosoms—this foul swine
> Is now even in the centry of this isle,
> Near to the town of Leicester, as we learn.
> From Tamworth thither is but one day's march.
> In God's name cheerly on, courageous friends,
> To reap the harvest of perpetual peace
> By this one bloody trial of sharp war. (5.2.1–16)

Richmond actually fulfills the promise of renewal, order, prosperity, of "summer fields and fruitful vines" (5.2.8).

In the closing speech of the play, Richmond describes the resurrection of England after the horrible butchery of the Wars of the Roses:

> Inter their bodies as become their births.
> Proclaim a pardon to the soldiers fled
> That in submission will return to us,
> And then, as we have ta'en the sacrament,
> We will unite the White Rose and the Red.
> Smile heaven upon this fair conjunction,
> That long have frowned upon their enmity.
> What traitor hears me and says not amen?
> England hath long been mad and scarred herself;
> The brother blindly shed the brother's blood;
> The father rashly slaughtered his own son;
> The son, compelled, been butcher to the sire.
> All this divided York and Lancaster,
> Divided in their dire division,
> O, now let Richmond and Elizabeth,
> The true succeeders of each royal house,
> By God's fair ordinance conjoin together.
> And let their heirs—God, if thy will be so—
> Enrich the time to come with smooth-faced peace,
> With smiling plenty and fair prosperous days.
> Abate the edge of traitors, gracious Lord,
> That would reduce these bloody days again
> And make poor England weep in streams of blood.
> Let them not live to taste this land's increase

> That would with treason wound this fair land's peace.
> Now civil wounds are stopped, peace lives again:
> That she may long live here, God say amen. (5.5.15–41)

Again, Richmond speaks of prosperity and happiness, a union of the divided houses of York and Lancaster, smiling, fair, prosperous days. After the sacrificial division of England, she will be raised again and reunited. The arc of the play moves from winter to summer, from division to reunion, from butchery to resurrection. Richmond comes, according to Marjorie Garber, as "a Christian ruler who defeats . . . the energetic anarchy of Antichrist, the devil Richard."[21] Under Richard, the chaos of the king's soul stretches out to encompass the whole land; under Richmond, order is restored.

The assured, self-conscious villain of Act 1 has turned into a scared rabbit, frightened now of himself. At the beginning, he was in control, stage-managing plots and inductions dangerous for his own purposes. He has realized through the course of the play that he is not in control. He ends the play pathetically crying for help: "A horse! A horse! My kingdom for a horse!" (5.4.13). There is more in heaven and earth than any Machiavel dreams of in his political philosophy. There is a God in heaven distributing rewards and punishments, doing justice. Those who seek to trap with lies and plots will eventually find themselves held fast by those very traps.

Review Questions

1. How is Clarence's death retribution for his sins? King Edward's?
2. How does Richard change in the later Acts of the play?
3. What happens to Buckingham? Why?
4. Who is Richard's main opponent?
5. How does language break down in the last two Acts?
6. What are the women lamenting?
7. What does Richard dream about on the night before battle?
8. Who is Richmond? Summarize his speeches in Act 5.

---

21. Garber, *Shakespeare After All*, 159.

Thought Questions

1. Why does Stanley (Earl of Derby) refuse to join Richmond (4.4.456–97)?
2. How does Richmond describe Richard's reign (5.2.1–16)? Read Psalm 80 and discuss the parallels.
3. Before the battle, Richard tells his men "conscience is but a word that cowards use" and "Our strong arms be our conscience" (5.3.310, 312). Discuss these lines in relation to the conversation of the Murderers in 1.4. Discuss these lines in relation to Richard's dream earlier in Act 5.

3

Crawling Toward the Grave

King Lear

TODAY, *KING LEAR* IS widely considered Shakespeare's greatest tragedy and even his greatest play.[1] Earlier generations recoiled at its raw, dark violence, but modern critics and audiences see these features as strengths, signs of authenticity. Especially in the mid-twentieth century, *Lear* was seen as a precursor to bleak modern drama. It has been called a "tragedy of penance" that takes place in an "imbecile universe" in which there is no hint of "charity, resiliency, or harmony."[2] Another reader says it's "impossible to retain *any* concept of an ordered universe" since the play promotes "the reflection that any system of order results in very strange notions of justice."[3] Some find a more hopeful note in the final scenes, claiming that Lear dies happy, thinking that Cordelia is still alive. Others say the play begins and ends in a world without hope of resurrection.

---

1. Two texts of Lear exist. One was published in 1608 and is known as the "Quarto" edition; the other was included in the "First Folio" collection of Shakespeare's plays, published in 1623. There are considerable differences between the two plays, and most editions are based on the Folio text, with some additions from the Quarto. Some scholars think we should study the plays separately. Since they appear to represent two stages of Shakespeare's composition of the play, each tells the story in a particular way. I use the conflated text found in *The Complete Pelican Shakespeare*.
2. Stampfer, "Catharsis."
3. Brooke, *Shakespeare*.

Lear can't seem to escape its first scene. It begins with Lear divesting himself of all the accouterments of kingship, renouncing his daughter Cordelia because she can say "Nothing" to express her love for her father, and sending faithful Kent, who defends Cordelia, into exile. The play ends on the same note. Shortly before the final scenes, Lear impatiently drives Kent from his sight ("Prithee away") and weeps over his beloved Cordelia, who is again silent, this time in death. Significantly, Lear dies calling out for someone to help him unbutton his robe (5.3.307). The wheel turns. The tide moves in, the tide moves out. Vanity of vanities, all is vanity. Critics take Gloucester's comment as the play's theme: "As flies to wanton boys, are we to th' gods; / They kill us for their sport" (4.1.37–38).

Lear, it appears, ends without the comic upturn that is often found in Shakespearean tragedies. There's no Malcolm coming to put shattered Scotland back together, no Richmond to toss Richard III from his horse, no rescue of Rome as in *Coriolanus*, nor even a Fortinbras to restore rotten Denmark.

This ending is Shakespeare's invention. Holinshed's *Chronicle*, one of Shakespeare's main historical sources, records that Lear was restored to power, with Cordelia alive and fully in her father's good graces. Edmund Spenser gives a brief synopsis of the story in *The Fairie Queene*:

> Next him king Leyr in happie peace long raind,
> But had no issue male him to succeed,
> But three faire daughters, which were well vptraind,
> In all that seemed fit for kingly seed:
> Mongst whom his realme he equally decreed
> To have diuided. Tho when feeble age
> Nigh to his vtmost date he saw proceed,
> He cald his daughters; and with speeches sage
> Inquyrd, which of them most did loue her parentage.
>
> The eldest Gonorill gan to protest,
> That she much more then her owne life him lou'd:
> And Regan greater loue to him profest,
> Then all the world, when euer it were proou'd;
> But Cordeill said she lou'd him, as behoou'd:
> Whose simple answere, wanting colours faire
> To paint it forth, him to displeasance moou'd,
> That in his crowne he counted her no haire,
> But twixt the other twaine his kingdome whole did shaire.
> (2.10.27–28)

In Spenser's version, Cordelia gives the kingdom back to her father and reigns after him. Eventually, her sisters' children rebel and imprison Cordelia, "Till wearie of that wretched life, her selfe she hong" (2.10.32). In Shakespeare's play, Lear never returns to the throne. Cordelia is hung in prison, not by her own hand but on orders from Edmund.

Shakespeare also adds the subplot involving Gloucester and his sons, Edmund and Edgar. *King Lear* is structured by the similarities and differences between two families:

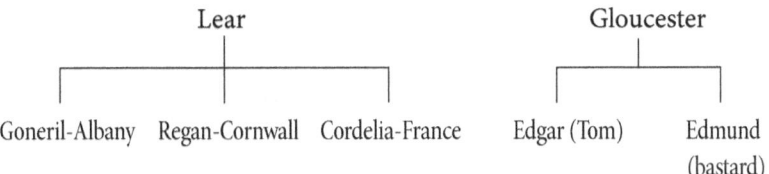

The bastard Edmund betrays his father as Goneril and Regan mistreat Lear. Edgar and Cordelia are both misunderstood and falsely accused, become outcasts, but finally reconcile with their fathers.

Again and again, the play raises hope only to frustrate it. Gloucester's son Edgar, disguised as "Poor Tom," a homeless and insane wanderer, no sooner finishes saying "things could not get worse" than he sees his father tottering across the heath with blood-stained bandages on his vacant eyes (4.1.1–12). Near the end, the Duke of Albany prays for Cordelia's safety; then, immediately, "Enter Lear with Cordelia in his arms," howling at the heavens (5.3.254–55). Albany inherits the kingdom, but he cedes it back to King Lear. Moments later, Lear dies. Every time we feel things might at last turn around, our hopes are sadistically dashed.

Lear's use of comic conventions has similar effects. There are comic elements in Shakespeare's other great tragedies. *Hamlet* lurches toward farce and has inspired zany offshoots like Tom Stoppard's *Rosencrantz and Guildenstern Are Dead*. Even austere *Macbeth* has its drunken porter. But no other tragedy has so much in common with comedy as *King Lear*.

Spatially, the movement of the play is reminiscent of comedy. As we will see, Shakespearean comedies are often stories of escape or exodus. Lovers are frustrated by city and home, whose rules inhibit the lovers' desires, its structures of authority are suffocating, its authority figures (notably fathers) are tyrants. The solution? Run to the woods, to a pre-political and pre-social Eden where the characters can shed their old skin and be renewed.

King Lear shares this structure with *A Midsummer Night's Dream, Cymbeline, The Tempest* and other comedies and romances. *Lear* begins in a disordered world, where child struggles against father and father against child, an apocalyptic world of blood, fire, and vapor of smoke. Lear and his small band of outcasts venture out into the heath, a natural setting that, in a comedy, would be a place of regeneration. Instead of a moonlit green world, they enter a stormy, nightmarish landscape. They go from apocalyptic frying pan into apocalyptic fire. Their return to nature doesn't appear to renew to the social and political world, for the play ends in disaster. We know from the comedies that Eden lies outside the walls of the human city. *Lear* shows that hell is outside as well.

Lear's Fool, moreover, plays the role fools normally do in Shakespearean comedy—to highlight the folly of the world by speaking wisdom disguised as humor. *Lear* has a prominent fool because its world is a "great stage of fools." Because Lear's world is bleak, though, the Fool's jests are too true to be funny. Jokes that are funny in the drawing room of Illyria (*Twelfth Night*) echo ominously in the empty world of *Lear*.

Following the conventions of Roman New Comedy and anticipating P. G. Wodehouse, Shakespeare's comedies frequently turn on mistaken identities. Two characters—a master and servant, let's say—exchange clothes and names, or a woman puts off her "woman's weeds" and dresses as a boy. Comedy traces the amusing confusion that ensues. *Lear* uses this device more than other tragedies. *Hamlet* is all about acting, with Hamlet acting out an antic disposition, Claudius acting as if Denmark is safe and he is a legitimate king, and the Players acting out the murder of Hamlet's father. *Lear*'s characters actually *adopt* alternative identities. Hamlet playing mad Hamlet is still Hamlet, but Kent becomes Caius and Edgar becomes Poor Tom and pretends to be a fisherman after his father "falls" from the cliffs of Dover.

Lear teases us with comic conventions and raises expectations of a comic resolution, only to pull out the props from under us. The play is a tragedy, but these comic elements give it the feel of black comedy. For a long time, Shakespeare's version of *King Lear* was too untidy and unsettling for theater audiences. In 1681, Nahum Tate rewrote the play, restoring Holinshed's original comic ending, a marriage between Cordelia and Edgar. Tate's version of the play dominated the stage until the early nineteenth century.

Tate didn't need to rewrite the play, since Shakespeare's version of the story fits the pattern of tragedy I discussed in chapter 1. On the surface, the play seems absurd, but it has a clear moral structure. In the world of *Lear*, offenses against order cause disorder; Lear's kingdom descends to chaos because of a primal sin. No passage in Shakespeare expresses this theme so fully as the speech of Ulysses in *Troilus and Cresida* 1.3. Ulysses describes the effects of Agamemnon's foolish leadership of the Greek warriors at Troy, and his analysis is so relevant to *King Lear* that it must be quoted at more than polite length:

> The specialty of rule hath been neglected;
> And look, how many Grecian tents do stand
> Hollow upon this plain, so many hollow factions.
> When that the general is not like the hive
> To whom the foragers shall all repair,
> What honey is expected? Degree being vizarded,
> Th' unworthiest shows as fairly in the mask.
> The heavens themselves, the planets, and this center
> Observe degree, priority, and place,
> Insisture, course, proportion, season, form,
> Office, and custom, in all line of order.
> And therefore is the glorious planet Sol
> In noble eminence enthroned and sphered
> Amidst the other, whose med'cinable eye
> Corrects the influence of evil planets,
> And posts, like the commandment of a king,
> Sans check to good and bad. But when the planets
> In evil mixture to disorder wander,
> What plagues and what portents, what mutiny,
> What raging of the sea, shaking of the earth,
> Commotion in the winds, frights, changes, horrors,
> Divert and crack, rend and deracinate
> The unity and married calm of states
> Quite from their fixture? O, when degree is shaked,
> Which is the ladder of all high designs,
> The enterprise is sick. . . .
> Take but degree away, untune that string,
> And hark what discord follows. Each thing meets
> In mere oppugnancy. The bounded waters
> Should lift their bosoms higher than the shores
> And make a sop of all this solid globe;
> Strength should be lord of imbecility,
> And the rude son should strike his father dead;
> Force should be right; or rather right and wrong,
> Between whose endless jar justice resides,

> Should lose their names, and so should justice too.
> Then everything includes itself in power,
> Power into will, will into appetite;
> And appetite, an universal wolf,
> So doubly seconded with will and power,
> Must make perforce an universal prey
> And last eat up himself. (1.3.78–124)

Macbeth's famous "sound and fury" speech offers another perspective on *Lear*. Learning of his lady's death, Macbeth responds with Stoic resignation:

> She should have died hereafter:
> There would have been time for such a word.
> Tomorrow, and tomorrow, and tomorrow,
> Creeps in this petty pace from day to day
> To the last syllable of recorded time,
> And all our yesterdays have lighted fools
> The way to dusty death. Out, out, brief candle,
> Life's but a walking shadow, a poor player,
> That struts and frets his hour upon the stage
> And then is heard no more. It is a tale
> Told by an idiot, full of sound and fury,
> Signifying nothing. (5.5.17–28)

Macbeth's speech is as bleak as anything in *Lear*, but it is hardly the play's final word on the world. It's the speech of a murderer who has drenched himself in blood. The closing lines of *Macbeth* stand in striking contrast. Malcolm, the legitimate king returned to Scotland, promises to do all that is necessary to restore his land "by the grace of Grace" (5.6.111). No doubt the world is absurd to Macbeth, but Macbeth has made it so.

These two passages are relevant to *Lear*. Ulysses would have recognized that the state of Lear's world—wolfish appetite devouring itself—is the result of "untuning" the string of degree. The turmoil Ulysses describes is similar to the disorders of which Gloucester complains (1.2.104–18). Lear is another Macbeth, or, better, he is Duncan and Macbeth rolled into one—both king and regicide. He is Adam, and his "original sin" makes his world a bleak and hopeless place.

Assaults on order breed disorder. But that's not the whole story. Disorder has a mysterious power to redeem. Suffering, even suffering one brings on oneself, can purify. In *Lear* as in other Shakespeare plays, there is a power at work beyond the moral or technical cause and effect of nature, the power of grace.[4]

King Lear is a tragedy of sin and judgment. But what *is* Lear's original sin? Ay, there's the rub.

Review Questions

1. Why do readers and viewers think *King Lear* is "absurd"?
2. Give examples of how *Lear* raises and destroys our hopes.
3. What comic conventions does Shakespeare use in *Lear*?
4. Why are there two texts of *King Lear*?
5. Where did Shakespeare get the idea for his play? How does his version differ from earlier versions?
6. How are the stories of Lear and Gloucester similar?
7. How did Nahum Tate's play differ from Shakespeare's?
8. What is the moral structure of *Lear*?
9. What does the play say about the effect of suffering?

Thought Questions

1. How is *King Lear* similar to the biblical book of Job? How is it different?
2. Read Holinshed's account of Lear's reign online, or Sir Philip Sidney's account in *Arcadia*. How do these versions of the story differ from Shakespeare's?
3. The 2018 Amazon Original production of *King Lear* begins with scenes of a modern cityscape at night, and the play includes cars, guns, and other modern devices. What effect does this have on the way the play works on the audience?

---

4. Harold Goddard brilliantly emphasizes this dimension of the play in his analysis in *Meaning of Shakespeare*, 2:136–71.

4. Watch the first scene of two different film versions of *King Lear*. How do they differ? What do the differences tell you about how the filmmaker understands the play?

Untune that String, Act 1

As the curtain parts, Lear is gathering his family and court to disclose his "darker purpose." All three of his daughters are there, along with Goneril's husband, the Duke of Cornwall, and Regan's husband, the Duke of Albany. Gloucester and Kent, Lear's advisors, are also in attendance. Act 2 ends with nearly the same assembly. In Act 2, scene 4, Goneril and Regan are together for the first time since the opening scene, along with Lear, Cornwall, Gloucester, and Kent (in disguise as Caius). The main missing person is Cordelia, banished to marry the King of France. Acts 1–2 are framed by scenes of banishment. Act 1, scene 1 ends with a double banishment, of Kent and Cordelia, and Act 2, scene 4 ends with the effective banishment of Lear and his small band out into the night.

Within this frame, the rest of the scenes are arranged symmetrically:

> A. Lear's family gathered; two banishments, 1.1
>   B. Edmund frames Edgar, accusing him to his father, 1.2
>   C. Oswald's contempt for Lear, 1.3–5
>   D. Edmund and Edgar separate, 2.1
>   C'. Oswald and Kent fight; Kent in stocks, 2.2
>   B'. Edgar plans to disguise himself, 2.3
> A'. Lear's family gathered, without Cordelia; Lear banished, 2.4

In Act 1, scene 2, Edmund plants suspicions about Edgar in his father's mind, while in Act 2, scene 3, Edgar plots his disguise to avoid the traps set by his brother. "Edgar I nothing am," he says, echoing the repetition of "nothing" in the opening scene. In Act 1, scenes 3–5 Oswald, Goneril's servant, treats Lear with disrespect, and in Act 2, scene 2, Oswald and Kent fight at Regan's house and Kent ends up in the stocks. At the center of this structure is Act 2, scene 1, where Edmund and Edgar part ways and the disintegration of Gloucester's house begins.

Many readers see Lear as pampered and petulant, a slightly demented old man used to being flattered and getting his own way. But there are hints he's been a stable, wise, even cunning king.[5] Kent is a blunt advisor,

---

5. Craig, *Of Philosophers and Kings*, 113–32.

but he says he's never had to oppose Lear until he disinherits Cordelia and pronounces over her a terrible curse of barrenness. "Be Kent unmannerly / When Lear is mad" (1.1.146–47). Lear will go mad during the play, but if he were always as bull-headed as he is in the opening, Kent would have been dismissed from court long ago. Besides, Lear knows his daughters, and rightly favors the wise, true, and affectionate Cordelia. If Lear loved flatterers, wouldn't he prefer Goneril and Regan?

If Lear *is* wise, though, why is he dumb enough to set up a "love competition" by offering his daughters land in exchange for telling him how much they love him? We have to assume that Lear hasn't told everyone what he's up to. Lear has, as he says, a "darker purpose," and even Kent and Gloucester, his closest advisors, aren't sure what he's on about (1.1.1–7).

If we read carefully and put the pieces together, the plan seems to be this: Lear doesn't have a son, so there is no obvious heir to the throne. If there's no succession plan at his death, his sons-in-law are likely to fight for power and split the kingdom. Lear preempts that future by splitting up the kingdom during his lifetime, but he splits it up in a particular fashion. He plans to retain the title of king and to live with Cordelia. As long as he lives, Albany and Cornwall will remain his vassals, though they will exercise power in the king's name in their own territories. Cordelia is about to marry, and we can surmise that Lear plans to give the crown to her husband. He seems to favor the duke of Burgundy for that position. When Lear dies, Albany and Cornwall will remain in a subordinate position to their brother-in-law. If this is his intention, it's a shrewd one. Of course, there's *always* the possibility of civil war. But Lear's plan has a chance to provide for an orderly succession, while satisfying Cornwall's and Albany's ambitions and making sure Lear's wisest daughter becomes queen.

The "love test" makes sense as part of this plan. In medieval societies, "love" isn't a romantic but a political emotion and virtue. A vassal shows his "love" for his lord by being loyal to his feudal vows and providing the service he promises. Lear has already decided which territories to give his daughters. Their inheritance doesn't really depend on the love they express here. Lear uses the contest for another, "darker purpose." When Lear calls on his daughters to declare their love, he's calling on them to swear fealty, in a formal setting, in the presence of witnesses. As long as he lives, they're bound to him by bonds of love. He knows they'll try to butter him up, exaggerating their love. That's part of his trap. The more extreme their declarations of love, the more closely they're bound to their father. When he dies, they will be bound by his decisions about the succession. Again, it is not a foolproof way to prevent civil war. There *is* no foolproof way to prevent civil war. But it's a reasonable effort to secure Lear's kingdom.

Lear hasn't told anyone, including Cordelia. He doesn't want to telegraph his plan, which would allow his daughters to shape their speeches ahead of time, working in loopholes. By springing the test on them, he secures their open declarations of undying loyalty. He knows they'll try to outdo one another, and they do. Goneril and Regan prove to be "monsters of ingratitude," and their monstrosity is brought into high relief by contrast with their declarations of love.

But Lear miscalculates. He expects Cordelia to pick up on his darker purpose, to discern the real aim of the game. He intends to give her the largest and most important portion of the kingdom, which will become the future "capital" for Cordelia and her husband. She doesn't have to say *much*. She doesn't have to imitate her sisters' transparent flattery. But she has to say *something*. "Nothing" is the one thing Lear can't tolerate.[6] By refusing to declare her love, Cordelia refuses to declare fealty, to honor Lear as king and father. Her silence shames Lear in his own court. There can be no doubt of her loyalty and love. Cordelia has expressed her love for her father many times. Now, when he asks her to proclaim it to the world, she refuses. Perhaps *she* was lying all along. Perhaps, Lear thinks, he misjudged her. Perhaps Cordelia, not Goneril or Regan, is the flatterer. Lear flies into a towering rage, renouncing all "paternal care, / Propinquity, and property of blood" he shares with Cordelia (1.1.114–16).

Cordelia's silence destroys Lear's entire plan. In retrospect, Lear's plot appears foolish. His "darker purpose" plunges England into darkness. Instead of being a buffer between his sons-in-law, he puts them into direct rivalry. Instead of having a secure base with Cordelia, he has to move back and forth between his other daughters. Instead of passing on a unified crown, he tells Cornwall and Albany: "This coronet part betwixt you" (1.1.140). *That* is a prescription for political disaster. A divided coronet is a string out of tune. Behold what discord follows.

As soon as Cordelia and Kent are banished, the action moves toward *Lear's* banishment. He banishes his faithful daughter and faithful advisor at the beginning of Act 1; at the end of Act 1 Lear himself leaves

---

6. Craig, *Of Philosophers and Kings*, 126.

Goneril's house after she complains about the conduct of his knights. At the end of Act 2, he leaves Regan's house, abjuring all roofs (2.4.207). By the end of Act 2, we have seen multiple banishments:

> 1.1: Lear banishes faithful Kent and Cordelia.
> 1.4: Lear leaves the house of Goneril and Albany.
> 2.1: Edmund convinces Edgar to flee his father's house.
> 2.2: Regan and Cornwall take over Gloucester's house.
> 2.4: Lear leaves Gloucester's house.

Ultimately, Gloucester will be banished from his own house. These developments reveal Lear's other miscalculation: He knows Goneril and Regan are wicked, but he doesn't realize just how wicked they are.

The first two Acts also trace the divestment of King Lear, which is worked out through varied uses of the word *nature*.[7] Lear uses the word first. To Lear, the love contest seems natural and just: "That we our largest bounty may extend / Where nature doth with merit challenge" (1.1.52–53). Here "nature" refers to the affections and respect a child is supposed to pay to his or her parents. "Nature" is the foundation of family and political order.

But there's another, nearly opposite, view of nature at work in the play. In his first soliloquy, Edmund addresses the goddess nature: "Thou, Nature, art my goddess; to thy law / My services are bound" (1.2.1–2). Edmund sets nature and custom in opposition. For an illegitimate son like Edmund, custom is a "plague." The rules of legitimacy are merely customary, not natural. By every "natural" measure, he's the equal of his brother: "my dimensions as well compact, / My mind as generous, and my shape as true" (1.2.7–8). For Edmund, nature doesn't provide a support for social hierarchy and custom, but instead corrects the injustices of custom. He appeals to nature in order to *undermine* the order of family and kingdom. When his father complains about Goneril and Regan's "unnatural" treatment of their father, Edmund agrees: "Most savage and unnatural" (3.3.7). As soon as his father leaves the stage, he foretells that he, the younger, "will rise when the old dost fall" (3.3.24). Nature doesn't require him to honor his father but the opposite.

These two ideas of nature play off one another throughout the play. Lear condemns his daughters' ingratitude as "unnatural" (2.4.278). Being Lear's flesh, they should respect him. Their cruelty makes turns them from flesh to a "disease that's in my flesh," "a boil, / A plague-sore, or

---

7. See Frye, *On Shakespeare*, 104–5.

embossed carbuncle / In my corrupted blood" (2.4.221–24). As he loses his grip on reality, Lear is afraid "I will forget my nature" (1.5.31), that is, his nature as king, father, general. But Lear's descent from "natural" kingship is a descent to a "natural" state in Edmund's sense, nature *opposed* to social custom and hierarchy. "Nature" can survive on a minimum of food, drink, and shelter. In this sense, natural man isn't social, but bestial. If we reduce human life to nature's needs, "man's life is cheap as a beast's" (2.4.264–67). Overcome by the unnatural evil of his daughters, Lear becomes a beast, in order to be raised again as something more than a natural man.

In modern English, "kind" has a double meaning. On the one hand, a "kind" is a group or species, usually of living things. Things of the same "kind" share the same "nature." On the other hand, a "kind" person is gentle and sensitive to the needs of others. For Shakespeare, the two senses of the word are linked. A kind person is one who treats his own kind well. Cruelty or unkindness is unnatural, a violation of the kind of beings we are, a violation of the obligations we owe to those of our "kind." Lear claims he's treated with "unkindness" (1.4.6); he means he's being treated unnaturally. An unkind person is outside humankind, more at home in the realm of monsters.

Ingratitude fits into this framework. By nature, children owe their parents gratitude, since their parents have, in Cordelia's words, "begot, bred, and loved" them. Filial ingratitude is unkind, not only because it's cruel but because it places a child outside the realm of man*kind*. When Lear exclaims, "Monster ingratitude!" he isn't letting off steam. He's offering a precise description of the dehumanizing effect of ingratitude. "Dehumanizing" is too weak. Ingratitude rests in the "marble hearts" of "fiends," or devils (1.4.254). "To have a thankless child," he says, is "sharper than a serpent's tooth" (1.4.284–85). Ingrates are of the devil's party. To be treated with ingratitude is to take the first step on the path of madness.

Lear's miscalculation ends with his early abdication. He gives up the position "nature" gives him and nature (in Edmund's sense) begins to overthrow custom. His unkindness will remove him from humankind, as his daughters reveal their own unkind, ungrateful, unnatural natures. From the moment that Lear removes his crown and kingship, he starts down a path that leads toward "nothing," a key word in the opening scene. When Lear demands that Cordelia express her love for him, she has "nothing" to say, and the exchange between Cordelia and Lear hammers the point home:

CORDELIA
    Nothing, my lord.
LEAR
    Nothing?
CORDELIA
    Nothing.
LEAR
    Nothing will come of nothing. Speak again (1.1.87–90).

Like the repetition of "murder" when Hamlet meets his father's ghost, the repetition establishes a motif that runs through the opening scenes.

Lear repeats Cordelia's "nothing" to Burgundy: "Nothing. I have sworn. I am firm" (1.1.250). Cordelia finds a true lover in the king of France, who considers her "most rich being poor, most choice forsaken, and most loved despised" (1.1.256–57). She is nearly a Christ figure, a despised Beloved. For France, Cordelia's honesty and beauty are sufficient dowry. She has all she needs. Something *did* come from her "Nothing."

Though Lear says *Cordelia* will receive nothing for saying nothing, "nothing will come of nothing" more accurately describes *his* future. The king who *gives* nothing, the king who wants *only* to receive, ends with nothing. Nothing comes from his "Nothing." Lear voluntarily deprives himself of authority, and Goneril and Regan progressively deprive him of soldiers, servants, and finally shelter and sanity. Goneril and Cornwall put Kent in stocks, even though he arrives at Gloucester's house as the king's representative and messenger (2.2), an act so defiant that Lear can't believe his daughter ordered it: "'Tis worse than murder / To do upon respect such violent outrage" (2.4.22–23).

This stripping of Lear comes to a climax in an exchange with Regan and Goneril, who are debating how many soldiers Lear needs in his entourage. Regan insists that he cannot come to her house with more than twenty-five, and Lear appeals to Goneril for more:

GONERIL
    Hear me, my lord.
    What need you five-and-twenty? ten? or five?
    To follow in a house where twice so many
    Have a command to tend you?
REGAN
    What need one? (2.4.260–68).

Anguished, Lear cries "O, reason not the need!" If man is allowed no more than he *needs*, "man's life is cheap as beast's" (2.4.259–62). Exactly so. Lear's needs have been "reasoned" out of existence, and a moment later, Lear is driven from the house and sent into the outer darkness. Eventually he sheds his last ragged pieces of clothing. He's reduced to "nothing" but his essential, bestial self. He's reduced to "natural" man.

As he's driven from his daughters' homes, Lear is also removed from fellowship and communion. As with Macbeth, Lear's isolation is a direct result of his own actions, his miscalculations and foolish abdication. He fails to discern the true feelings of Regan and Goneril, just as he misreads the genuine love behind Cordelia's "nothing." As a result, he pushes away the only ones who are truly loyal to him, the two members of his court who tell him the truth—Cordelia and Kent—and associates himself instead with "treachers."

King Lear's identity is bound up with his status as king. He is what he is because he's surrounded by subjects, courtiers, advisors, because he can summon knights to fight for him. In Goneril's house, as he loses status, he begins to lose himself. Goneril's servant Oswald treats him with indifference and contempt, refusing to come when summoned. Lear demands, "Who am I, sir?" and Oswald answers, "My lady's father" (1.4.78–79). Lear is demoted from king to a place below his own daughter. In a frenzy, he asks if anyone recognizes him:

> Does any here know me? This is not Lear.
> Does Lear walk thus? speak thus? Where are his eyes?
> Either his notion weakens, his discernings
> Are lethargied—Ha! waking? 'Tis not so.
> Who is it that can tell me who I am? (1.4.220–24)

Is a king still king when no one treats him as king? And if a king is no longer a king, who *is* he? The Fool has the best answer: "Lear's shadow" (1.4.225). No wonder Lear fears he will go mad (1.5.43–44), for what's the difference between a shadow and nothing?

Gloucester's family is also disintegrating to nothing. Act 1, scene 2, where Edmund begins his plot against father and brother, is structured chiastically:

> A. Edmund's first soliloquy.
>   B. Edmund with Gloucester, accusing Edgar.
>   C. Edmund's second soliloquy.
>   B'. Edmund with Edgar, sowing suspicion that Gloucester is suspicious of Edgar.
> A'. Edmund's third soliloquy.

The structure beautifully reinforces the substance. Edmund is present the whole time, the single continuity of the scene. He surrounds the scene, just as his plot encircles Gloucester and Edgar like a tightening noose. At the same time, Edmund is in the *middle* of the scene, dividing his father from his brother.

Gloucester knows things aren't right in the kingdom, but he blames the sun, moon, and stars:

> These late eclipses in the sun and moon portend no good to us. Though the wisdom of nature can reason it thus and thus, yet nature finds itself scourged by the sequent effects. Love cools, friendship falls off, brothers divide. In cities, mutinies; in countries, discord; in palaces, treason; and the bond cracked 'twixt son and father. This villain of mine comes under the prediction, there's son against father; the king falls from bias of nature, there's father against child. Machinations, hollowness, treachery, and all ruinous discords follow us disquietly to our graves. (1.2.104–12)

Gloucester is staring at the very horrors he lists, for he's speaking to Edmund, the real treacherous son. But he can't see them.

Edmund is wiser and more clear-sighted. He knows that the problem is not in the stars but in ourselves. After listening to his father's ruminations on astrology, he muses on fate and free will:

> This is the excellent foppery of the world, that when we are sick in fortune, often the surfeits of our own behavior, we make guilty of our disasters the sun, the moon, and stars; as if we were villains on necessity; fools by heavenly compulsion; knaves, thieves, and treachers by spherical predominance; drunkards, liars, and adulterers by an enforced obedience of planetary influence; and all that we are evil in, by a divine thrusting on. An admirable evasion of whoremaster man, to lay his goatish disposition on the charge of a star. (1.2.118–28)

That Edmund is himself of "goatish disposition," that he is the epitome of "whoremaster man," does not alter the orthodoxy of his statement, which captures both the Christian notion of freedom and the Christian doctrine of original sin. Lear's world is a "great stage of fools," for sure; but it is so because man—the king especially—has chosen folly over wisdom and loved darkness rather than light. Man is not evil by "spherical predominance" or through a "divine thrusting on." Man is evil, and the world disordered, because of an original fall.

Edmund often conducts his villainy secretly, through letters. In the second scene, he pretends to put away a letter when his father enters, insisting that it's "nothing." This only rouses his father's interest: "The quality of nothing hath not such need to hide itself. Let's see. Come, if it be nothing, I shall not need spectacles" (1.2.32–36). Edmund claims the letter expresses his brother's opinion that "sons at perfect age, and fathers declined, the father should be as ward to the son, and the son manage his revenue" (1.2.74–76). The letter is literally "nothing." Edgar didn't write it, and he doesn't hold the opinions Edmund claims. By a sort of black magic, Edmund is able to make something of this nothing, a something that will bring his family and father to nothing. In the end, nothing comes from nothing, but along the way to a final nothing, evil nothings give birth to catastrophic somethings.

Review Questions

1. Explain the structure of Acts 1–2.
2. Why does Lear do what he does? What is his plan?
3. Why does the "love test" fail?
4. How does Lear himself "come to nothing"?
5. Explain the interlocked ideas of nature, kind, and gratitude.
6. Describe the structure of Act 1, scene 2.
7. Who is Edmund? What is his view of "nature"?
8. What does Gloucester think of astrology? What does this say about his character?

Thought Questions

1. Where is the region of Cornwall? Where does the "Duke of Albany" rule? How do these geographic details help explain what Lear is up to?
2. What gods does King Lear invoke? What does this say about the setting of the play?

3. Lear tells France and Burgundy that Cordelia's "price is fallen" (1.1.202). What does he mean? What does this say about Lear's view of his daughters and their marriages?

4. Edmund hides a letter from his father, which casts suspicion on Edgar (1.2.31–46). What other letters does Edmund send in the course of the play? Why does he write so many letters? What does he do with his letters?

5. Edmund says our bad fortune is "often the surfeits of our own behavior" (1.2.120–21). What does he mean? How does his comment reflect the action in the opening scenes of the play? How is Edmund himself a "surfeit" of his father's bad behavior?

6. What instructions does Goneril give Oswald (1.3)? Why?

7. Lear curses Goneril with sterility (1.4.271–85). How might Lear suffer from his own curse?

Unaccommodated Man, Acts 3–4

The Fool is one of the comic elements that give this dark play its strange power. Shakespeare knows he's violating tragic conventions, but that's the point. When we see a "Clown" on stage, we want to laugh. The fool *does* make us laugh, though mournfully rather than mirthfully. The Fool first appears in Act 1, scene 4, and he comments on the action until Act 3. After that, he disappears, and there is a hint that he died offstage at some point. While he's onstage, his insights, disguised as jests, are crucial for feeling our way through the play.

The Fool's first exchange, with Kent (disguised as Caius) and Lear, is a good example of the method in his madness (1.4.94–130). He initially addresses Kent, offering him his fool's cap. Kent must be a fool himself to want to follow a man like Lear, who has been reduced to nothing, a stranger in his own kingdom who is snubbed by his daughter's servants. Kent is foolish for "taking one's part that's out of favor" (1.4.97). The Fool later says Lear "has banished two on's daughters," while doing the third, Cordelia, a favor by sending her away. In fact, of course, Lear has done the opposite. He hasn't banished Goneril or Regan. But the Fool sees what's coming. The exchange between the Fool and Kent occurs before Goneril pushes her father out of her house, but the Fool suspects there are more banishments to come. He doesn't hear Goneril tell Oswald to insult Lear: "Put on what weary negligence you please, / You and your fellows" (1.3.12–13). The Fool doesn't need to hear her. He can tell from Oswald's behavior that banishment is on the horizon.

When Kent asks why he should wear a fool's cap, the Fool answers "an thou canst not smile as the wind sits, thou'lt catch cold shortly" (1.4.98–99). The winds have shifted, in favor of Goneril and Regan and their husbands and against Lear. If Kent were wise, he would learn to smile and cozy up to Lear's daughters. If he doesn't learn do to that, he'll find himself out in the wind, in danger of catching cold. The Fool's mockery turns literal in Act 3, when Lear, Kent, and the Fool are forced out into the wind and rain.

Though the Fool begins with jokes at Kent's expense, he eventually turns his attention to his real target, Lear. He tells Lear he wishes he had "two coxcombs and two daughters." When Lear asks, "Why, my boy?" the Fool answers: "If I gave them all my living, I'd keep my coxcombs for myself. There's mine; beg another of thy daughters" (1.4.105–6). At the very least, this means that Lear was a fool to divide his kingdom between his daughters. The only thing he has left is his fool's cap. Eventually, he will lose even that. On the heath, he disrobes completely, becoming a mere bare forked animal. Lear is outraged when he realizes the Fool is calling him a fool: "Does thou call me fool, boy?" (1.4.145). The Fool reasonably responds: "All thy other titles thou hast given away; that thou wast born with" (1.4.146–47). Lear plays the lead on the "great stage of fools," a natural-born fool.

The Fool is not merely critical. In the "speech" he teaches Lear, he gives practical advice. Don't show all that you have, or speak all you know, or lend all you possess. In short, keep something back. Lear failed to do this, giving "all," as he repeatedly complains, to his daughters. But Lear dismisses the lesson with "This is nothing, fool" (1.4.125). He means to say the speech is meaningless, but the word *nothing* is a pregnant one. Lear doesn't see the irony. He thinks the Fool's advice is nothing, but it's the opposite. It offers a way of keeping something; if Lear follows the Fool's counsel, he won't end with "nothing." Lear repeats the axiom he spoke earlier to Cordelia: "Nothing can be made out of nothing" (1.4.129–30). He still doesn't realize that his axiom applies to him more than anyone else in the play.

Later in the scene, the Fool accuses Lear of making "thy daughters thy mother; . . . thou gav'st them the rod, and put'st down they breeches" (1.4.167–69). Lear threatens to whip him, because the Fool's joke stings.

Lear thinks his daughters have acted unnaturally, like monsters who deny their parents. The Fool sees the real truth: *Lear* is the one who has violated nature, by putting himself under the care of his daughters and planning to crawl, like an infant, toward death. When his daughters invert the natural hierarchy of parent and child, they're following their father's lead. Untune the string holding together father and daughter, and behold what discord follows.

Lear's tragedy is not Lear's alone. The fact that the *king* comes to nothing means that the kingdom too descends into the void. These two dimensions to the play are directly connected, and both arise from Lear's original sin. When he gives up his throne and crown, Lear hopes his peaceful division of the kingdom will prevent a future violent division (1.143–45). In fact, his divestiture makes conflict inevitable. Without a tamer on the throne, the beasts break out of their cages and send the righteous into to caves and hovels. The disorder Gloucester foresees actually happens, not because of the stars but because of Lear's folly.

In a sense, Lear gets exactly what he asks for. When Cordelia refuses to flatter him, he rejects her with terrible curses, abdicating as a father just as he has abdicated as a king:

> Here I disclaim all my paternal care,
> Propinquity, and property of blood,
> And as a stranger to my heart and me
> Hold thee from this for ever. The barbarous Scythian,
> Or he that makes his generation messes
> To gorge his appetite, shall to my bosom
> Be as well neighbored, pitied, and relieved
> As thou my sometime daughter. (1.1.114–21)

Lear believes Cordelia is worse than the barbarian who "makes his generations messes," feeding on the father who gives her all. In reality, he throws himself at the mercy of genuine Scythians, Regan and Goneril, who gorge their appetites on their father's wealth, who "digest" portions of his kingdom (1.1.93–94), who prove to be "pelican daughters" (3.4.76). Animal imagery clusters around Goneril in particular. She is a kite, wolf, boar, and tiger, and her own husband says in her world "humanity must perforce prey on itself, / Like monsters of the deep" (4.2.49–50).

Appetite for power is joined to run-of-the-mill and rather tawdry sexual lust. Goneril and Regan, partners in reducing Lear to nothing, become rivals for the love of Edmund, who plays both like a master musician. Edmund's rise to prominence depends partly on his skill in playing to the sisters' lusts. In the fallen world after Lear's withdrawal, it is fitting that Edmund, the bastard child of appetite who is wholly governed by goatish appetites, should worm his way to prominence.

The social and political results of Lear's folly come to a climax in Act 3, whose structure underlines the fact that bestiality and barbarity rule Lear's kingdom. Scenes on the heath focusing on Lear and his company alternate with scenes of the court focusing on Edmund, Cornwall, and Regan:

> 3.1–2: Kent searches for and finds Lear.
> > 3.3: Gloucester tells Edmund he has letters from France.
> 3.4: Lear, Kent, and Fool discover Edgar (disguised as Poor Tom).
> > 3.5: Edmund betrays his father to Cornwall.
> 3.6: Gloucester visits Lear on the heath.
> > 3.7: Cornwall and Regan torture Gloucester for helping Lear.

On the surface, it appears that the "community" on the heath is the community of beasts and barbarians; they are, after all, "unaccommodated" with house or clothing. But the scenes' structure makes it clear that the real barbarism is elsewhere. The "civilized" world is the house of horrors. Edmund plots against his father (3.3), treacherously accusing him of being a traitor and finally receiving his father's title and property as a reward (3.5). The disinherited bastard inherits everything. It seems Edmund's prayer has been heard: "Now, gods, stand up for bastards" (1.2.22). In the last scene in the court, Cornwall and Regan savagely pluck out Gloucester's eyes, while Cornwall is fatally wounded in the scuffle (3.7). *These* are the civilized? *This* is "natural"? A world of fools and madmen, stripped of "lendings" of civilization, is more humane than the world of the "sane."

The blinding of Gloucester is so horrible a scene that many productions leave it out, sending it offstage.[8] That is a mistake, both dramatically and thematically. Dramatically, it removes the scene that best unveils the savagery of Lear's family. We're shocked by the brutality of the scene, but that is the effect Shakespeare wants. He wants us to find the whole pack of them appalling.

Thematically, the scene is even more important, as if fits into a thread about eyes and sight. Goneril is the first to mention sight, when she tells Lear her love is "dearer than eyesight, space, and liberty" (1.1.56). Later in the same scene, Lear rages at Kent for stepping between the "dragon

---

8. The next several pages are deeply indebted to the analysis of Goddard, *Meaning of Shakespeare*, 2:143–47.

and his wrath" (1.1.123), and eventually dismisses him with "Out of my sight!" (1.1.160). Kent sees the real problem: "See better, Lear, and let me still remain / The true blank of thine eye" (1.1.161–62). Lear's folly is the product of faulty eyesight. If he could see well, he'd regard Kent as the apple of his eye and see that Kent has hit the bullseye with his warning.

Similarly, Gloucester is blind to the true nature of his sons, but he goes through an excruciating process of purging and renewal, of blindness that leads to sight. He admits to Cornwall and Regan he sent the king to Dover to protect him: "Because I would not see thy cruel nails / Pluck out his poor old eyes; nor thy fierce sister / In his anointed flesh stick boarish fangs" (3.7.57–59). Cornwall immediately picks up Kent's reference to eyes. Because Gloucester wants to save the king's eyes, Cornwall says, "Upon these eyes of thine I'll set my foot" (3.7.69). Almost instantly, Gloucester has the overwhelming insight that he has been wrong about his sons. When Regan tells him Edmund provided evidence of Gloucester's treason, he confesses his follies: "Then Edgar was abused. / Kind gods, forgive me that and prosper him" (3.7.92–93). The world has gone topsy-turvy: Gloucester is punished as a traitor for *helping the king*!

Cornwall and Regan drive Gloucester out of his own house. "Let him smell / His way to Dover" (3.7.94–95) is Regan's taunt. An old man finds Gloucester wandering and offers to guide him, since "you cannot see your way" (4.1.17). Gloucester's response shows he understands the moral effect of his blinding:

> I have no way, and therefore want no eyes;
> I stumbled when I saw. Full oft 'tis seen
> Our means secure us, and our mere defects
> Prove our commodities. O dear son Edgar,
> The food of thy abused father's wrath,
> Might I but live to see thee in my touch
> I'd say I had eyes again. (4.1.18–24)

As soon as Gloucester mentions Edgar, Edgar approaches him, still in the guise of Poor Tom, and offers to take him to Dover. Gloucester has begun to see, with Edgar providing the healing touch. The sensuous Gloucester who makes crude jokes about Edmund's illegitimacy ("there was good sport at his making") has become merciful, giving his purse to Edgar with the hope that "distribution should undo excess, / and each man have enough" (4.1.72–73).

Gloucester has one more lesson to learn. He complains that we are playthings to the gods and believes in astrology and spherical predominance. His resignation to fate leads to despair. He asks Edgar to take him to the cliffs of Dover so he can throw himself off. Edgar has no intention of helping his father commit suicide and instead sets up a ruse. He pretends they are ascending to the bluff and says he hears the sea. Gloucester hears nothing and protests that the ground is level. Edgar suggests that Gloucester's blindness has marred his other senses: "your other senses grow imperfect / By your eyes' anguish" (4.6.5–6). It's more typical, of course, for other senses to compensate for blindness, and the scene makes it clear that Gloucester's hearing is perfectly good. He even recognizes that Edgar's "voice is altered" and that he speaks "in better phrase and matter than thou didst" (4.6.7–8). For blind Gloucester, the world is coming into focus.

Meanwhile, Edgar paints a splendid portrait of the scene before him:

> How fearful
> And dizzy 'tis, to cast one's eyes so low!
> The crows and choughs that wing the midway air
> Show scarce so gross as beetles. Halfway down
> Hangs one that gathers samphire—dreadful trade;
> Methinks he seems no bigger than his head.
> The fishermen that walk upon the beach,
> Appear like mice; and yond tall anchoring bark,
> Diminished to her cock; her cock, a buoy
> Almost too small for sight. The murmuring surge
> That on th' unnumb'red idle pebbles chafes
> Cannot be heard so high. I'll look no more,
> Lest my brain turn, and the deficient sight
> Topple down headlong. (4.6.11–24)

Edgar tells Gloucester he's at the edge of the cliff and Gloucester leans forward to fall all the way to . . . the stage.

Edgar instantly changes persona, pretending to be a fisherman who saw Gloucester fall from the cliff. He tells Gloucester the beggar who accompanied him to the cliff edge was a devil tempting him to suicide:

> As I stood here below, methought his eyes
> Were two full moons; he had a thousand noses,
> Horns whelked and waved like the enridged sea.
> It was some fiend. Therefore, thou happy father,
> Think that the clearest gods, who make them honors
> Of men's impossibilities, have preserved thee. (4.6.69–74)

For the audience, Gloucester's fall is anti-climactic, even unintentionally funny. Not for Gloucester. It alters him. He'll no more complain against the gods, and he vows to be patient: "Henceforth I'll bear / Affliction till it do cry out itself / 'Enough, enough,' and die" (4.6.75–77). Edgar has saved his father, exploiting his father's deep belief in portents and spirits. He has delivered his father from a genuine demon, despair, by inviting his father to imagine a world where death is followed by resurrection, where someone can fall from a cliff, get up, dust himself off, and live on. Edgar saves him, we might say, by calling him from the world of sight, which he has already left behind, into a world of faith. His eyes cannot see, but Gloucester sees "feelingly" (4.6.149).

Now the blind man is ready to meet the madman, the man who has become every inch a king. For Lear has spent the night going through his own purgation, his own death and resurrection. Like Gloucester, he has begun to see better.

We should recall the title of this play, *King Lear*. Macbeth was a king, yet his play isn't *King Macbeth*. The full title of *Hamlet* is *Hamlet, Prince of Denmark*, but that title subtly hints at a division between Hamlet the man and his princely status. But Lear is *King* Lear, and the title suggests the play is about kingship.[9]

Shakespeare wrote many parts for kings, but most of them fail to reach true kingship. They are weak, or worldly, or villainous devils like Richard III. Lear, however, becomes "every inch a king." But his progress toward kingship is such a tortuous one we are liable to miss it.

We might think Lear is most royal in the opening scene, when he's still wearing his crown imperial and intertissued robe and exercising his absolute power with absolute corruption, banishing Kent and Cordelia with a dragon's breath. He looks every inch a king. But he calls himself "every inch a king" only in the fourth Act when he appears in a very different guise. Eyeless Gloucester hears the king's voice and cries "Is't not the king?" Lear answers, "Ay, every inch a king!" (4.6.107). He no longer wears a crown but, in some performances, the Fool's cap. He no longer sparkles with jewels, but decks himself with flowers. Detached from the court and its networks of relations, Lear is no better than a beast: "If humankind cannot satisfy the individual's need for a sense of himself, how then is man different from a beast?"[10] "Man wears clothes" might be an

---

9. Goddard, *Meaning of Shakespeare*, 2:143.
10. Bevington, *Four Tragedies*, 521.

answer, but Lear comes to realize that the clothes are expendable, mere "lendings" that cover the "unaccommodated... forked animal" that he is. But Lear's vision of unaccommodated man enables him to see the world afresh.

Through his new eyes, Lear sees through the lies that kept him confident of his power:

> They flattered me like a dog, and told me I had white hairs in my beard ere the black ones were there. To say 'ay' and 'no' to every thing that I said! 'Ay' and 'no' too was no good divinity. When the rain came to wet me once, and the wind to make me chatter; when the thunder would not peace at my bidding; there I found 'em, there I smelt 'em out. Go to, they are not men o' their words. They told me I was everything. 'Tis a lie—I am not ague-proof. (4.6.96–105)

He also sees the difference between reality and social appearances. He recognizes how "clothing" can become a weapon of unjust power and privilege:

> a dog's obeyed in office.
> Thou rascal beadle, hold thy bloody hand!
> Why dost thou lash that whore? Strip thy own back.
> Thou hotly lusts to use her in that kind
> For which thou whip'st her. The usurer hangs the cozener.
> Through tattered clothings small vices do appear;
> Robes and furred gowns hide all. Plate sins with gold,
> And the strong lance of justice hurtless breaks;
> Arm it in rags, a pygmy's straw does pierce it. (4.6.158–67)

Now he knows he shares the same fragile humanity as the beggar and the slave. He's the sick one, and he prescribes physic to heal his great greatness:

> Poor naked wretches, wheresoe'er you are,
> That bide the pelting of this pitiless storm,
> How shall your houseless heads and unfed sides,
> Your looped and windowed raggedness, defend you
> From seasons such as these? O, I have ta'en
> Too little care of this! Take physic, pomp;
> Expose thyself to feel what wretches feel,
> That thou mayst shake the superflux to them
> And show the heavens more just. (3.4.30–38)

Lear, in short, progresses in his grasp of "nature." He sees the common nature he shares with all other men, and he sees what appear to be the "natural" garments of social life can be most unnatural. Passing through madness, he emerges as a picture of sanity. Having experienced bestial "nature," he's able to see human nature more clearly.

Lear has learned to season justice with mercy. During the mock trial he holds in the hovel where he spends the night, he shows clemency to lechers and adulterers. It is now that he becomes royal, now that he has passed unhoused through a stormy night. The heath is his Eden, where he receives a new Adam's nature. On the heath, he eats the tree of knowledge, his eyes are opened, and he can discern good and evil.

Though the Fool disappears, Lear has learned the Fool's lessons and become his own fool. Early on, he fights back "womanly" tears from staining his manly face (1.4.292–95). Lear suffers like Job but it takes time for him to acquire the patience of Job. Through his suffering, he comes to see the truth of Virgil's words: "here are the tears of things" (*Aeneid* 1.462). He counsels Gloucester to have patience in the face of trials:

> If thou wilt weep my fortunes, take my eyes.
> I know thee well enough; thy name is Gloucester.
> Thou must be patient. We came crying hither;
> Thou know'st, the first time that we smell the air
> We wawl and cry. I will preach to thee. Mark. . . .
> When we are born, we cry that we are come
> To this great stage of fools. (4.6.176–80, 182–83)

He's come to recognize his own folly, and the folly of man: "I am a very foolish fond old man" (5.1.62). Recognizing his folly, King Lear becomes wise, every inch a king.

Review Questions

1. What is the role of the Fool in *Lear*? Explain his method of fooling.
2. How does Lear's folly overturn proper family order?
3. What effect does Lear's folly have on his kingdom?
4. What is the point of the alternation of scenes between Gloucester's house and the heath, where Lear is riding out the storm?
5. What happens to Gloucester? How is he restored?

6. What does the play tell us about the nature of kingship?
7. What does Lear learn from his suffering? How does he come to "see better"?

Thought Questions

1. The Fool says a snail has a house on his back "to put's head in" and so he won't "leave his horns without a case" (1.5.29–30). How does the Fool's joke apply to Lear? In what sense does Lear have horns?
2. The Fool says Lear "hast pared thy wit o' both sides and left nothing i' th' middle" (1.4.177–83). What does he mean? Who or what are the "parings"?
3. Why do Regan and Cornwall leave their house to visit Gloucester (2.1.98–106)? How does their action anticipate their later treatment of Gloucester (3.7.39–41)?
4. Who kills the duke of Cornwall? (3.7.73–99). How is this similar to Kent's confrontation of Lear in Act 1, scene 1? How does this incident illustrate Gloucester's description of the state of England? (1.2.104–88).
5. What does Lear do during his night on the heath (3.6.35–80)? How does this fit with the play's treatment of kingship?
6. The 2018 Amazon Original production of *King Lear* changes the order of scenes in Acts 3–4. Why?

The Promised End, Act 5

Act 4 has the sense of an ending. After the mayhem of Act 3 (Lear going mad on the heath, the brutal blinding of Gloucester), Act 4 begins to mend the world. Edgar saves Gloucester, and Lear is brought inside, out of the storm. It is day, Lear has slept, and he is in new clothes: He is *re*accommodated man. As he awakes, he speaks of being brought up from the torments of the grave: "You do me wrong to take me out o' th' grave. / Thou art a soul in bliss; but I am bound / Upon a wheel of fire" (4.7.45–47). He has been recalled to life, redeemed from the tortures of hell or purgatory, by Cordelia, his Beatrice, his savior. Lear and Cordelia are reconciled, sealed by Cordelia's unutterably poignant gift of forgiveness:

> LEAR
> Do not laugh at me;
> For, as I am a man, I think this lady
> To be my child Cordelia.
> CORDELIA
> And so I am! I am!
> LEAR
> Be your tears wet? Yes, faith. I pray weep not.
> If you have poison for me, I will drink it.
> I know you do not love me; for your sisters
> Have (as I do remember) done me wrong.
> You have some cause, they have not.
> CORDELIA
> No cause, no cause. (4.7.70–76)

The daughter Lear renounced is now, tenderly, "my child." When Lear confesses that Cordelia has some cause to hate him, Cordelia, who has identified herself by the name of God ("I am, I am") puts Lear's sin behind her, as far as the east is from the west. She redeems from the curse (4.6.202–3) and has been about her "father's business" (4.3.23–24), echoing Jesus' words to his parents (Luke 2).

We seem poised for a comic ending. Cornwall has already died, killed by a servant. Add in the deaths of Edmund, Goneril, and Regan, and the world will be glad. Act 5 obliges. Edgar gets his just revenge by defeating and killing Edmund in single combat. Rivals for Edmund's love, the sisters destroy one another. Goneril poisons Regan, then takes her own life when Edmund dies. Characters who persevere in loyal love, particularly Kent and Edgar, are vindicated and live to tell the story.

But *Lear* is a tragedy, and that means that innocents are caught up in the mayhem. Cordelia's reticence at the beginning is, perhaps, a slight fault, but it doesn't deserve death. Lear reconciles with Cordelia, but he has favored two monstrous daughters who helped to promote Edmund, stepped aside from his public responsibilities, and led England into a dark age. Lear isn't wholly redeemed because he never recognizes the full extent of the damage he's done.

Lear's ambiguous repentance is evident in another poignant scene with Cordelia. They have lost the battle and been captured. Cordelia rages. She could accept her fate, but for the fact that Lear suffers. She wants to "outfrown false Fortune's frown" (5.3.6), but Lear calms her:

> No, no, no, no! Come, let's away to prison.
> We two alone will sing like birds i' th' cage.
> When thou dost ask me blessing, I'll kneel down
> And ask of thee forgiveness. So we'll live,
> And pray, and sing, and tell old tales, and laugh
> At gilded butterflies, and hear poor rogues
> Talk of court news; and we'll talk with them too—
> Who loses and who wins; who's in, who's out—
> And take upon's the mystery of things
> As if we were God's spies; and we'll wear out,
> In a walled prison, packs and sects of great ones
> That ebb and flow by th' moon. (5.3.8–19)

In one sense, this is the culmination of Lear's ascent to true kingship. A king is truly royal only when he can smile with detachment at the turmoil of political life, when he can "talk of court news" as if he were talking about the "ebb and flow by th' moon." On the other hand, Lear's willingness to retreat to a cage repeats his original fault, his initial abdication that plunged England into chaos. Kings must live within the paradox: They must act, decisively, without believing their actions finally determine outcomes. Lear hasn't kept that balance. His original deed, once done, cannot be undone.

Lear's whole attention is concentrated on his wrongs to Cordelia, and there is never a hint that he repents for wrongs done to Kent, to Gloucester, to the entire kingdom. When Lear is hysterical with grief over Cordelia's death, Kent attempts to comfort him and is met with an abrupt dismissal: "Prithee away" (5.3.274). When Edgar reminds Lear that he is speaking to "noble Kent, your friend," Lear is recalcitrant: "A plague upon you murderers, traitors all" (5.3.274–75). He does recognize Kent later in the scene (5.3.288), but when Kent attempts to describe his tenacious loyalty to the king—he has "from your first of difference and decay . . . followed your sad steps" (5.3.294–95)—Lear barely listens. Lear never accepts responsibility for the political disasters of which he was the ultimate author; he never realizes England has become a "gored state" (5.3.327).

And so, instead of ending with Act 4, the play ends with the numbing horror of Act 5. Lear carries Cordelia's body onto the stage howling like a beast. It's another near miss: Earlier, Edmund sent a letter instructing his henchmen to make her death look like suicide. Defeated in single combat by his brother Edgar, he confesses and urges Albany to send someone to rescue her. It's too late. "She's gone forever," Lear says, "I know when one is dead, and when one lives. / She's dead as earth" (5.3.265–68). But he holds out hope. He asks for a mirror to test whether she's breathing, and he sees the feather he holds up to her nose stir: "She lives," and if so, "it is a chance which does redeem all sorrows / That ever I have felt" (5.3.271–73). He can't hear her speak, but that's no surprise: "Her voice was ever soft, / Gentle, and low," as when she softly answered "nothing" when asked to heave her heart into her mouth (5.3.278–79). He dies in a wild zigzag between despair and ecstasy:

> And my poor fool is hanged: no, no, no life?
> Why should a dog, a horse, a rat, have life,
> And thou no breath at all? Thou'lt come no more,
> Never, never, never, never, never.
> Pray you, undo this button. Thank you, sir.
> Do you see this? Look on her! Look, her lips,
> Look there, look there—(5.3.312–18)

This is madness, we say. Her lips aren't moving, nor is there mist on the mirror or a stirring of the feather. Lear was right the first time. Cordelia *is* dead as earth.

Then we pause and look again. "Is this the promised end?" Kent asks (5.3.269). Is this the apocalypse, the last day? Edgar replies that it may be the "image of that horror" (5.3.270). It's a day of wrath and carnage, like the coming day when the wicked will be sent to torment. "This is a dull sight," Lear says when he sees the corpses of Goneril, Regan, and Edmund heaped on the stage (5.3.288). It's a horror, but a just one. Right has triumphed, and to this extent it's the image of the sorting-out of judgment day. But the sorting-out is only *part* of judgment day, and not the most important part. Goats are sent to outer darkness, but the sheep enter into the joy of the Father. Judgment day is also resurrection day, and the final scene of *King Lear* is hardly a fitting image of that day without hope for resurrection. Is this the promised end? Perhaps so. Perhaps Lear knows something we don't.

Lear sees through new eyes. He knows Cordelia and calls her a "spirit," and recognizes Gloucester and Kent. He sees through the flattering lies that buttressed his hubris, sees past the gold-plated sin and knows the beadle who beats the whore lusts for her. His pomp has taken its medicine so he can see, and pray to, the poor naked wretches he has neglected during his reign. "See better, Lear," Kent told him at the beginning. He does, and perhaps he sees better than we do.

Perhaps he dies in the same way Gloucester dies and rises on the "cliffs" of Dover: As he dies, he leaves the world of sight and enters a world of spirits. In that world, Cordelia lives, and the future life of "the promised end" is so certain that she lives even now. Nothing comes from nothing. So Lear assumes. But the promise of the end is otherwise: From the nothing of death, from the darker purpose of the grave, comes something of great constancy.

Review Questions

1. How does the end of Act 4 tie up the threads of the play? How does Act 5 satisfy and complicate the ending?
2. In what state is King Lear in Act 5?
3. How does Cordelia treat her father?
4. What does Lear want to do with Cordelia?
5. How does the play's end display the moral structure of the universe?
6. What does Lear believe is happening as he dies?
7. How does the play's closing scene provide a glimpse of "the promised end"?

Thought Questions

1. How does Edgar challenge Edmund to single combat? (5.1.39–51). Why is this a fitting way for Edgar to act?
2. What does Lear say when Regan suggests he ask Goneril for forgiveness (2.4.150–54)? Compare Lear's words to Cordelia (5.3.10–11). How has Lear changed between those two incidents?
3. As he dies, Edmund says "The wheel is come full circle" (5.3.176). What does he mean? How does this compare to his speech about the "foppery of the world" in 1.2?
4. Lear pronounces "A plague upon you murderers, traitors all" (5.3.275). What does he mean? Is his statement truthful?

5. Edgar disguises himself as Poor Tom by sticking nails into his flesh (2.3.15–16). Why? What does this remind you of?
6. David Bentley Hart has written this about *King Lear*. Explain what Hart means, and discuss.

> Were *Lear* an Attic tragedy, it might well end upon the heath, at the height of the protagonist's madness and at the point of his greatest and most demonic (that is, ennobling) despair, where he arrives at a final exhaustion of passion. Certainly there would not be the strange and beautiful reunion with Cordelia, overbrimming with imagery of resurrection and talk of forgiveness, because this scene of reconciliation (which strains after an eschatological hope) makes the subsequent death of Cordelia more terrible than anything in Attic tragedy: precisely because the spectator has been granted a glimpse of the joy that tragic wisdom is impotent to adumbrate—the restoration of the beloved—the death that follows is seen to be absolutely without meaning, without beauty, imparting no wisdom, resistant to all assimilation into any metaphysical scheme of intelligibility or solace.[11]

---

11. Hart, *Beauty of the Infinite*, 393n229.

4

The Course of True Love

A Midsummer Night's Dream

THE FAMOUS SEVENTEENTH-CENTURY DIARIST Samuel Pepys once went to see *Midsummer Night's Dream* at the King's Theatre. He didn't like it. He called it "the most insipid ridiculous play that ever I saw in my life," though he admitted it had some "good dancing and some handsome women," which nearly made it worth watching.[1]

Pepys had a point. It *is* a ridiculous play, with its fairies and love potions and slapstick comedy and ass-headed Bottom in bed with the fairy Queen Titania. We laugh, but it is too bizarre for our laughter to be entirely comfortable. Watching the final play-within-a-play, Hippolyta says it is the "silliest stuff" she's ever seen. What, if anything, is the point of it all?

Shakespearean comedy is never mere light entertainment. Shakespearean comedy is animated by a two-sided "belief."[2] On one hand, Shakespeare is convinced human beings are capable of making a mess of life. On the other hand, Shakespeare knows human beings are incapable of resolving the messes we make. If things are going to turn out well, we need help from somewhere beyond ourselves. We need "grace."

Grace takes different forms in different sorts of plays. As Peter Saccio observes, comedy is about desire, especially the desires of lovers to be with one another.[3] Comedy is also about the obstacles that stand in the

---

1. See *The Diary of Samuel Pepys* at www.pepysdiary.com/diary/1662/09/29/.
2. Salingar, *Shakespeare and the Traditions of Comedy*, 22.
3. Saccio develops this in an audio course, *Shakespeare: The Word and the Action*.

way of our desires. As Mick Jagger told us long ago, we can't always get what we want. We cannot always be with the person we want to be with. Our desires are frustrated, and as long as our desires are frustrated, there can be no happily ever after. If the desires of lovers are always frustrated, the human race will be stopped in its tracks. The world must be peopled.

In Shakespeare's comedies, there are two primary kinds of obstacles, internal and external. External obstacles are more obvious. A young woman is in love with a young man, but her father thinks the young man is childish, irresponsible, shiftless, and horny. Even if he's an okay guy in general, every dad thinks, he is nowhere near good enough for *my* daughter! Dad disapproves, and he becomes an external obstacle to the lovers. Or: A young man sees a beautiful young woman and falls in love. He tells his best friend, who also sees the beautiful young woman and falls in love with her. This is the story of Chaucer's *Knight's Tale*, where Palamon and Arcite, imprisoned in Theseus's Athens, both spy Emily through a narrow window that looks out on a garden. It is impossible for both young men to have her, so they fight it out. They become external obstacles to each other. Or: the obstacle can be a law, a family rule, or social custom. Romeo wants Juliet, but Capulets and Montagues are feuding in fair Verona. A white man falls in love with a black woman in Jim Crow Alabama, and the law and social disapproval of interracial marriage conspire against the lovers.

External obstacles can lead to tragedy, as they do in *Romeo and Juliet*. In comedies, the lovers evade tragedy and get what they desire—each other. But the path to their destination is a winding one. According to Saccio, the solution to external obstacles is flight. If Dad disapproves, the lovers elope. If the families are feuding in Verona, the lovers run away to Venice, where anything goes. If the law or social custom is an obstacle, the lovers flee to a place beyond the reach of the law. In every case, they flee to a safe place. In Shakespeare's plays, the safe place is usually a natural environment. Dad lives in the city, and that's where the law operates. Flight from the law or from parental authority means flight from the city into a "green world," a forest or a rural region where the lovers can have what they want without interference. They leave the city for the bright innocence of Eden. To put it in biblical terms, the comic response to external obstacles is *exodus*.

Sometimes the obstacles are *internal*. Boy likes girl, but girl likes somebody else. Girl likes boy, but boy is a sadistic flirt, who gets his kicks by making girls like him and then rejecting them. Boy likes girl, but girl is what Shakespeare calls a "shrew," angry and embittered. Here the problem is not a parent, a law, a social custom, or family tradition. The problem is not outside the lovers. The problem is the lovers themselves, or one of them. To get what they want, one or both of them have to change.

Internal obstacles are resolved by invasion. Someone has to come from outside to break through the logjam. A Petruchio has to arrive in Padua, ready to "wive it wealthily" by taming a shrew. An Olivia has to be thrown shipwrecked on the beach of Illyria and enter Duke Orsino's service, disguised as a pageboy (*Twelfth Night*). In biblical terms, lovers break through internal obstacles by *incarnation*.[4]

A Midsummer Night's Dream opens with a perfect storm of external obstacles. Hermia is in love with Lysander, and he with her, but everyone and everything is stacked against them. Hermia's father, Egeus, disapproves. He wants Hermia to marry Demetrius, a rival lover. Duke Theseus, ruler of Athens, backs up Egeus and threatens to bring the law down on Hermia with full force. Parental disapproval, the law, a rival lover—they form a wall between the lovers. The play is, at least in one dimension, about the resolution of these obstacles, so that Hermia can marry Lysander. It's about how they break down the dividing wall.

Naturally, the solution is flight into a green world, the world of the forest. That flight sets up the major spatial and thematic contrast of the play. Act 1 takes place in the city. Acts 2–3 take place in the wood. From the middle of Act 4 to the end of the play, the characters are back in the city. This geographic contrast is overlaid with thematic contrasts:

City	Wood
Day	Night
Awake	Asleep
Sight	Dream
Reason	Passion
Law	Magic
Duke Theseus	Oberon, King of the Fairies
Reality	Illusion

---

4. Take note of the happy assonance: *Ex*ternal obstacles are solved by *ex*odus, *in*ternal obstacles by *in*carnation.

When they enter the wood, the lovers do not just enter a natural setting. They enter a dream world of night, ruled by the magic of Oberon and Titania, a world where weavers can turn into asses and lovers betray lovers in an instant. The light of the wood is Luna, who inspires lunacy. The wood is the world of lovers, poets, madmen (cf. Theseus' speech in 5.1, discussed below).

These contrasts not only frame the play as a whole, but recur periodically throughout the play. Theseus talks about bedtime a lot, but we never see anyone asleep in Athens. In the city, it's always daylight, with everyone awake and alert. When Hippolyta wants to take some leisure, she heads out for a hunt with Theseus. In the wood, Titania looks for her luxuriant bower where her fairies can give her a pedicure and a massage. In the wood, the lovers fall asleep and awake repeatedly. Each time, it's a death and resurrection.[5] Demetrius falls asleep loving Hermia and awakes in love with Helena; Lysander falls asleep loving Hermia, awakes to love Helena, falls asleep again, and awakes in love with Hermia. Hermia has a nightmare of an attack from a serpent and awakes to find Lysander gone. Harmony is established among the lovers when they all fall asleep and awake at the same time. Each time they sleep, they are like Adam in Eden, put into deep sleep so he could awake to a lover's face.

For Elizabethans, the association between "wood" and "madness" is partly verbal. When Demetrius first enters the wood, he tells Helena, "here am I, and wood within this wood" (2.1.192). As Marjorie Garber points out, "'Wood,' derived from the Old English word *wod*, means 'mad' or 'lunatic.'" There is a similar pun on "wood" and "wooed." Demetrius "is maddened, and also 'wooed' (by Helena), within the wood." In short, "to be wood within the wood is also to become part of the wood, to take on its qualities, to become transformative and changeable as the wood itself."[6]

Dreamlike transformations happen in the wood, but they aren't all of the same kind. Some are symbolic, marked by changing names and descriptions, while others are literal, such as the male lovers' change of affection or Bottom's transformation. But the play raises the question of whether the transformations are in fact transformative, and this question is most pointedly raised in connection with Bottom: Does he *become* an

---

5. Thanks to my friend, Dave Shaw, for pointing out how crucial these transitions are in the play. "Crucial" is a pun, by the way, since it comes from *crux*, "cross." See below.

6. Garber, *Shakespeare After All*, 217.

ass? Or does his assization merely manifest what was already true about him? With Bottom, the answer seems to be the latter, but then we are tempted to ask whether the same is true of the other characters. Is Lysander's apparently magical change into a lover of Helena really a change, or does it manifest something hidden in the previous situation? Does Titania's infatuation with an ass unmask something about her or change her? The fact that Titania and Oberon are engaged in a conflict over an Indian changeling boy, throwing the wood into chaos, suggests the possibility that her desires are disordered from the beginning. Are her desires already bestial when the play begins? Does the wood make a person wod? Or does the wood merely make the wodishness obvious?

The play's spatial structure raises questions about what we might call Shakespeare's "philosophy of life." Does he think human beings are mainly rational creatures or primarily creatures of imagination? Does he think law rules, or should law give way to magic? What's more human—waking or sleeping, light or the cover of darkness? Is Shakespeare a man of the city or a man of the wood? Is he a rationalist or a romantic? *A Midsummer Night's Dream* doesn't favor one or the other, but a marriage of the two. We can't live in the wood, but we can't live in the city if it is only a place of law. The city needs the magic of dreamland if it is going to be a truly human city.

This twofold spatial contrast is overlaid with a triadic arrangement of characters. There are three stages in the play, and three stage "directors." In Athens, Theseus manages the civic stage, giving orders, threatening punishments, deciding what entertainment will amuse the court on the night of his wedding. Oberon, king of the fairies, is the stage manager of the wood, with Robin Goodfellow, the Puck, serving as assistant manager.[7] Oberon stages a humiliation for his estranged Queen Titania, and Puck improvises by putting a donkey head on Bottom. Oberon sends Puck to smooth out the distressed love quadrangle. Sometimes Puck improvises too much and needs to untangle the knots later. But in the end, Oberon orchestrates a play for his own, and Puck's, amusement. The third stage is the troupe of "rude mechanicals" who practice a play to show during Theseus's wedding celebration. Peter Quince is the official director, but Bottom keeps taking over.

We're invited to compare the three stages, and the third is the key to the play. The players are low on the scale of being, heavy and slow

---

[7]. As in the play, I will treat "Puck" as a name, but in Elizabethan lore a "puck" is a type of fairy.

especially in comparison to the fairies. Even their names are grossly physical (Snout, Bottom). But the low characters, and particularly Bottom, "point up by contrast the shortcomings of the aristocrats." Bottom moves from weaver to actor to ass to the "sweet-faced lover" Pyramus with "unflagging zeal, equanimity, and enthusiasm." He alone discerns that "reason and love keep little company together nowadays."[8] As often in Shakespeare, we need to pay closest attention to the low and weak things of the world, because they're liable to confound the wise and high.

Review Questions

1. What does Leo Salingar mean when he says Shakespearean comedy is guided by a "belief"?
2. Describe the plotline of an "exodus" comedy. What is an "incarnation" comedy?
3. Discuss the significance of the two places in *Midsummer Night's Dream*, the city and the forest.
4. Explain the pun on "wood" in the play.
5. What are the three "stages" in the play? Who are the three "stage directors"?

Thought Questions

1. Research the mythology about Theseus. Who is he? Does the Theseus of mythology resemble Shakespeare's Theseus?
2. What sources did Shakespeare use in writing *Midsummer Night's Dream*? Why is this significant?
3. What does the title tell you about this play?

---

8. Garber, *Shakespeare After All*, 225.

Act 1: Love and Law in Athens

Overall, the first four Acts are organized in a chiastic pattern, in which the second half of the play repeats the first half in roughly reverse order.

>A. Theseus and Egeus demand that Hermia marry Demetrius, 1.1
>>B. Rivalry among lovers, 1.1
>>>C. Conflict between Oberon and Titania, 2.2
>>>>D. Titania and Bottom; lovers' confusions, Act 3
>>>C'. Resolution of rivalry among lovers, 4.1
>>B'. Resolution of Oberon-Titania conflict, 4.1
>A'. Theseus overrules Egeus, 4.1

Within this larger pattern, the play opens with a rhythmically structured scene:

>A. Lovers' dialogue: Duke Theseus and Hippolyta, 1.1.1–19
>>B. Interruption: Egeus complains against his daughter Hermia, 1.1.20–126
>
>A'. Lovers' dialogue: Lysander and Hermia, 1.1.127–79
>>B'. Interruption: Helena, 1.1.180–225
>
>Coda: Helena's soliloquy, 1.1.226–51

The drama really starts with Egeus's abrupt entry, "full of vexation" (1.1.22). It's easy to skim over the quiet opening dialogue between Theseus and Hippolyta. That would be a mistake. Shakespeare is always careful about how he opens his plays. Importantly, the wedding of Theseus and Hippolyta frames the entire play. The play begins with their conversation about their upcoming wedding, and it ends on the wedding day. Within Act 1, the dialogue between Theseus and Hippolyta parallels the dialogue of Hermia and Lysander. The first romance of the play, and the one that sets the frame for all the others, is the romance of Theseus and Hippolyta.

Theseus is impatient to get to his wedding day, which is "four happy days" away (1.1.2). That's also the day when Hermia is supposed to decide whether or not to marry Demetrius, as her father demands (1.1.83–90). Since the play ends on the wedding day of Theseus and Hippolyta, it seems that the action takes place over the intervening days. That doesn't fit other time references in the play. At the end of Act 1, Hermia and Lysander decide to leave "tomorrow night" (1.1.164), and the events of the middle acts occur on the night of their escape from Athens. The internal chronology of the play appears to be:

Day 1	Egeus's appearance before Theseus
Day 1	Hermia and Lysander plan to leave the city
Day 2, night	Hermia and Lysander meet in the wood
Day 2, night	Action of Acts 2–4
Day 3, morning	Theseus finds lovers

When the hunting party finds the lovers, Theseus says it is the day when Hermia is supposed to give her response to the court (4.1.134–35). But it's the third, not the fourth day. Hermia should have another day to decide, and there should be another day before the wedding.

This isn't the only time confusion in *Midsummer Night's Dream*. In Act 5, Theseus says at the beginning of the play-within-the-play that there are "three hours" till bedtime. As soon as the play is over, however, he announces that it is midnight. "Tedious" as the mechanicals' play may be, it's also "brief," not three hours long.

These problems may be insoluble. But the discussion has brought something important to our attention. The play's resolution occurs on the *third* day, which is also a wedding day. In Christian history, the "third day" is the day of Jesus' resurrection. That detail may turn out to be significant.

The moon is waning, moving toward the darkness of the new moon, the few days each month when the moon is invisible to the naked eye. When it reappears "like to a silver bow / New-bent in heaven" (1.1.9–10), it will be Theseus's wedding day. In Theseus's view, the moon moves too slowly, like an old woman who refuses to die. He compares himself to a young man watching his "stepdame or dowager" use up his inheritance (1.1.5). This is the first of many references to the moon and moonshine in the play. Most of the action takes place when the moon has waned to darkness. The mechanicals puzzle about how to represent moonlight, since their play about Pyramus and Thisby also takes place at night.

Moon rules the night, and so is associated with the world of the wood, the world of dreams, magic, and passion. The moon is the source of lunacy, the madness of the madman, the poet, and the lover. The moon represents everything Athens is not, and yet even the daylight world of Athens has to await the moon. The moon is a classic symbol of inconstancy. Unlike the sun, it contracts and grows from night to night. If the play takes place under the sign of the moon, it is a play of fluidity, constantly changing desires and affections, and metamorphosis. The play passes through night to a new day as it passes through the utter darkness of moonlessness to the beginning of a new moon. From waning moon to new moon to that "silver bow"—it's a passage through death into life, a passage through the chaos of the wood to the fresh harmony of a city renewed, a passage which reaches its destination on the third day.

Comedies typically end with weddings. *A Midsummer Night's Dream* does. But it also *begins* with talk of a wedding. That might seem to make the play static: We have to find some way to occupy the tedious time before the wedding. Theseus's final words to Hippolyta indicate something else needs to happen in the intervening time:

> Hippolyta, I wooed thee with my sword,
> And won thy love doing thee injuries,
> But I will wed thee in another key,
> With pomp, with triumph, and with reveling. (1.1.16–19)

Some ancient myths claim Theseus kidnapped Hippolyta while visiting the Amazons, much as Paris abducted Helen from her husband Menelaus. Others say Hippolyta fell in love with Theseus and betrayed her subjects by leaving with him. In both versions of the story, Hippolyta's sister Antiope attacked Athens to rescue her, and Theseus's Athenian armies defeated the Amazons in war. Hippolyta became the only Amazon to marry.

Shakespeare seems to believe the first version of the story, that Theseus took his bride by force. But Shakespeare's Theseus is aware he cannot continue to force Hippolyta. Love can't be coerced. You can't love at the point of a sword. He wooed by the sword, but he needs to wed in "another key." Like every marriage, only more so, the marriage of Theseus and Hippolyta is a reconciliation of opposites, a harmony of rivals. Throughout the play, we will discover various oppositions that must be reconciled if Athens is to flourish.

As soon as Theseus speaks of the new "key" of his life, Egeus appears, demanding that Theseus force his daughter to do what Theseus himself doesn't wish to do: To wed by the sword. Theseus's reaction to Egeus shows that he still needs to learn something about love. The play is framed by the wedding of Theseus and Hippolyta, king and future queen of Athens, but their love will be something of great constancy only if the duke learn the lessons the other lovers have to teach.

As noted above, this scene plunges us into a complex romantic tangle. Hermia and Lysander are in love, but Hermia's father insists she marry Demetrius. Duke Theseus promises to support Egeus, even to the point of sentencing Hermia to death if she disobeys her father. Theseus warns he could sentence Hermia to a lifetime of virginity, singing "hymns to the cold fruitless moon" (1.1.73), another reference to moonlight. Those who "master so their blood," who control their passions in a life of perpetual virginity, are blessed. But the rose that turns to perfume is "earthlier happy" than the rose the withers on the "virgin thorn" and "dies in single blessedness" (1.1.74–77).

Virginity remains a theme throughout the play. Even at night, even alone in the woods, Hermia insists on sleeping at a distance from Lysander, which is more fitting for a "courteous gentleman" and a maid. Demetrius tries to scare Helena off by threatening to steal her virginity. Later, Titania sees the watery-eyed moon, dropping tears that make the flowers weep, as a sign that the moon laments "enforced chastity" (3.1.192–96).

Both Hermia and Theseus speak of love by referring to "eyes." Hermia wants her father to look "but with my eyes" (1.1.56), but Theseus insists Egeus is a "god" to Hermia and therefore "your eyes must with his judgment look" (1.1.57). Whose eyes will make the final judgment about Hermia's lover? Here's the problem of the play: Whose judgment, whose desire, determines the course of love? Does Hermia get to follow her own eyes, or does she have to submit her desires to the eye of another? Helena, who is madly in love with Demetrius, denies the primacy of the eye. Love is a fantasy, an airy nothing constructed by the mind and projected on the object of love:

> Things base and vile, holding no quantity,
> Love can transpose to form and dignity.
> Love looks not with the eyes, but with the mind,
> And therefore is winged Cupid painted blind. (1.1.232–35)

In Helena's allegory, Cupid has wings, and so love often acts with "unheedy haste" (1.1.237). Cupid is a child, a figure of love's innocence that is "oft beguiled" by the promises of "waggish boys" (1.1.239–40). Cupid is blind, and so is love. In Helena's opinion, we don't love what our eyes see at all. We love what our minds *fool* us into seeing.

The love quadrangle is ultimately sorted out. Hermia ends up with Lysander, Helena with Demetrius. Demetrius is the main problem: He needs to be converted from Hermia to Helena, whom he once courted. It's sorted out through the eyes, but only because Puck puts the love potion on Demetrius's eyes. The resolution suggests an answer to the dilemma of the first scene: Love doesn't come from our own eyes, or from the eyes of a father, or from the imagination. Love comes unbidden from a different world. It's a kind of magic. Love invades, like a gift of grace.

Lysander is philosophical about the troubles he and Hermia face. He tells Hermia that every tale and history confirms that "The course of true love never did run smooth" (1.1.134). He offers examples of the obstacles to true love, and Hermia laments each of his examples, forming a braided dialogue:

> LYSANDER
> ... either it was different in blood—
> HERMIA
> O cross! too high to be enthralled to low.
> LYSANDER
> Or else misgraffed in respect of years—
> HERMIA
> O spite! too old to be engaged to young.
> LYSANDER
> Or merit stood upon the choice of friends—
> HERMIA
> O hell! to choose love by another's eyes. (1.1.125–40)

Even when social status, age, and friends converge, love is cut short by war, death, or sickness. Love is "momentany as a sound, / Swift as a shadow, short as any dream." It's lightning on a dark night that "unfolds both heaven and earth" for the merest instant before "the jaws of darkness do devour it up" (1.141–48).

Hermia accepts Lysander's lesson and raises it to a theological level. "O cross!" she cries, and a moment later adds, "true lovers have been ever crossed" (1.1.150). A cross is as "customary" (1.1.153) in love as thoughts, dreams, sighs, hopes, wishes, tears. Athenian pagan though she is, Hermia somehow knows about the cross. "Let us teach our trial patience" (1.1.152), she says, because love, if it is true love, is always born in pain. Bear the cross, because love, if it is true love, is "ever crossed."

Before she met Lysander, Hermia's world was a childhood paradise. Lysander's love, and the conflicts it produced, have made the city a hell (1.1.204–7). She hopes for the bliss of consummated love, but the course of true love doesn't run smooth. More often than not, it takes the lovers through hell before raising them to heaven.

It's easy to forget the play takes place in Athens, since the characters hardly resemble classical Athenians. Athens is the city of reason, a pre-Christian world of law and good order. But this world is threatened by the very law that maintains order. For true order to be established, something else must intervene. If it doesn't, the lovers will end tragically, like Pyramus and Thisby in the play performed in Act 5: The wall of law, of the father's will, leads to the lovers' death. Unless the wall is broken down, Athens will not survive.

The names of the various lovers point to their symbolic, and particularly their astrological, significance. Hermia (Hermes) is Mercury, and Helena (= Selene) is associated with the moon. Mercury is in a higher sphere than the moon, and this perhaps points to the social or moral status of the two women, with Hermia at a higher level than Helena. "Lysander" appears to come from the Greek, combining the verb *luo* (= "loose") and the noun *ander* (= "man"). "Lysander" means "Freedman." Demetrius is linked with the goddess Demeter, who rules the vegetable cycle of sowing and harvest and is associated with the sun. James Jordan suggests the union of Hermia and Lysander is a union of high and low, while the union of Helena and Demetrius is a union of sun and moon.[9] Their weddings symbolize the harmony of the universe, with its marriages of opposites.

Before Act 1 is over, we're introduced to another group of Athenians, the "rude mechanicals" who are practicing a play to celebrate the wedding of Theseus and Hippolyta. Peter Quince is supposed to be in charge, but Bottom the weaver dominates the troupe. He wants to play every character, raises objections about the production, comes up with solutions to the various theatrical dilemmas that Quince poses. Their play is Bottom's play, much as *Midsummer Night's Dream* is itself Bottom's play.

Bottom's name is appropriate to his profession as a weaver. A bottom is a part of a loom, the reel around which thread is wound. For Shakespeare's audience as for us, bottom also names a body part, the buttocks. And this Bottom/butt will turn into a donkey or "ass." Elizabethans spoke of the buttocks as an "arse," from the old English "aers." At some point the "r" dropped out to make our "ass." It's not clear when that shift took place, possibly as late as 1800. Perhaps, though, Shakespeare's audience would already make the association, with Shakespeare's help, and making a further link between ass = donkey and ass = butt.

Bottom's role in the play is unusual, even unique, in Shakespeare. Unlike many other plays, *A Midsummer Night's Dream* has an ensemble

---

9. Jordan, private conversation on an unremembered date.

cast. There's no single dominant figure, as in the great tragedies (Hamlet, Macbeth, Othello, Lear). Many of the comedies have one or two dominant characters (Petruchio and Kate). Who, though, is the protagonist of *Midsummer Night's Dream*? Neither of the male lovers is distinctive enough to fit the bill. Theseus is absent most of the play. Oberon and Titania are more important to the action than Theseus is, but Oberon and Titania are overshadowed by Puck. Bottom comes as close as anyone to being the dominant character. He's certainly the most memorable.

Besides, Bottom is the only character to connect the three groups and three "stages." He begins among the thespian commoners, but he is caught up in Oberon's magic and has more intimate interactions with the fairies than any other human character. He's closer to the queen of magic than any of the high-born nobles of the city. At the end, he's on stage playing Pyramus before Theseus and Hippolyta and carrying on a dialogue with the audience. Lowly Bottom stands in the middle between fairy and human. He joins the wood and the city in one man.

Bottom is also one of the few human characters who has the stage to himself. Helena ends Act 1, scene 1 with a soliloquy, and Oberon has a brief moment alone on stage after he sends Puck to fetch the magic flower (2.1). Hermia wakes up alone in a nightmarish fright (2.2). None has so much time alone onstage, or so long a soliloquy, as Bottom (4.1.199–217). It's one of the most memorable soliloquies in the play and, for all its humor, reaches an almost mystical height. In a play with "dream" in the title, Bottom's speech is notable for its attention to the mysteries of dreams.

No doubt Shakespeare had had some experience with actors like Bottom, who wants to hog the stage, to play every part, to be writer, director, cameraman, and star all rolled into one. But there's more going on than a playful swipe at actors. Bottom *does* play all the parts, ranging from man to animal to fairy back to man. He encompasses the whole chain of being.

Bottom's self-introduction is also notable. Initially, he seems to know all about "The most lamentable comedy and most cruel death of Pyramus and Thisby" (1.2.11–12): "A very good piece of work," he assures his friends (1.2.13). Within a few lines, it becomes clear that he has not the faintest idea of what the play's about: "What is Pyramus? a lover, or a tyrant?" (1.2.19). Told that Pyramus "kills himself, most gallant, for love" (1.2.20), Bottom describes his acting preferences:

That will ask some tears in the true performing of it. If I do it, let the audience look to their eyes. I will move storms; I will condole in some measure. To the rest. Yet my chief humor is for a tyrant. I could play Ercles rarely, or a part to tear a cat in, to make all split. (1.2.21–25)

Tyrants and lovers—those are the coordinates within which the play moves. The play begins with Egeus tyrannizing over Hermia, with Theseus's support. Bottom can play the tyrant too. Once he's transformed into an ass, he begins ordering the fairies around like a two-bit Oberon. Bottom's most memorable role, though, is as lover—not Pyramus, but the ass-head who is doted on by Titania. Bottom not only connects with every group of characters in the play. He's a comically distorted mirror to reflect the tyranny and love that dominate life in the Greek city-state.

Review Questions

1. Why is the opening conversation of Act 1 important?
2. Explain the significance of the wedding coming at the beginning of the play.
3. Give two examples of temporal confusions in *Midsummer*.
4. Discuss the moon symbolism in *Midsummer*.
5. What is the romantic dilemma at the beginning of the play?
6. Explain the importance of "eye" symbolism in the play.
7. Why does Hermia say lovers are "ever crossed"?
8. How is Bottom's role unique in the play?

Thought Questions

1. Hermia swears by "that fire which burned the Carthage queen" that she will meet Lysander in the wood (1.1.168–74). Who is the "Carthage queen"? Why is it ironic that Hermia would swear by her?
2. Why does Helena decide to tell Demetrius about Hermia's and Lysander's flight? (1.1.226–51). Does her reasoning make sense?

3. If you were casting a film of *A Midsummer Night's Dream*, who would you get to play Bottom? Quince? Flute? Starveling? Snug? Puck?

4. Watch clips of three actors playing Bottom. How are they different? What does this tell you about the director's or actor's understanding of the play?

Act 2: "Wod" in the Wood

As we move from the end of Act 1 to the beginning of Act 2, we move from one of the play's worlds to another, from the city to the forest. And that means we move from day to night, from law to magic, from waking to dream, from cool reason to the madness of lovers and poets. Hermia and Lysander go to the wood bearing a lovers' cross. At least at the beginning, the wood is an even heavier burden.

Athens has some magic. Love is a kind of civic magic, magic that threatens good order and decorum within the city walls. That, at least, is how Egeus accounts for Lysander's courtship of Hermia:

> This man hath my consent to marry her.
> Stand forth, Lysander. And, my gracious duke,
> This hath bewitched the bosom of my child.
> Thou, thou, Lysander, thou hast given her rhymes
> And interchanged love tokens with my child;
> Thou hast by moonlight at her window sung
> With feigning voice verses of feigning love,
> And stol'n the impression of her fantasy
> With bracelets of thy hair, rings, gauds, conceits,
> Knacks, trifles, nosegays, sweetmeats—messengers
> Of strong prevailment in unhardened youth.
> With cunning hast thou filched my daughter's heart,
> Turned her obedience (which is due to me)
> To stubborn harshness. (1.1.26–38)

In Egeus's mind, gifts of love like poems, music, and songs in the moonlight are a form of witchcraft, designed to "filch" hearts and turn daughters against their fathers, their "gods."

Egeus is a withered old man. We have a hard time imagining how he ever mounted the passion to father Hermia. But he's not wrong. Love is a kind of magic, with nearly supernatural power. Children grow up dependent on parents or other caretakers. Dependence can become a habit too strong to break. Some thirty-year-olds *do* live in their parents' basement. To grow up, children need power to break out of the ruts of childhood. If, as Theseus says, parents are "gods" to their children, children need *divine* power to break free. That is the power of love. It is, as the Song of Songs puts it, the very fire of Yahweh (8:6). No wonder withered old men want to tamp it down and keep it well under control. Passion disrupts.

In Athens, the magic of love clashes with the demands of law. In the wood, love magic has free rein. That doesn't make it a pleasant place. The opening dialogue of Act 2, between a fairy and the shape-shifter who goes by the names "Robin Goodfellow" and "Puck," recounts some of Puck's pranks. He's a "merry wanderer of the night," a jester to make Oberon smile, who spooks horses, makes a "gossip" (an old woman) spill her ale, pulls a stool from the "wisest aunt." If this is the world of magic, you can see why Athens passes laws to keep it in check. Magic is unpredictable. It does cause disorder, and Puck is the incarnation of its chaotic force.

Puck is an annoying but comparatively harmless trickster. No one *really* gets hurt. The magic of Oberon and Titania is of a different order. Puck introduces us to the conflict between them before the fairy king and queen appear on stage. Elizabethans believed fairies often kidnapped human children to bring them into the fairy world. These children are known as changelings. Titania has a changeling boy from the daughter of an Indian king. As she later tells the story, the boy's mother, a devotress of Titania, died in childbirth, and Titania swore to raise the boy in his mother's honor. Oberon wants the boy, and the conflict between them throws the natural world into disorder. As Titania says,

> Therefore the winds, piping to us in vain,
> As in revenge, have sucked up from the sea
> Contagious fogs which, falling in the land,
> Have every pelting river made so proud
> That they have overborne their continents.
> The ox hath therefore stretched his yoke in vain,
> The plowman lost his sweat, and the green corn
> Hath rotted ere his youth attained a beard;
> The fold stands empty in the drowned field,
> And crows are fatted with the murrion flock;
> The nine-men's morris is filled up with mud,
> And the quaint mazes in the wanton green
> For lack of tread are undistinguishable.

> The human mortals want their winter cheer;
> No night is now with hymn or carol blessed.
> Therefore the moon, the governess of floods,
> Pale in her anger, washes all the air,
> That rheumatic diseases do abound.
> And thorough this distemperature we see
> The seasons alter: hoary-headed frosts
> Far in the fresh lap of the crimson rose,
> And on old Hiems' thin and icy crown
> An odorous chaplet of sweet summer buds
> Is, as in mockery, set. The spring, the summer,
> The childing autumn, angry winter change
> Their wonted liveries; and the mazed world,
> By their increase, now knows not which is which.
> (2.1.88–114).

Under normal circumstances, each season has its own fashion: Green in spring, bright yellow in summer, muted oranges and browns in autumn leading to the pure white of winter. But the seasons now wear the wrong clothes. Times are out of joint. There aren't any hymns or carols to brighten the night. It's winter, but never Christmas. Titania charges that "this same progeny of evils comes / From our debate, from our dissension; / We are their parents and original" (2.1.115–17). As so often in Shakespeare, personal conflict has cosmic echoes.

Oberon and Titania are rivals for the changeling boy. As a result, the differences of nature dissolve into a chaotic mess. In Athens, rivalry has a similar effect. Lysander and Demetrius are rivals for Hermia, and they become twins, the differences between them erased. Helena regards Hermia as a rival and wants to take on her beauty, her face, her eyes. She wants to become Hermia to win the love of Hermia's lover (1.1.181–93).[10] Rivalry blends opposites. In order to arrive at true love and companionship, rivals have to be differentiated. They need to become opposites before they can be reconciled as opposites. As the play moves forward, rivals are first separated, so they can be united later. Painful as the separations are, they are necessary to undo the chaotic effects of rivalry.

Oberon's demand for the boy seems petty. His desire for the boy seems a childish wish, no more than a wish to have what he can't have. His desire for the boy mimics Titania's desire and puts them into violent conflict. There are, however, higher stakes in their debate. Oberon chides

---

10. See Girard, *Theater of Envy*, 40–49.

Titania with the question, "Am I not thy lord?" (2.1.63). As king and husband, he has the right of command, and Titania should obey. Titania's refusal is disorderly and causes further disorder. Here we hear echoes of Egeus's demand that Hermia honor him as "god," and Theseus's warning about flouting proper authority. The sylvan world of love has structures of authority too.

The other issue is implied rather than stated. The changeling is a *boy*, and Oberon wants him as his "henchman," a member of the king's court. The male world of the Fairy King is the right place for a male child. He's no longer an infant, no longer dependent on his stepmother, and Titania violates right order by insisting on keeping the boy in her feminine world. It's time for him to enter the path of manhood.

This aspect of their conflict also has an echo in the human drama. Hermia and Helena were intimate friends in their childhood, sharing everything. They've become women, their desires directed to men, and those desires divide what was once a "double cherry" (3.2.209). In other plays, men have to leave behind the men's club of friends and fellow soldiers in order to assume their place with a bride. In *Midsummer*, the women are faced with the same choice. Like the changeling, they must grow up, and that means suffering on the "cross" of love and "dying" to their idyllic childhood world.

Since the nineteenth century, critics have seen Titania as a veiled depiction of Queen Elizabeth, who escaped Cupid's arrow and continued in "maiden meditation, fancy-free."[11] Elizabeth was often thought of as an Amazon during her reign, since she was in the odd position of being a woman ruling men. Others have been more inclined to link Elizabeth with the human women. In contrast to Hermia, for whom the prospect of perpetual virginity is a curse, Elizabeth was able to use her virginity to increase her power, playing both the roles of queen and of potential bride.

---

11. Annabel Patterson catalogues some of the writers who linked Titania and Elizabeth: "As the moon goddess, Diana, Cynthia, or Phoebe, [Elizabeth] was celebrated as the Belphoebe of Spenser's *Fairie Queene*, and the Cynthia of Ben Jonson's *Cynthia's Revels* and Ralegh's *The Ocean's Love to Cynthia*, all texts of the 1590s when Elizabeth was approaching or in her sixties. . . . Further, as the title of Spenser's poem indicates, the myths of the classical moon-goddess also merged, for the unique moment of Elizabeth's reign, with fairy legends of Titania and Oberon. Even in Ovid's *Metamorphoses*, Titania was another name for Diana (3:173); during a royal progress of 1591 the 'Fairy Queen' presented Elizabeth with a chaplet that she had received from 'Auberon, the Fairy King'; and after her death Thomas Dekker referred to Elizabeth as Titania in his *Whore of Babylon* (1607)" (*Shakespeare and the Popular Voice*, 54–55).

Elizabeth saw herself as the bride of England, wearing her coronation ring in place of a wedding ring. She wrote in 1563 that while marriage works for a "private woman ... it is not meet for a Prince." Freed from the obligations of a husband, she could devote herself wholly to her people.[12]

Whether or not his claim on the changeling is just, Oberon wants his revenge. It needs to fit what he sees as Titania's crime. She is monstrous, unnatural, and unkind toward Oberon. He'll trick her into manifesting her monstrosity by falling in love with some vile thing. He reminds Puck of a magic flower, endowed with the love-power of Cupid because it was struck by Cupid's arrow. Usually, Cupid's arrow enters a person through the eye (the sight of a lover) and moves from there to the heart, inspiring the passionate pain that Oberon describes as "love's wound" (2.1.167). In the incident Oberon recounts, Cupid misses his target and wounds the flower, which gives the flower the power to wound the heart.

While Puck flashes off to get the magic flower, Demetrius and Helena appear, searching for Lysander and Hermia. It's the first time we've seen these characters together, and it's painfully funny to watch. Demetrius's only desire is to find Hermia, and he does everything he can—reject, scold, threaten—to get Helena to leave him alone. Helena's attachment is puppyish, as she herself acknowledges: She wants nothing more than to be Demetrius's spaniel (2.1.203, 205).

Dogs are proverbially faithful. The classic name "Fido" comes from the Latin *fideles*, "faithful." Helena's comparison of herself to a dog alerts us to the sexual dynamics of the play. For all the romantic topsy-turmoil, two things stay firm: The women. Hermia loves Lysander at the beginning, loves him when he leaves and rejects her, loves him when he's restored to himself. Helena never once gives up Demetrius, no matter how badly he treats her. All the romantic shuffling and reshuffling happens because the *guys* change. Their eyes aren't constant. That is fairly typical Shakespearean "feminism": Men are notoriously fickle, women as constant as, well, as a faithful spaniel.

The appearance of the lovers in the wood touches off a rollicking sequence of events. Act 2, scene 2 is organized in a chiastic structure:

---

12. Garber, *Shakespeare After All*, 216–17.

Titania with court, settles in for sleep;
Oberon anoints her eyes, 2.2.1–34
   A. Lysander and Hermia, 2.2.35–65: ends with them sleeping
      B. Puck anoints Lysander's eyes, 2.2.66–83
         C. Helena and Demetrius, 2.2.84–87:
            Demetrius still trying to get away
      B'. Lysander wakes to see Helena, 2.2.88–144:
         Lysander chases Helena
   A'. Hermia, 2.2.145–56: awakes to find Lysander gone

Lovers are separated, reunited, and separated again. One lover chases a lover who is chasing a lover. They form a big, fruitless circle of pursuit. Demetrius looks for Hermia, Hermia looks for Lysander, Lysander pursues Helena, and Helena wants to find Demetrius. It feels like nothing so much as the recurring dream of the chase, where you're trying and failing to escape a witch or a vicious dog, or trying and failing to catch up with a friend.

Let's look at the sequence of events in more detail. Helena and Demetrius enter the wood together, but almost by accident. Demetrius wants to be left alone to chase Hermia. Lysander and Hermia come into the wood as a unit, carrying out their plan to escape the reach of Athenian law. But the wood is a labyrinth, and Lysander's first words express his fatigue and his confusion: "to speak troth, I have forgot our way" (2.2.35–38). He means it literally: He doesn't know the path through the woods. But he will soon lose the way in a metaphorical sense. The wood is hard to track, and the cycle of pursuit turns the wood into a fun house of desperate confusions.

As they prepare to rest, Lysander says they should sleep together: "One turf shall serve as pillow for us both, / One heart, one bed, two bosoms, and one troth" (2.2.41–42). It's the kind of line a young man would try out when he finds himself alone with an attractive girl. Hermia protests that a "virtuous bachelor and a maid" should put some distance between themselves, for the sake of "love and courtesy" (2.2.59, 56). When Puck finds them, and misjudges the situation, he thinks Lysander is a "lack-love" and a "kill-courtesy" for sleeping so far away from Hermia (2.2.77). Puck has the situation exactly backward: Love and courtesy keep them from lying too close together.

Hermia lies down on the bank of a stream, while Lysander sleeps some distance away. It's a small separation, a sign of the purity of their love, but that gap creates the possibility for further separation. Puck mistakenly, or puckishly, puts the love potion on Lysander's eyes and exits. Demetrius and Helena appear, and Demetrius quickly continues his pursuit of Hermia, without seeing her on the ground in front of him. Helena finds Lysander and, fearing he's dead, wakes him. Seeing through eyes opened by the magic flower, he instantly expresses his love for Helena: "I do repent / The tedious minutes I with [Hermia] have spent. / Not Hermia, but Helena I love" (2.2.111–13). Helena is a dove in comparison to the "raven" Hermia (2.2.114). Lysander's tastes have matured, so that he no longer wants the food that once delighted him. Reason overcomes his will, and "reason says you [Helena] are the worthier maid" (2.2.116). Lysander could learn some wisdom from Bottom: "reason and love keep little company together nowadays" (3.1.138–39). Helena is sure that Lysander is mocking her, and she runs away again, now not only pursuing Demetrius but escaping Lysander. Lysander follows. What was once a short distance between pillow and pillow, bed and bed, has become a chasm, and a widening one.

It's a slapstick scene of romantic confusion. But we shouldn't minimize the tragic possibilities. Hermia ends Act 2, scene 2 alone, awaking in terror:

> Help me, Lysander, help me! Do thy best
> To pluck this crawling serpent from my breast.
> Ay me, for pity! What a dream was here!
> Lysander, look how I do quake with fear.
> Methought a serpent eat my heart away,
> And you sat smiling at his cruel prey.
> Lysander! What, removed? Lysander! lord!
> What, out of hearing gone? No sound, no word?
> Alack, where are you? Speak, an if you hear.
> Speak, of all loves! I swoon almost with fear.
> No? Then I well perceive you are not nigh.
> Either death, or you, I'll find immediately. (2.2.145–56)

Serpents, adders, snakes, and poisons are diabolical images in Shakespeare. Claudius kills King Hamlet by pouring poison in his ear, a variation on Adam and Eve, who died because they listened to a serpent's poisoned words. Hermia sees some satanic power is stealing her heart. She'll later accuse Demetrius of being a serpent who killed Lysander, and Lysander will try to shake Hermia loose like a serpent: "Hang off, thou cat, thou burr! Vile thing, let loose, / Or I will shake thee from me like a serpent!" (3.2.260–61). Who has poisoned whom? None of them suspects they're all poisoned by an outside power, Oberon's love potion, administered by Puck.

Hermia's nightmare isn't real. There's no *actual* serpent. Yet in the wood dreams speak more truly than waking reason. Someone has drawn near to separate this Eve from her Adam; like Adam, Lysander has abandoned his bride, in pursuit of a phantom love inspired by the love potion. For Hermia, the night is a lovers' cross, which she has to bear. Perhaps, though, this wooden cross will prove her salvation.

Hermia's frantic cries for Lysander anticipate the doggerel of the final play-within-a-play. We remember her speech later when we hear Bottom as Pyramus lament the night that hides Thisby from him: "O night, O night, alack, alack, alack" (5.1.171). We're reminded of Hermia's speech again when Thisby discovers Pyramus's body, and falls into a frenzy of grief:

> Asleep, my love?
> What, dead, my dove?
> O Pyramus, arise!
>   Speak, speak. Quite dumb?
>   Dead, dead? A tomb
> Must cover thy sweet eyes.
>   These lily lips,
>   This cherry nose,
>   These yellow cowslip cheeks,
>   Are gone, are gone.
>   Lovers, make moan.
> His eyes were green as leeks. (5.1.319–30)

Thisby's speech ends with her suicide. Hermia gets up to run after Lysander. But the resemblance hints at the tragic potential of the lover's confusion. Blocked desire *can* lead to death. Rivals in love do kill each other. Despairing lovers do commit suicide. Some walls aren't broken down in time.

This play's title contains the word *dream*. The entire play takes place in a dreamscape and is framed by references to dreams. Hippolyta assures Theseus they will "quickly dream away the time" before the wedding (1.1.8), and Puck's epilogue excuses any offense in the play by urging the audience to think they've been asleep and dreaming (5.1.415–30). Within the play, only two characters actually have and recount dreams. Hermia's is the first, the nightmare of the serpent. Bottom has the second, and that dream is about to begin.

Review Questions

1. What kind of magic exists in Athens? What problems does this create for the city?
2. Who is Puck?
3. What is the quarrel between Oberon and Titania about? Why is the quarrel significant? What effects has their quarrel had on the natural world?
4. How does Shakespeare allude to Queen Elizabeth in *Midsummer*?
5. How do the male characters differ from the female characters?
6. Discuss or diagram the "circle of pursuit" in Act 2.
7. How does the demonic imagery fit into the play?
8. Who are the literal dreamers in the play?

Thought Questions

1. Oberon wonders why Titania would "cross" her Oberon (2.1.119). How is this connected with the other uses of "cross" in the play?
2. Titania sleeps in a bower of flowers and herbs (2.1.248–54). How is this connected with the flower Oberon calls "love-in-idleness" (2.1.168)?
3. Helen refers to Apollo and Daphne (2.1.231). What is she talking about? How is it relevant to the scene?
4. What do the fairies sing to Titania as she falls asleep? (2.2.9–24). Given what happens later, why is their song significant?
5. According to Helena, which of Hermia's features is most beautiful? (2.2.88–102). How does this fit with imagery elsewhere in the play?

Acts 3–4: What Eye Hath Not Heard

The arrangement of scenes in Acts 3–4 is significant. On the surface, it looks as if the scenes with Bottom and Titania are interspersed with the romantic scenes. Demetrius and Helena, and then Lysander and Hermia, arrive in the forest. Their affections are altered and they begin a dizzying circular pursuit through the maze of the woods. Then Titania falls in love with ass-headed Bottom. Finally, the lovers' rivalry is resolved. On this reading, Bottom's story is embedded within the larger frame of the romantic drama.

When we examine Acts 3–4 together, the relationship between these two subplots is the opposite. Although the lovers have been introduced and the romantic confusions have already begun to arise, Bottom's encounter with Titania initiates a new movement within the play, one that frames the two central Acts:

    A. Bottom with the mechanicals, 3.1
      B. Bottom and Titania, 3.1
        C. Lovers confused, 3.2
      B'. Titania released from charm, 4.1
        C'. Theseus discovers lovers reconciled, 4.1
      B". Bottom awakes from his dream, 4.1
    A'. Bottom with the mechanicals, 4.2

Within this structure, the quarrels of the lovers form a subnarrative within the story of Bottom. More space is devoted to the lovers, but their storyline is nestled within the other storyline.

With the reappearance of Bottom and the mechanicals, the three sets of characters and stages intersect, now in the woods. The lovers are subject to the whims of the fairies, but they never see them or even suspect their presence. Confined to Athens and its surrounding grounds, Theseus, Hippolyta, and Egeus never come into the wood or have any links with the fairies. As noted above, Bottom is the only character who bridges the fairy-human divide.

Yet Bottom isn't an inert bridge, but a means of reconciliation and re-harmonization. The seasons are out of joint, and nature is in turmoil, because of the conflict between Oberon and Titania over the changeling boy. Bottom isn't aware of his role in resolving that conflict, but he's crucial. Oberon's vengeance is exhausted by tricking Titania into falling for a donkey-headed human. In Act 4, scene 1, Oberon releases her from her spell and she agrees to give him the changeling boy. Nature gets put back together, and Bottom is at the center.

Act 3 opens with the mechanicals setting up a stage on a "green plot" near a hawthorn patch that will serve as their "tiring house," the dressing room. The play presents problems for the literal-minded day laborers.

Bottom is worried the play will be too frightening for the gentleladies in the audience. Lions and suicides aren't suitable to such an audience. Starveling goes so far as to suggest leaving the killing out, but Bottom has another solution: Break the fourth wall of the stage, address the audience directly, and assure everyone that no animals or people have been harmed in the production of the play. They fret over moonlight for similar reasons: How can they capture moonlight and carry it into the theater? Or a wall, for that matter? They consult an almanac to determine whether they can rely on *real* moonlight and decide to appoint actors to "present" both moonlight and wall.

Shakespeare intends his audience to laugh at the simple-minded characters, but there are deeper issues at work here. The players, more than the lovers, recognize the potential dangers of illusion and fantasy. They know imagination poses dangers as well as delights. As Garber puts it, "Role-playing is dangerous. . . . The condition of being an actor is a condition akin to the performance of magic. . . . The dangers of the irrational can be combated only by a safe retreat to reality," only by breaking the frame and informing the audience that "he is Snug the joiner."[13] Athenian law can turn tyrannical, even murderous. But imagination is dangerous too, if left to play without its playmate reason.

As soon as they begin to practice, Puck enters, first as audience or "auditor," but then as "actor." In fact, he becomes the director. Above, we noticed that the lovers are separated and reunited in various combinations. Bottom too is first separated from his comrades and then united with a new collection of characters, Titania and her fairy attendants.

Puck puts an ass's head on Bottom and then squeezes the magic juice into Titania's eyes, so she falls in love with the ass-man. When Bottom wakes her by singing, she says her eye is "enthralled to thy shape," and adds, "On the first view . . . I love thee" (3.1.134, 136). Bottom responds with some of the best lines of the play: "Methinks, mistress, you should have little reason for that. And yet, to say the truth, reason and love keep little company together nowadays" (3.1.137–39). From the opening scene, the play has asked whose eyes do or should determine love: A father's? A lover's? Titania's experience makes it clear that we must be *given* eyes to love, and Bottom confirms the point: Love isn't subject to the scrutiny and examination of reason. Titania is under a spell, but she's right about Bottom: "Thou art as wise as thou art beautiful" (3.1.142).

---

13. Garber, *Shakespeare After All*, 231.

Act 3, scene 2 is a long, complex scene and dramatizes the primary complications of the plot and the beginning of its resolutions. It alternates between the lovers and the fairies:

   A. Puck reports to Oberon, 3.2.1–40
      B. Demetrius and Hermia enter & argue, 3.2.41–87
         (Hermia exits; Demetrius sleeps)
   A'. Oberon and Puck, 3.2.88–121
      B'. Lysander and Helena; Demetrius awakes and Hermia comes back, 3.2.122–344
   A". Puck and Oberon, 3.2.345–400
   Coda: Puck sorts lovers out, 3.2.401–63

Out in the wood, Lysander, Demetrius, Hermia, and Helena meet up, for the first time since the beginning of the play (3.2.122–344). The dynamics of the scene replicate the opening scene. In 1.1, Lysander and Demetrius compete for Hermia; in 3.2, due to Puck's mistake, the two men compete for Helena. In the opening scene, Egeus claims to own his daughter Hermia; in 3.2, Lysander implies that he has property rights to Hermia's love, which he cedes to Demetrius.

Some of the imagery of 1.1 is repeated too. Hermia and Lysander list tears among "Fancy's followers," one of the normal effects of love; in 3.2, Helena complains the men are mocking her to bring tears to her eyes. When Lysander describes the evils that befall lovers, Hermia responds with exclamations: "O spite! O hell!" Helena uses the same words when she thinks everyone has agreed to tease her. Hermia charges that Helena is a "thief of love," echoing Egeus's charges against Lysander in the opening scene.

When the lovers meet in the wood, though, the duke and Egeus aren't present. Neither Athenian law nor paternal authority is operative. Instead, the lovers quarrel and fight under the gaze of Oberon, king of the fairies. This isn't a court of law, but a place of magic. The rivalries of the lovers knot up into tighter tangles. Hermia and Helena come to see each other as rivals. Helena thinks Hermia has broken their childhood covenant and joined with the boys to mock her. While Lysander and Demetrius trudge off to duel, Helena taunts Hermia about her short stature and Hermia threatens to scratch Helena with her fingernails. This is not the escape the lovers sought when they fled from Athens. But in the nighttime world of magic, not the daylit world of Athens, obstacles are removed and harmony is restored. Puck restores right sight to all the lovers, and all is put right. One is tempted to offer a Pauline gloss: What the law could not do, fairies have done.

But the city isn't left behind. Before the end of Act 4, scene 1, the court is fully reconstituted. Theseus and Hippolyta are hunting, with Egeus in their entourage, accompanied not by the music of fairies but by the "musical confusion / of hounds and echo in conjunction" (4.1.109–10). At the edge of the wood, they find the four lovers, waking from their chaotic night, "amazed" as Lysander puts it (4.1.145). Egeus repeats his charge: Hermia's presence outside the city is proof of her intention to run away with Lysander. Both should be punished. But the wall that divided the lovers is gone. Demetrius's desire for Hermia "melted as the snow" and now seems a childish toy by comparison with his love for Helena. He admits he was "betrothed" to Helena before he saw Hermia and has now returned to his "natural taste" (4.1.159–75). Theseus renders judgment: He denies Egeus's demand and offers the couples to join his marriage to Hippolyta. A single royal marriage becomes a triple marriage, and the harmony established in the wood is endorsed by the ruler of the city. Now that the lovers have come to the "third day," they enter into a new life.

As the members of the court leave for Athens, the lovers discuss the experience of the night. What happened seems to Demetrius like "far-off mountains turned into clouds" that dissolve and blow away. Hermia sees everything double, as with a "parted eye" (4.1.186–98). The eye she wanted to guide her father's decision for Lysander has been doubled and parted and reunited. The lovers can't even figure out whether they're awake or asleep, until they compare their memories of the duke's appearance. If they all agree, it cannot have been a dream, and they head back to the city to prepare for their weddings.

One Athenian is still asleep in the wood, Bottom the weaver. He began the central section of the play, rehearsing with his fellows. He closes out the scenes in the wood with a comic attempt to express what he's seen and done. He wakes up calling for Quince, Flute, Snout, and Starveling. Hearing nothing, he concludes they've been "stolen hence," but the syntax of the opening line suggests that he, or his life, is the thing that has been stolen. And it has. Mystics everywhere will tell you they lose themselves in the object of their meditation, whether that is the All-Soul, the Buddha, or the wounds of the Son of God. "God's my life" (4.1.202) echoes the mystical Pauline claim: "I no longer live, but Christ lives in me" (Gal 2:20). Bottom's life, like Paul's, has been wrenched from him, and is no longer his own.

If it seems a stretch to find an apostolic echo in the words of Bottom, we need only read further, because there can be no doubt that Bottom is speaking words he's heard and half-understood and half-remembered. He's had a "rare vision," so deep that one would have to be an "ass" to try to expound it:

> God's my life! Stolen hence, and left me asleep? I have had a most rare vision. I have had a dream, past the wit of man to say what dream it was. Man is but an ass if he go about to expound this dream. Methought I was—there is no man can tell what. Methought I was, and methought I had—But man is but a patched fool if he will offer to say what methought I had. The eye of man hath not heard, the ear of man hath not seen, man's hand is not able to taste, his tongue to conceive, nor his heart to report what my dream was. I will get Peter Quince to write a ballad of this dream. It shall be called "Bottom's Dream," because it hath no bottom; and I will sing it in the latter end of our play, before the duke. Peradventure, to make it the more gracious, I shall sing it at her death. (4.1.199–217)

In with and under the comic synesthesia, the confusion of senses (eye hears, ear sees, hand tastes) is Paul's description of the wisdom of God paradoxically revealed in the foolishness of the cross: "Things which eye has not seen and ear has not heard, and which have not entered the heart of man, all that God has prepared for those who love Him" (1 Cor 2:9). Bottom is unaware, but he chose a fitting voice, for he is precisely one of the foolish things that surpasses human wisdom.

What is it that Bottom has discovered? Part of his wisdom lies in his refusal to attempt to explain it. When he rejoins his friends in the city (4.2), he tells them he's had an experience he cannot share with them. He could "discourse wonders," but there will be "not a word of me" (4.2.28, 32). For a chatterbox like Bottom, keeping a secret is a superhuman act of discipline. But he knows he cannot express what he knows. He's brushed up against mysteries, and unlike the lovers he is content in his ignorance. He has experienced something close to what theologians describe as the "learned ignorance" of mystical experience. An encounter with the fairies, like love itself, keeps little company with reason. Before the magic of love, we can only stand in awe.

The Pauline reference might point us in a different direction. From the outset of the play, we've known true love doesn't run in a smooth course. Love is beset by various crosses. Suffering is as much a part of love as sighs, sexual excitement, tears of worry. When Paul describes the things that the eye has not seen or the ear heard, he's talking about the surprising wisdom of God displayed in the crucifixion of Jesus. In the cross, God shows that his weakness is stronger than men, his folly wiser than human wisdom. Bottom has touched this mystery. Reason and love keep little company together nowadays, he observes to Titania. What *does* keep company with love, true love, is suffering. Bottom has somehow stumbled on the reality that Hermia hinted at early on: O cross! Bottom has learned that love is redeemed only by the wood, only if the reasonable Athenians are willing to run "wod" in the wood.

Review Questions

1. Explain the structure of Acts 3–4.
2. How does Bottom reconcile Oberon and Titania?
3. What is the serious point in the inability of the "mechanicals" to stay in their stage roles?
4. How is Act 3, scene 2 similar to Act 1, scene 1? How are they different?
5. How does Act 4, scene 1 bring the lovers' plot to resolution?
6. What is Bottom's dream about?

Thought Questions

1. What is Bottom singing about when he wakes up Titania (3.1.120–28)? What is significant about his song?
2. What are the names of the fairies that attend on Bottom? (3.1.170–91). What do their names tell you about them, and about fairies in general?
3. Explain Hermia's discussion of sight and hearing in 3.2.177–83.
4. What does Lysander call Hermia when he's infatuated with Helena?
5. What do Hippolyta and Theseus have to say about the sound of their hounds (4.1.111–25)? Why is this discussion significant?

THE COURSE OF TRUE LOVE   123

Act 5: The Dividing Wall

Act 5 is one long scene, organized in this way:

> A. Human rulers: Theseus and Hippolyta reflect on the lovers' stories
>   B. Lovers enter
>   B'. Theatrical love story: Pyramus and Thisby
> A'. Fairy rulers: Oberon, Puck, and Titania bless Theseus's house

The rival lovers have been reconciled. Every Jack, from Theseus on down, has found his proper Jill. There is no more action, and the final act celebrates the triple wedding with feasting and entertainment. Theseus is not a man of imagination, but a man of reason. Unlike Hippolyta, he doesn't believe the lovers' account, even though they all agree on details. They're telling nothing but "antique fables" and "fairy toys"(5.1.3). It's just what we expect from lovers:

> Lovers and madmen have such seething brains,
> Such shaping fantasies, that apprehend
> More than cool reason ever comprehends.
> The lunatic, the lover and the poet
> Are of imagination all compact.
> One sees more devils than vast hell can hold;
> That is, the madman. The lover, all as frantic,
> Sees Helen's beauty in a brow of Egypt.
> The poet's eye, in a fine frenzy rolling,
> Doth glance from heaven to earth, from earth to heaven;
> And as imagination bodies forth
> The forms of things unknown, the poet's pen
> Turns them to shapes, and gives to airy nothing
> A local habitation and a name. (5.1.4–17)

Theseus's last lines are justly famous. Poets and artists do just what Theseus says: From the imagination, the storehouse of images in the soul, where they form things unknown in nature, they bring forth *bodies*—solid sculptures, colorful paintings, heartaching music, enthralling poetry and story. All these are "bodied forth" and take bodily shape, just as, we might say, the eternal Word becomes flesh. Poets and madmen have nothing to work with, but they can give shape to nothing, locate it, name it. They are like the Creator, who speaks what he imagines into solid being.

Theseus's speech is such a lovely and compelling description of artistic creation that we forget he's a skeptic about art. He's not impressed that artists can echo God's original creation from nothing. His emphasis is on the *nothing*. Imagination tricks us into seeing something when nothing is there. It tricks us into thinking joy must have a bringer of joy, and that a bush seen in the night shadows might be a bear. Theseus has yet to learn the lesson he should have learned from the lovers: Cool reason and law in Athens can't explain or resolve conflicts of love. Athens must be reconciled to the wood, day to night, reason to passion. If Athens is going to survive, the wall that separates the city from the wood must come down. Hippolyta is more attuned to the lovers' experience. She believes airy nothings can become something.

There *are* signs of hope for Athens. For starters, Theseus does allow the mechanicals to put on a play, despite Philostrate's repeated efforts to convince him the play is "nothing." He's skeptical about imagination, and his skepticism is evident in his sneering jeers at the players. He's more a critic than an audience member, pointing to the flaws in the design and execution of the tragedy. Still, Theseus is generous, willing to accept anything that is offered in "simpleness and duty" (5.1.83). The play may indeed be nothing, but

> The kinder we, to give them thanks for nothing.
> Our sport shall be to take what they mistake,
> And what poor duty cannot do, noble respect
> Takes it in might, not merit.
> Where I have come, great clerks have purposed
> To greet me with premeditated welcomes;
> Where I have seen them shiver and look pale,
> Make periods in the midst of sentences,
> Throttle their practised accent in their fears,
> And, in conclusion, dumbly have broke off,
> Not paying me a welcome. Trust me, sweet,
> Out of this silence yet I picked a welcome,
> And in the modesty of fearful duty
> I read as much as from the rattling tongue
> Of saucy and audacious eloquence.
> Love, therefore, and tongue-tied simplicity
> In least speak most, to my capacity. (5.1.89–105)

The play is, like the entire play, a "coincidence of opposites," billed as both "brief" and "tedious," as "tragical mirth." It depicts the story of Pyramus and Thisby, lovers separated by their families, as Hermia and Lysander were separated by Egeus. The two lovers whisper to one another through a chink in the wall that divides their families. One moonlit night, they plan a rendezvous at Ninus's tomb. A lion, bloody from a kill, greets Thisby and tears away her shawl. Thisby escapes, but Pyramus finds her bloody shawl and thinks her dead. In despair, he kills himself. When Thisby returns to find his body, her heart shatters and she kills herself. It is a tragedy of misperception.

Opening themselves charitably to the play, the members of the court are moved in spite of themselves. Pyramus's lament over Thisby is bad poetry, silly on the face of it. Theseus comments that Bottom might move him to tears, if at the same time he learned of the death of a dear friend. Hippolyta sees beyond the bad performance and feels the force of Pyramus's lament: "Beshrew my heart but I pity the man" (5.1.285). In some productions, Thisby's dying speech (quoted above) has a sobering effect on the audience. Not only Hippolyta, but all the court, pauses before Theseus resumes his mockery. That seems right, dramatically and thematically. The play holds up, as Hamlet says, a "mirror to nature." It shows the lovers and the court what *might* have been if the fairies had not intervened. Hermia and Helena must see themselves in Thisby; Lysander and Demetrius must think they could have ended like Pyramus.

The mechanicals' play is ended. The bodies of Pyramus and Thisby lie on the stage. No one is left but Moonshine, Lion, and Wall, which, Theseus jokingly says, will bury the dead. Pyramus rises to speak. Bottom can't keep still and has to explain. Whatever might be said for Moonshine and Lion, Wall isn't left: "the wall is down that parted their fathers" (5.1.345–46). With their deaths, the lovers have broken down the wall of hostility and reconciled their families and the city.

It's a toss-off line, another of Bottom's endless interruptions and asides. But we need to be attentive. Bottom has had a vision beyond expression. He's slept in the bower of the Fairy Queen and been touched by the transforming magic of the wood. Despite his name, he's not a bottom-dweller, but the wisest character in the play. When he speaks of a dividing wall broken down, we can't help but hear another echo of the apostle Paul:

> For He Himself is our peaces, who made both groups into one and broke down the barrier of the dividing wall, by abolishing in His flesh the enmity, which is the Law of commandments contained in ordinances, so that in Himself He might make the two into one new man, thus establishing peace, and might reconcile them both in one body to God through the cross, by it having put to death the enmity. (Eph 2:14–16)

Act 5 is a marriage scene. The third day, Theseus's wedding day, has finally arrived, and along with the duke and (now) duchess, Athens celebrates the noble weddings of Lysander and Hermia, Demetrius and Helena. Out in the wood, Oberon and Titania have given up their quarrel and renewed their love. Bottom is reunited with his friends. After a night in the labyrinth of the wood, morning brings reconciliation and peace. It's a perfect comic ending, with multiple weddings.

These actual weddings and reconciliations point to thematic reconciliations. At a large level, the marriages reconcile different civilizations. As Duke of Athens, Theseus represents Greek civilization with its philosophy, art, smooth order. Queen of the Amazons, Hippolyta represents what is wild and untamed. She's queen of a race of women who refuse to bow to men. That she's now marrying Theseus shows that she's really a *former* Amazon, but she brings her untamed Amazonian nature into Athens.

As noted above, the names of the lovers suggest that they come from different classes. Lysander is perhaps a "Loosed Man," a freed slave, lower on the social scale than Demetrius. Hermia is shorter in stature than Helena, a point of contention between them, but her name suggests an association with Mercury, in a higher heavenly sphere than "Helena," associated with the moon. The weddings reconcile the sexes in lifelong love, but they're also reconciling Athenian society across class boundaries. Theseus has to overcome the objections of Philostrate, his snobbish master of ceremonies, to bring the mechanicals onto the stage. The fact that their play is "preferred" and performed before the court is a sign of the reconciliation of Athens.

The final sign of hope for Athens comes in the closing lines. The play is ended, and the lovers are off to bed. As they leave, Puck, Oberon, and Titania appear, spreading light, music, dancing, and blessing through the house. Oberon pronounces a benediction not only on the wedding bed but on the future children of all the newly married couples:

> Now, until the break of day
> Through this house each fairy stray.
> To the best bridebed will we,
> Which by us shall blessed be,
> And the issue there create
> Ever shall be fortunate.
> So shall all the couples three
> Ever true in loving be,

> And the blots of Nature's hand
> Shall not in their issue stand.
> Never mole, harelip, nor scar,
> Nor mark prodigious, such as are
> Despised in nativity,
> Shall upon their children be. (5.1.393–406)

Puck apologizes to the audience of *Midsummer Night's Dream*, breaking the fourth wall as decisively as the mechanicals did in their play. The final words of the play come from Puck.

Here is something we had not known, nor expected. We get some hints that Oberon once pursued Hippolyta, and Titania Theseus, but throughout the play humans and fairies have kept to their separate worlds. In the final scene, we learn they are intertwined. All unknown and unseen, the fairies of the wood make their way through the city, spreading the goods of the forest within the duke's house. Here is the hope for Athens—not reason nor law alone, but reason and law infused with fairy power. This is the hope for any city, that it is safe in the hands of grace. At the end if not at the beginning, city and wood are reconciled, joined as one flesh. The walls that separated lover and lover are down, but only because fairy magic has breached the wall separating city and forest.

Review Questions

1. What weddings take place in Act 5?
2. Discuss Theseus's opening speech in Act 5. Is he right?
3. What is the plot of the play-within-a-play? What effect does it have on Theseus's court?
4. What is significant about Bottom's line about the "wall is down"?
5. What is Puck's final song about?

Thought Questions

1. What other plays does Theseus have to choose from (5.1.44–60)?
2. Read the Prologue speeches for the play (5.1.108–17, 126–50). What makes the poetry funny?

3. What ancient lovers do Pyramus and Thisby name (5.1.194–98)? Are they good models of love?

4. How does Puck describe the night (5.1.363–82)? Why does he have a broom?

5

Tempests Are Kind

Twelfth Night

TRAGEDY ENDS IN DISASTER for the principal character or characters. In tragedy, the gods are dangerous and whimsical, the characters' mistakes and wrongs spin out of control and engulf innocent bystanders. Some characters survive the final catastrophe, but the only victors are death and the grave, who smiles because he's fat with new corpses. Threats appear in comedies too, but the threats are overcome. In a comedy, the last state is better than the first. Instead of ending with multiple funerals, comedies end with multiple marriages.

It's an old prejudice to think tragedy is more profound than comedy. The ancients believed comedy skims the surface of reality, while tragedy, grim as it is, gets to the truth deep down things, because the truth is grim.

Christianity changed all that.[1] The Bible records a comic history, moving from creation to fall to final advent, from Eden's garden to the garden city that comes from heaven. History doesn't degenerate from better to worse, from good to bad. Jesus the *last* Adam improves on the first. According to Christian belief, comedy shows the real world, the world as it really is, the world heading toward glory and the joy of an eternal wedding feast, a world that ends not with a dirge but a dance.

Shakespeare wrote in the tradition of Christian comedy, and few of his plays bring that tradition to as high an expression as *Twelfth Night*.

---

1. See my *Deep Comedy*.

It was one of his last comedies, and in it he pulls out all his tricks and motifs, wordplay, and plot twists to dramatize a world where comedy is the truth deep down things.

Like *Midsummer Night's Dream*, *Twelfth Night* is structured around two locations. *Midsummer* moves between the city of Athens and the fairyland of the forest. In Athens, romance and desire crash into various obstacles, but in the forest Oberon and Puck complicate, then untie, Athenian knots. Athens—the city of law, reason, and democracy—can be what it should be only if it's seasoned with the grace of Faerie.

Twelfth Night moves between two noble houses in the kingdom of Illyria. The first belongs to Duke Orsino, ruler of Illyria. Early in the play, Orsino is joined by a young page boy, Cesario, with whom he rapidly develops a close attachment. Other courtiers appear, but they are minor characters. Orsino is able to rule the country adequately, but there's something sickly in the air. He spends most of the play moping like a lovesick teenager over Lady Olivia, who presides over the second house.

Lady Olivia's house is more densely peopled and is itself divided in two. Olivia's cousin, Sir Toby Belch, is a long-time guest, and creates a realm of "uncivil rule" (2.3.114) among the servants and guests. Sir Andrew Aguecheek, Toby's constant companion, has come to court Olivia. A weak and foolish but *rich* knight, Andrew funds Toby's late-night revels, which they share with Feste the Fool, a sometime resident of Olivia's house. Despite her position in Olivia's inner circle, the maid Maria is Toby's ally and a symptom of the house's disorder. Olivia's steward, Malvolio (his name means "ill will"), mediates between Olivia and the chaotic "downstairs" characters, bringing their misdeeds to Olivia's attention and delivering Olivia's messages to Sir Toby and the others. In revenge, Maria, Toby, and Andrew devise a cruel trick to take Malvolio down several pegs.

Through the course of the play, the two houses are put in order. As always in Shakespeare, the path to order runs through a valley of chaos.

> Act 1: Both houses disordered.
> Acts 2–3: Disorder heightened.
>   Act 2: Ends with gulling of Malvolio.
>   Act 3: Malvolio acts on the false letter.
> Act 4: Olivia's house ordered by marriage; Andrew and Toby tamed.
> Act 5: Orsino's house ordered by marriage: disguises removed.

Here as in *Midsummer*, the course of true love is anything but smooth.

Until Act 5, Orsino and Olivia remain in their separate houses. The comedy, complications, and resolutions emerge from characters who mediate between the two locations. One is Feste, a wandering fool, who has a history with Olivia's family but visits Orsino's house regularly. The other mediator is Cesario, who is not really Cesario but Viola, a young woman who disguises herself as a page after being shipwrecked in Illyria. Falsely believing she lost her brother, Sebastian, in the wreck, she thinks she has to fend for herself. As Cesario, she becomes Orsino's messenger of love to Olivia. Adding these mediators, we might graph the geography of the play as follows:

Orsino's house	**Mediators**	**Olivia's house**
Orsino, Cesario	Cesario, Feste	Olivia
		+
		Malvolio, Feste
		+
		Toby, Andrew, Maria, Fabian, Feste

In *Midsummer* and in *Merchant of Venice* (see chapter 6), the major locations represent a cluster of contrasting themes, attitudes, ways of life. The forest (in *Midsummer*) and Belmont (in *Merchant*) are Edenic locations, associated with moonlight, music, and magic. To escape the dangers of Athens or Venice, characters retreat or flee to the green world.

Neither house in *Twelfth Night* is Edenic; neither offers redemption. On the contrary, both are initially pervaded by an atmosphere of melancholy, self-love, and perplexity. Olivia has sworn to mourn her dead brother for seven years by wearing black, refusing to see the sun, and renouncing the company of men. Orsino pines for Olivia, his desire strengthened by her resolute refusal to receive him or hear his suit. He so enjoys wallowing in his tears that he doesn't seem to *want* her to love him back. These internal obstacles—Olivia's sorrow and Orsino's self-indulgence—lock them in a motionless non-dance of unrequited love.

Such a static situation is ripe for incarnational invasion. Viola breaks through the impasse, though initially creating more rather than less chaos. The structure of the first Act introduces Viola as mediator between the houses:

A. Orsino's house: Orsino pines for Olivia, 1.1
    B. The ship captain helps Viola find a place at Orsino's, 1.2
        C. Olivia's house: Toby, Maria, Andrew, 1.3
A'/B'. Orsino's house: Viola disguised as Cesario, 1.4
        C'. Olivia's house: Viola speaks to Olivia on Orsino's behalf, 1.5

Viola literally appears in the middle (1.2) between scenes in Orsino's house (1.1) and Olivia's house (1.3). In terms of structure as well as in terms of plot, Viola is a "go-between."

There's a deeper layer to Viola's role as mediator. As Orsino's messenger, she catches the eye of Olivia, who is instantly "infected" with desire. Meanwhile, Cesario/Viola falls in love with her master. Viola is doubly frustrated. She cannot fulfill Olivia's desires because she's a woman herself; she cannot fulfill her own desires because Orsino thinks she's a boy. Nor can she reveal her true identity without destroying the relationship she already has with Orsino. Viola thus comes to bear the afflictions of both of the noble characters: Like Orsino, she pines with frustrated desire; like Olivia, she mourns for a dead brother. She isn't a mere go-between. She is a mediator indeed, bearing the pains of those whom she connects.

It may be helpful to think about the plot geometrically. Before she arrives, Orsino is in love with Olivia, while Olivia deliberately shuts herself off from the possibility of new love. Each is stuck dead in a dead past. Viola breaks open the situation by becoming both a lover (of Orsino) and an object of love (from Olivia). Her appearance turns a static two-way romance into a romantic triangle:

Olivia
Orsino   ←   Viola

The triangle is comically confused, but romantic triangles are unstable, potentially tragic. This triangle is unnatural, since Olivia is unwittingly infatuated with another woman. A fourth must be added, so nature can return to her bias. If the romance is to end with a harmonious dance, the triangle has to be squared.

As a third wheel, Viola can't bring the situation to comic resolution by herself. Her brother Sebastian must rise from his "watery tomb" (5.1.229). Sebastian seems to be a minor character in the play, but he holds the key. Shakespeare designed the plot to highlight his centrality.

Viola tells the captain of the ship about "my poor brother" who is "in Elysium" (1.2.7, 4), but she doesn't name him. When Sebastian first appears on stage in Act 2, we don't know who he is, until he names himself to Antonio (2.1.15), who has rescued him from the sea (2.1.20–21). Then Sebastian disappears from the stage until the middle of Act 3, when he and Antonio part company. Act 4, however, belongs to Sebastian. He meets Feste, defends himself against Sir Toby and Sir Andrew, and is introduced to Olivia, who mistakes him for Cesario/Viola and whisks him off to a priest to get married before he changes his mind (4.3). We in the audience know Sebastian is alive and on his way to visit Orsino. The other characters don't know, and much of the comedy arises from that gap between our knowledge and the characters'.[2]

At that point, all of the confusions of the play are still in place. Viola is still in disguise. Toby, Maria, and Feste persist in their terrible prank on Malvolio. Olivia has mistaken Sebastian for Cesario. Yet once Sebastian is installed as master of Olivia's house, the plot begins to bend toward a happy ending. Sebastian beats down the disorders of Toby and Andrew, something Olivia couldn't accomplish. Revealed as Viola's brother, Sebastian unveils Viola. Because Sebastian appears, the play ends with weddings, each Jack (Sebastian, Orsino, even Toby) finding his Jill (Olivia, Viola, Maria). The resurrection of Sebastian proves Viola's imagination true. It shows tempests are kind, and salty tears are rich in fulfilled love.

The title sets this play in a context of festivity. In the Christian calendar, Twelfth Night is the evening of the last day of the twelve-day Christmas season. But the festivity isn't pure joy. Twelfth Night is the *final* night of Christmas, and so the feast is tinged with the melancholy sense that the fun is nearly done. That melancholy seems most evident in Feste the Fool, who sings of the brevity of love and beauty (e.g., 2.3.37–50). Party hearty as we may, the party doesn't last forever, and neither do we. "Youth's a stuff will not endure" (2.3.50).

Though Twelfth Night ends Christmas season, it begins another season, Epiphany, which celebrates the coming of the Magi to visit the Christ child (Matt 2). That points to a theme of manifestation, which links to the disguises that pervade the play and the unveilings and recognitions at its climax.

In Elizabethan England, many festivals had a "saturnalian" dimension. Normal order was turned upside down, and everyday constraints

---

2. Scholars describe this gap as "dramatic irony."

were thrown aside. Elizabethans celebrated Twelfth Night by making a boy bishop for the day and acting out a Feast of Fools, a burlesque of the Mass. As Marjorie Garber summarizes, "In England, Twelfth Night was a feast of misrule, a festival of eating and drinking, during which masques and revels were presented. A large cake with a bean or a coin baked into it was served to the assembled company, and the person whose slice of cake contained the coin became the Christmas King, the Lord of Misrule."[3]

These upside-down customs were probably on Shakespeare's mind, because the play is topsy-turvy from start to finish. Olivia falls for Viola, and in some productions Orsino and Cesario come close to kissing. We laugh, but our laughter is uncomfortable because we know something about the situation the characters don't know. Sir Toby is a lord of misrule who humbles the stiff steward Malvolio, who is "a kind of Puritan" (2.3.130). The play is "a Revels," a "suspension of mundane affairs during a brief epoch in a temporary world of indulgence." For a brief time, Illyria is "a land full of food, drink, love, play, disguise and music."[4] As John Hollander says, the play forces us to ponder the "morality of indulgence": Is it good to let off steam now and again, or should we keep strictly to the rules at all times? And it poses a more subtle question: Are self-indulgence and "Puritanism" perhaps two sides of the same coin, competing forms of excess?

Review Questions

1. How did Christianity change people's views on comedy?
2. What are the two main locations of *Twelfth Night*? How are they similar? How are they different?
3. Is *Twelfth Night* a comedy of exodus or incarnation?
4. What is the state of Olivia's house?
5. Explain the role of "mediators" in the play.
6. Discuss the significance of the structure of Act 1.
7. What is Sebastian's role in the plot?

---

3. Garber, *Shakespeare After All*, 506.
4. Hollander, "*Twelfth Night* and the Morality of Indulgence," 76.

8. What is "Twelfth Night" on the Christian calendar? What does that have to do with the play?

Thought Questions

1. Where did Shakespeare get the story for *Twelfth Night*? How did he change it?
2. What is the subtitle of *Twelfth Night*? What does this say about the play?
3. The names "Orsino," "Olivia," and "Viola" are quite similar to each other. Viola and Olivia have identical letters, with a slight difference in arrangement. Why did Shakespeare give his main characters such confusing names? What effect does this have on the audience?

The Food of Love, Act 1–2

The structure of the first Act highlights the similarities and differences between the two houses. Scenes alternate between Orsino's home (scenes 1, 4) and Olivia's (scenes 3, 5). We learn each is ruled by a self-indulgent head: Orsino indulges his frustrated love, and Olivia wallows in excessive grief for her father and brother. Olivia has the wisdom to diagnose the soul of her steward, Malvolio: "You are sick of self-love" (1.5.86). She's right about Malvolio, but her diagnosis applies just as well to her and Orsino. Everyone in the dreamworld of Illyria is sick with self-love and tastes "with a distempered appetite" (1.5.86–87).

Yet the two houses are different in other respects. Despite his passion, Orsino controls his house and kingdom. Olivia's house, by contrast, is in disarray. Act 1, scene 3, provides our first glimpse of Olivia's house, and Olivia herself doesn't appear at all. The scene is dominated by the rambunctious guests, Toby and Andrew, and by Olivia's maidservant, Maria. Olivia can't control her house because Olivia is herself out of control. We don't meet Olivia until scene 5, and then we watch her fall in love with a page boy we know is a woman. Malvolio looks like the steady man in the house, but we learn later he's angling to become master of the house by marrying Olivia. It is not good for either Orsino or Olivia to be alone, but even their combined self-love cannot redeem Illyria. Both houses need an injection of a love greater than *self*-love. They both need a love willing to sacrifice self.

The structure of the Act also suggests that "upstairs" and "downstairs" are more similar than different. Toby's excesses are more obvious. He drinks too much, and in the middle of the day, brawls and pranks, and sings in the middle of the night, sleeps till noon, if he sleeps at all. But the refined characters are as excessive as he. Orsino and Olivia have excess of passion, while Sir Andrew has become so "refined" he's barely a man at all. Some viewers side with the subversives, with Toby and his crew. Others will side with the civilized characters. Shakespeare's point, though, is to expose the similarity between them. Uncontrolled appetite and attenuated civilization are but two forms of excess.[5]

Orsino expresses his excess in the first lines of the play: "If music be the food of love, play on" (1.1.1). Rarely has an opening so deftly summarized the world of a play as this line from Duke Orsino at the beginning of *Twelfth Night*. Music and food are symbolic of the delights of love. The first line introduces music, food, love, and their complex interplay—all in a single line of iambic pentameter. As Orsino's speech continues, he anticipates the movement of the play. Why does he want more music?

> Give me excess of it, that, surfeiting,
> The appetite may sicken, and so die.
> That strain again, it had a dying fall;
> O, it came o'er my ear like the sweet sound
> That breathes upon a bank of violets,
> Stealing and giving odor. Enough, no more;
> 'Tis not so sweet now as it was before.
> O spirit of love, how quick and fresh art thou,
> That notwithstanding thy capacity
> Receiveth as the sea, nought enters there,
> Of what validity and pitch soe'er,
> But falls into abatement and low price
> Even in a minute. So full of shapes is fancy
> That it alone is high fantastical. (1.1.2–15)

Orsino seems a lover of the art of music. Not so. He wants so much music that he loses his joy in music. Music doesn't pull him out of himself. He gorges on music, because his passion is hungry like the ocean, digesting everything (2.4.100–101), transforming music into another fuel for his self-indulgence.

---

5. Goddard, *Meaning of Shakespeare*, 1:294–306.

Orsino's speech lays out a "theory" about festivity. Revels end as "the reveler . . . becomes satiated and drops heavily into his worldly self again."[6] That's the destiny for most of the main characters: They get their fill of food or drink or self-indulgent sentiment or disorderly pranks. Appetite sickens and dies by its own indulgence.

By showing characters whose passions die by being filled, Shakespeare offers an alternative to the moral "comedy of the humours" written by his contemporary Ben Jonson. Jonson's plays taught moral lessons. The theory of the humours has some similarities with our personality tests and Enneagram. A person with a particular balance of fluids (humours) has a certain kind of personality: He's sad because he has an excess of melancholic humor, or steady and calm because of phlegmatic humour. In Jonson's plays, characters acted out their dominant humour, and the plays were intended, in Jonson's words, to anatomize "the times deformitie," to depict the illnesses of early seventeenth-century England. Jonson's humour-dominated characters become caricatures, inhuman and ultimately bestial.

Several characters in *Twelfth Night* mention the humours, but the only character who *believes* in humours is Malvolio, and he's a morally stunted personality. Shakespeare's characters seem more real because they aren't mere examples of personality types.

Like the Puritans of Shakespeare's time, Malvolio wants to stamp out revels and suppress popular entertainments such as the theater. The play shows this won't work. Appetites and desires *do* need to be held in check. If you love drink too much, you'll become a Toby. If you're fearful, you'll be an Andrew. But passions aren't overcome by restraint and suppression. Paradoxically, appetite is overcome by limited indulgence. Toby's delight in pranks dies because one prank goes too far. Shakespeare seems to send his contemporaries an anti-Puritan "message": Don't suppress revels. Let the people have their fun. Leave them be. No one can drink forever. Shakespeare doesn't endorse the unruly revels in Olivia's house. But he knows even Toby Belch eventually has to sober up.

That's one side of the argument. But Shakespeare tends always toward the Aristotelian mean, favoring neither an excess or defect of any human passion or pleasure. After all, there is a worrying dimension to Orsino's theory of desire. If indulgence eventually leads to satisfaction, and satisfaction to loss of appetite, what will happen if Orsino *does* win

---

6. Hollander, "*Twelfth Night* and the Morality of Indulgence," 76–77.

the heart of Olivia? Will his oceanic passion devour her too, so that she disappears? Will he grow bored of her as he grows bored of his music? Can desire be strong over the long run? Once again, the play is nudging us toward a different kind of desire that doesn't swing wildly from extreme to extreme.

We leave Orsino working himself up into a lather of melancholy and are introduced to Viola, shipwrecked on the shores of Illyria, certain that her brother Sebastian has died. From the captain, she hears of Orsino's love for Olivia, and the reason for Olivia's refusal:

> A virtuous maid, the daughter of a count
> That died some twelvemonth since, then leaving her
> In the protection of his son, her brother,
> Who shortly also died: for whose dear love,
> They say, she hath abjured the sight
> And company of men. (1.2.36–41)

Valentine has already informed Orsino that "The element itself, till seven years' heat, / Shall not behold her face at ample view." Olivia is a nun of lamentation, living "like a cloistress" within a veil and watering her chamber "with eye-offending brine" (1.1.26–33).

The captain's story about Olivia touches Viola deeply. Like Olivia, she has lost a brother, and before that a father. Valentine's reference to Olivia's "briny" tears connects the two women even more closely, since Viola weeps for a brother who was lost in the briny sea. It's no wonder Viola is immediately tempted to join Olivia in her cloister: "O that I served that lady, / And might not be delivered to the world, / Till I had made mine own occasion mellow, / What my estate is" (1.2.41–44). Remarkably, she takes a more daring course. Instead of renouncing the company of men, she disguises herself *as* a man and enters the very world of men that Olivia avoids. Instead of retreating into the shadows, Viola plunges into the sunshine. That brash "incarnational" decision is Illyria's only hope.

As I noted above, Viola doesn't name Sebastian to the captain, but he hovers in the background. His death is the reason for Viola's plan, and she even sees her disguise as a way of keeping her brother alive. Much later, she says, "I my brother know / Yet living in my glass," that is, in her mirror (3.4.364–65). Sebastian is dead but lives in Viola's image. The plot will turn on whether or not that image of Sebastian materializes.

The conversation between Viola and the captain introduces a crucial theme into the play: chance or providence. "Perchance," Viola tells the captain, Sebastian "is not drowned." The captain agrees: "It is perchance that you yourself were saved." If it happened once, Viola reasons, it may happen again: "so perchance may he be," and the captain comforts her "with chance" by telling her how he last saw Sebastian (1.2.5–8). When Shakespeare uses the same word in three successive lines, we should pay attention. "Murder, murder, murder," say Hamlet and his father's ghost like a haunted chorus. "Nothing, nothing, nothing, nothing," Lear and Cordelia tell one another at the outset of *King Lear*. Perchance, perchance, perchance, comforting chance. Viola has suffered a tragedy, but perhaps it will turn to comedy. Sebastian is dead; perchance he will live again; perchance the sea that took him will turn kind and give him back. Perchance even the storm and shipwreck are overseen by a kind providence.

Twelfth Night is hardly unique among Shakespeare's comedies in the centrality of disguises, mistaken identities, and deceptions. In this play, the deceptions are many and multi-layered. Several wear disguises or perpetuate deceptions; others are victims of deception or disguise; importantly, some are *both* perpetrator and victim.

Sir Toby is at the center of various deceptive plots. From the beginning of the play and throughout, Toby tricks Sir Andrew Aguecheek, an absurdly unknightly knight who is romantically pursuing Olivia, into believing he is promoting Andrew's suit before Olivia, long after it's clear, even to Andrew, that he's not in Olivia's league.

Toby knows exactly what kind of man he's dealing with. He defends Andrew to Maria by saying he "plays o' th' viol-de-gamboys, and speaks three or four languages word for word without book, and hath all the good gifts of nature" (1.3.24–26). As soon as Andrew appears, it's clear he's nothing like the man Toby describes. He doesn't even understand English: "Accost," Toby says, encouraging Andrew to "front [Maria], board her, woo her, assail her" (1.3.53–54). "Is that the meaning of 'accost'?" asks a puzzled Sir Andrew (1.3.56). When Andrew announces he plans to leave the next day, Toby asks "why?" in French: "*Pourquoi*, my dear knight?" This man who allegedly "speaks three or four languages" is again baffled: "What is '*pourquoi*'? Do, or not do?" (1.3.86–87). Maria pegs Andrew from the beginning: "he's a fool, he's a great quarreler," and he would soon be dead if he didn't also possess the "gift of a coward to allay the gust he hath in quarreling" (1.3.28–31). To his credit, every now and then Andrew recognizes his own limitations: "I would I had bestowed that time in the tongues that I have in fencing, dancing, and bearbaiting. O, had I but followed the arts" (1.3.87–90). Most of the time, he's puffed with self-importance. If he thought Malvolio a Puritan, Andrew says, "I'd beat him like a dog" (2.4.131). He plans to impress Olivia with his valor, since "policy I hate" (3.2.28–29). "I warrant there's vinegar and pepper in't," he says of the challenge he writes to Cesario (3.4.137–38). It's all bluster and buffoonery.

Toby wants Andrew to stay only because Andrew funds the incessant parties. Andrew threatens to leave several times, and Toby tricks him into staying. Andrew is an easy mark. Toby's accomplice Fabian easily convinces Andrew that Olivia pays attention to Cesario "to awake your dormouse valor, to put fire in your heart and brimstone in your liver" (3.2.17–18). Toby easily persuades Andrew that a duel will win Olivia's heart: "Challenge me the count's youth to fight him; hurt him in eleven places. My niece will take note of it" (3.2.31–33). At the end, Sir Toby tells Andrew what he truly thinks of him: when Andrew offers help, Toby turns on him: "an asshead and a coxcomb and a knave, a thin-faced knave, a gull" (5.1.201–2). This is no recent opinion for Toby. Early on, he confides, "For Andrew, if he were opened, and you find so much blood in his liver as will clog the foot of a flea, I'll eat the rest of th' anatomy" (3.2.57–58).

Viola's deceptive disguise is more central to the play. She fools everyone in both houses and does so for most of the play. The duration of her disguise is rare in Shakespeare's comedies. In *The Merchant of Venice*, Portia disguises herself for a few scenes to save Antonio from Shylock's attack. Imogen in *Cymbeline* is in disguise only for a time, as is Julia in *Two Gentlemen of Verona*. In other plays, the disguised woman has a confidant: Portia and Nerissa go to the court of Venice together, and Imogen's disguise is Pisanio's idea in the first place. The captain is the only one who knows who Viola really is, but he disappears from the play after the second scene. Viola is utterly alone in a foreign land, a fake man among men.

At times, her disguise is the cause of dramatic irony. In her first conversation with Orsino, Orsino states his belief that Cesario will have better success wooing Olivia than "a nuncio's of more grave aspect" (1.4.28). Cesario is just the man for the job because of his womanly qualities:

> For they shall belie thy happy years
> That say thou art a man. Diana's lip
> Is not more smooth and rubious; thy small pipe
> Is as the maiden's organ, shrill and sound,
> And all is semblative a woman's part. (1.4.30–34)

By their second conversation, the audience knows Viola is falling in love with Orsino ("whoe'er I woo, myself would be his wife," 1.4.42), and the dramatic irony adds a painful overtone to the conversation. Viola reminds Orsino that Olivia has every right to reject his suit, just as a woman would have to accept Orsino's rejection. Orsino thinks there's no comparison. No woman, he says, could love as he loves:

> There is no woman's sides
> Can bide the beating of so strong a passion
> As love doth give my heart; no woman's heart
> So big to hold so much. They lack retention. . . .
> Mine is all as hungry as the sea,
> And can digest as much. Make no compare
> Between that love a woman can bear me
> And that I owe Olivia. (2.4.93–103)

Orsino speaks these words in the presence of a woman who has at least as strong a passion for him as he professes to have for Olivia. Besides, his words are self-contradictory. Here, he says women "lack retention." Earlier, he admits to Cesario "however we [men] do praise ourselves, / Our fancies are more giddy and unfirm, / More longing, wavering, sooner lost and worn, / Than women's are" (2.4.32–35). Which is it, my lord? The fact that he speaks out of both sides of his mouth—praising male constancy at one moment, admitting male "giddiness" at another—answers the question. His very insistence on men's "retention" is a sign of his lack of it.

Viola doesn't point out the contradiction. All she can do, disguised as she is, is to invent a "sister" who loved deeply but never professed her love:

> She never told her love,
> But let concealment, like a worm i' the bud,
> Feed on her damask cheek. She pined in thought,
> And with a green and yellow melancholy,
> She sat like Patience on a monument,
> Smiling at grief. Was not this love indeed? (2.4.110–15)

Indeed it was, and it is the very love Viola cannot speak. For her, "concealment" leads to green and yellow melancholy.

Even when Viola's disguise has more comic effects, it quickly slips into a bittersweet tone. After her first encounter with Cesario/Viola, Olivia sends Malvolio after Viola to return a ring. Malvolio is triply deceived, and the joke is largely on him: He believes he's returning a ring to Orsino, but Orsino sent no ring; he believes he's communicating Olivia's rejection of a suitor, but he is actually playing pander as Olivia *pursues* a suitor (Cesario); he believes he's talking to a man, but he is talking to a woman. Witty as the scene is, it ends with a speech from Viola that can only be called a lamentation:

> Disguise, I see thou art a wickedness
> Wherein the pregnant enemy does much.
> How easy is it for the proper false
> In woman's waxen hearts to set their forms!
> Alas, our frailty is the cause, not we,
> For such as we are made of, such we be.
> How will this fadge? My master loves her dearly;
> And I (poor monster) fond as much on him;
> And she (mistaken) seems to dote on me.
> What will become of this? As I am man,
> My state is desperate for my master's love.
> As I am woman (now alas the day!),
> What thriftless sighs shall poor Olivia breathe?
> O Time, thou must untangle this, not I;
> It is too hard a knot for me t'untie! (2.2.27–41)

The potential for a tragic outcome is acute, unless time proves to be an ally in untangling the knots Viola's deception has caused. If time is the tragic reality the ancients and many moderns believe, Viola's situation is hopeless. But Shakespearean comedy is guided by a "belief," the conviction that man is capable of jumbling things but absolutely incapable of sorting out the jumble. Viola is herself an agent of grace, but before she can reorder the disordered houses of Illyria she has to be rescued. It will take another incarnation, one that takes the form of resurrection.

Review Questions

1. What is Orsino's opening speech about? How does it anticipate the themes of *Twelfth Night*?
2. How does Shakespeare's attitude toward "revelry" differ from that of a moralistic playwright like Ben Jonson?
3. Whose side is Shakespeare on? Sir Toby's or Malvolio's?
4. Why does Viola identify with Olivia?

5. Discuss the role of chance or providence in the play.
6. How does Viola's disguise differ from disguises in other Shakespeare plays? Who else in *Twelfth Night* is "disguised"?
7. How is disguise a "wickedness"? What does Viola rely on to overcome that wickedness?

Thought Questions

1. Trevor Nunn's 1996 film version of *Twelfth Night* creates a war between Messaline, Viola's home city, and Illyria. Why would the screenwriter add that to the play?
2. Explain the exchange between Maria and Andrew (1.3.42–75). Do you get Maria's jokes? If you don't, does that make you as foolish as Andrew? Is that Shakespeare's intention?
3. Olivia ends Act 1 saying, "Fate, show thy force; ourselves we do not owe. / What is decreed must be—and be this so!" (1.5.299–300). What does she mean? How do Olivia's words fit with the themes of providence, fortune, and fate?

Folly, Madness, Wit, Wisdom, Acts 2–3

Twelfth Night is about wisdom and folly, and various forms of madness. It takes place in Illyria, "a land where folly holds sway." Orsino is "a melancholy poseur, gratifying an epicurean desire for surfeit of pleasures." He claims to love Olivia, but his love is really a form of self-love. He doesn't fantasize about how he can console Olivia in her bereavement, but about how much she'll love *him*: If she shows such devotion to a brother, "How will she love when the rich golden shaft / Hath killed the flock of all affections else / That live in her" (1.1.36–38). For her part, Olivia's grief is morbid.[7] She's as mad as he.

In a mad, mad, mad world, the only sane man is, of course, the *Fool* (or Clown) Feste, who exposes the follies around him. In an early exchange with Olivia, he proves she's more a fool than he:

---

7. Ghose, *Shakespeare and Laughter*, 109–10.

> CLOWN
> Good madonna, why mourn'st thou?
> OLIVIA
> Good fool, for my brother's death.
> CLOWN
> I think his soul is in hell, madonna.
> OLIVIA
> I know his soul is in heaven, fool.
> CLOWN
> The more fool, madonna, to mourn for your brother's soul being in heaven. Take away the fool, gentlemen. (1.5.62–67)

Feste shows that Olivia's mourning is as much a role as Viola's trousers and page-boy haircut.

Feste unmasks Orsino as deftly as he does Olivia. The duke fancies himself a lover of epic constancy, but Feste discerns his mind is "very opal." An opal appears to contain a flickering flame within, and so, from ancient times, opals have symbolized changeability. Feste suggests men who have the "constancy" of Orsino should be put to sea, "that their business might be everything, and their intent everywhere" (2.4.75–78). Feste doesn't know it, but Orsino compares his passion to the sea (2.4.100). Orsino doesn't realize the metaphor works against him: Rivers have banks and flow in one direction, but on the sea a ship can turn in any, or every, direction. Feste sees Orsino's mind is as mercurial as "the shifting hue of an opal" and "the changing moods of the sea."[8]

Feste exposes Orsino again when he sings for the duke. Orsino asks for an "old and plain" song he heard Feste singing, one that "dallies with the innocence of love, / Like the old age" (2.4.43–48). Feste sings, but it's not what the duke asked for:

> Come away, come away, death,
>   And in sad cypress let me be laid;
> Fly away, fly away breath;
>   I am slain by a fair cruel maid.
> My shroud of white, stuck all with yew,
>   O, prepare it!
> My part of death, no one so true
>   Did share it.

---

8. Ghose, *Shakespeare and Laughter*, 111.

> Not a flower, not a flower sweet
>   On my black coffin let there be strown;
> Not a friend, not a friend greet
>   My poor corpse, where my bones shall be thrown.
> A thousand thousand sighs to save,
>   Lay me, O, where
> Sad true lover never find my grave,
>   To weep there! (2.4.51–66)

This is a love song, but hardly a song of *innocent* love.[9] It's a song about a love that kills the lover, "slain by a fair cruel maid." The jilted lover doesn't even want his grave to be marked, because he doesn't want any lovers to weep over it. Feste mocks Orsino's overwrought expressions of love and belittles them. Orsino is a drama queen, sharing his lovesickness with everyone who will listen, but a *truly* distraught lover wants to lie down in a forgotten grave.

Orsino rules Illyria, and the land is only as steady as its duke. Feste recognizes folly when he sees it. Folly "does walk about the orb like the sun; it shines everywhere" (3.1.38–39). Language suffers. "To see this age!" Feste cries to Viola. "A sentence is but a chev'ril glove to a good wit. How quickly the wrong side may be turned outward!" (3.1.11–13). He is Olivia's "corrupter of words," who says things like, "Nothing that is so is so" (4.1.8–9). Feste isn't the *source* of folly. He only mirrors the folly around him. Not that it helps. Nobody listens, and Feste contents himself with begging an extra coin for a song or a snatch of repartee.[10]

Feste holds his mirror up to the audience too. The characters aren't the only ones playing parts. We do too.[11] We put on a face to meet the faces, disguise ourselves to attract attention or to sneak into forbidden territory. We have our know-it-all Facebook mask, our snarky Twitter costume, our life's-a-party Instagram getup. To us, as to the other characters, Feste poses the question: Who is the wise man? Who the fool? Take away the fool, gentlemen.

At a minimum, a sane person knows who he or she is. A madman stumbles in darkness, confused above all about himself. By this definition, the principal characters in *Twelfth Night* are mad. Nothing that is so is so. Ironically, the only character who seems completely sane, completely self-aware, is Viola, and she's the one in disguise, the one who

---

9. Downer, "Feste's Exposure of Orsino," 100–101.
10. Ghose, *Shakespeare and Laughter*, 112.
11. Ghose, *Shakespeare and Laughter*, 113.

can say quite literally: "I am not that I play" (1.5.177) and, more directly, "I am not what I am" (3.1.140). From within her disguise, she can see through the disguises of others: "you do not think you are not what you are," she tells the smitten Olivia (3.1.138). With the delightful paradox of comedy, the one who fools everyone is wise, the one embarked on a mad scheme is sane, the one who cannot speak her love loves most.

The biggest fool is Malvolio. In his first appearance in the play (1.5), Feste has a witty exchange with Maria, which ends with Feste's reflection on the relation of wits and fools:

> Wit, an't be thy will, put me into good fooling. Those wits that think they have thee do very oft prove fools, and I that am sure I lack thee may pass for a wise man. For what says Quinapalus? "Better a witty fool than a foolish wit." (1.5.30–34)

Just before Feste speaks, the stage direction indicates, "Enter Lady Olivia with Malvolio," our first glimpse of both Olivia and her steward. Who are the foolish wits? Feste will prove Olivia a fool, and the whole play proves Malvolio a greater fool.

I suggested above that Sebastian is the key character in the central Acts of the play. From another angle, Malvolio is the main attraction. In Act 1, he appears alongside Olivia, trading wits with Feste and running errands for his lady. In Acts 2–4, he appears without Olivia and begins to act on his own. He is present in most of the scenes of Act 2:

> 2.1: Antonio and Sebastian.
> 2.2: Malvolio attempts to return a ring to Viola.
> 2.3: Malvolio interrupts the nighttime revels of Toby and Andrew.
> 2.4: Orsino and Viola talk.
> 2.5: Gulling of Malvolio.

Malvolio is not as omnipresent in Act 3, but in a very long final scene (3.4, 379 lines) he acts on the instructions of the letter he discovers (cf. 2.5) and is taken to an asylum. Fittingly, Toby convinces Olivia that Malvolio is mad and tries to convince Malvolio too. What can only be described as Malvolio's torture is taken further in Act 4, when Feste visits him disguised as Sir Topas, a priest (4.2). The subplot of Malvolio is so large and dramatic that it threatens to obscure the main plot involving Orsino, Viola, and Olivia.

Malvolio is not without wit, dignity, competence, or righteous concern for order and decorum. He keeps pace with Feste in their insult battle (1.5.71–94). The turning point, and the primary revelation of his character, occurs in Act 2, scene 3, the first large scene in which Malvolio is the central character:

> A. Toby, Andrew, Feste drinking and singing, 2.3.1–66
>   B. Maria enters and rebukes them for their "caterwauling," 2.3.67–80
>   C. Malvolio enters, rebukes the men and Maria, exits, 2.3.81–115
>   B'. Maria hatches plot against Malvolio, exits, 2.3.116–64
> A'. Toby and Andrew continue party, 2.3.165–79

When Malvolio intervenes to put a stop to the midnight party, his rebuke hits the mark:

> My masters, are you mad? Or what are you? Have ye no wit, manners, nor honesty, but to gabble like tinkers at this time of night? Do ye make an alehouse of my lady's house, that ye squeak out your coziers' catches without any mitigation or remorse of voice? Is there no respect of place, persons, nor time in you? (2.3.81–86)

It's hard to argue with him. There's a time and place for everything, and midnight in Olivia's house isn't the time for heavy drinking and loud song.

Toby quickly deflates him: "Dost thou think, because thou art virtuous, there shall be no more cakes and ale?" (2.3.106–7). Even at his best, Malvolio's weaknesses are glaring. Earlier in the play, Olivia gently rebukes him for taking Feste's gibes too seriously: "To be generous, guiltless, and of free disposition, is to take those things for bird bolts that you deem cannon bullets" (1.5.87–89). Malvolio is wholly without humor precisely because he is "sick of self-love" (1.5.86). Joy requires self-abandonment, the opposite of self-importance and self-love.

Maria calls Malvolio a "Puritan" (2.4.130). It's an unfair characterization of the real Puritans, but by Shakespeare's time, "Puritan" had already taken on a popular connotation of "kill-joy." A Puritan, the joke goes, is one who cannot sleep at night if someone else is having fun. In any case, Maria doesn't think "Puritan" really describes Malvolio, who is no more than a "timepleaser; an affectioned ass, that cons state without book and utters it by great swarths; the best persuaded of himself; so crammed, as he thinks, with excellencies that it is his grounds of faith that all that look on him love him" (2.4.137–41).

The play doesn't side with Toby, but it's clear that Malvolio's virtues are monstrously misshapen. Neither excess of revelry nor excess of virtue is human or healthy.

Initially, Maria chides Toby and Andrew as severely as Malvolio, but when Malvolio turns the blame on her, she makes her choice and joins the rebels. She discerns that Malvolio's self-love and conceit make him a perfect target for the gulling. She discerns that his folly can be stoked up into a kind of madness. She imitates Olivia's handwriting in a love letter to Malvolio and leaves it in the garden for him to find. She knows he will "crush" it to make it apply to himself because she knows Malvolio sees everything colored by self-love.

The gulling scene (2.5) is masterfully constructed:

> Toby, Fabian, and Andrew discuss bearbaiting, 2.5.1–10
>   Maria gives instructions, 2.11–20
>   Malvolio enters and discovers the letter, 2.5.21–170
>   Fabian, Toby, and Andrew react, 2.5.171–76
>   Maria enters to debrief, 2.5.177–98

Malvolio is the center of attention in the long central section, but he's interrupted every few lines by comments and outbursts from Toby, Fabian, and Andrew, who eavesdrop from a box tree (2.5.13). The result is an intricately four-staged scene:

1. We watch Malvolio discover a letter.
2. We also watch and hear Toby, Fabian, and Andrew watch and hear Malvolio.
3. Both layers of the scene on stage are being stage-managed by Maria.
4. We, the audience, watch Maria manage the men who watch Malvolio.

Even before he sees the counterfeit letter from Olivia, Malvolio is fantasizing about being "Count Malvolio":

> Having been three months married to her, sitting in my state ... calling my officers about me, in my branched velvet gown; having come from a daybed, where I left Olivia sleeping.... And then to have the humor of state; and after a demure travel of regard, telling them I know my place, as I would they should do theirs, to ask for my kinsman Toby.... Seven of my people, with

an obedient start, make out for him. I frown the while, and perchance wind up my watch, or play with my—some rich jewel. Toby approaches; curtsies there to me. . . . I extend my hand to him thus, quenching my familiar smile with an austere regard of control . . . saying, "Cousin Toby, my fortunes having cast me on your niece, give me this prerogative of speech. . . . You must amend your drunkenness." (2.5.41–70)

One of the most striking things about this fantasy is how little Olivia enters into it. She is lounging on a bed somewhere, presumably exhausted from trying to keep pace with the sexual exertions of the oh-so-potent stud, Malvolio. To Malvolio, marriage is only an excuse to lord it over Sir Toby. Marriage isn't about love. It intensifies Malvolio's original sickness: He continues to be mortally sick with self-love.

This imagined future is ironic, given his obsession with keeping the house in "good order." There is nothing quite so disorderly as a steward who aspires to be lord of the manor. As a "lord of misrule," Sir Toby is a piker. *Malvolio* is the true master of chaos, a semi-tamed madman before he is tricked into acting like a wild madman.

Malvolio's self-absorption is evident in his interpretation of Maria's letter. Given the complexity of the scene, Malvolio reads the letter only in bits and pieces. It is addressed to "the unknown beloved" (2.5.87) and includes these rhymes:

> Jove knows I love,
>   But who?
> Lips, do not move;
>   No man must know. . . .
>
> I may command where I adore,
>   But silence, like a Lucrece knife,
> With bloodless stroke my heart doth gore.
>   M, O, A, I, doth sway my life. (2.5.92–103)

Malvolio naturally sees himself everywhere. "No man must know": "If this should be thee, Malvolio!" (2.5.97–98). "I may command where I adore": "Why, she may command me" (2.5.110–11). "M. O. A. I": After Malvolio "crushes" it a little, he makes it "bow to me, for every one of these letters are in my name" (2.5.131–32). Scholars have puzzled over the alphabetic riddle. Perhaps, though, it's deliberately nonsensical. Knowing Malvolio is a "Puritan," Maria expects him to twist the text, as the Puritans (in the view of other Christians) twisted the Scriptures to their advantage. Maria has read her prey well: he's a self-absorbed Procrustes, who cuts everything to conform to his fantasies.

The letter encourages Malvolio to grasp his destiny: "In my stars I am above thee, but be not afraid of greatness. Some are born great, some achieve greatness, and some have greatness thrust upon 'em" (2.5.135–38). Malvolio looks to "Fate" and "Fortune" to raise him higher, and resolves to obey the instructions of the letter: "Be opposite with a kinsman, surly with servants. Let thy tongue tang arguments of state. . . . Remember who commended thy yellow stockings and wished to see thee ever cross-gartered" (2.5.141–46). Malvolio isn't really submitting to fate. Unlike Viola, he doesn't wait for time to untie knots and prove his imagination true. He doesn't have the faith to wait, but instead scrambles to the top as fast as he can. Such pride can only lead to a fall.

Review Questions

1. Who is Feste? What is his role in the play?
2. How is language a sign of disorder in Illyria?
3. Who is Malvolio? What does his name mean? What kind of character is he?
4. What is Maria's plan to "gull" Malvolio?
5. What does Malvolio fantasize about?
6. What does the code "M.O.A.I." mean? How does Malvolio interpret it?

Thought Questions

1. "'Tis too late to go to bed now," Toby says after his all-nighter with Andrew and Feste (2.3.178–79; cf. 2.3.6–9). What does he mean? How do his words express the disorder of Olivia's house?
2. Andrew reminds Feste of his earlier discussion of Pigrogromitus and the "Vapians passing the equinocturnal of Queubus" (2.3.22–23). Who are these people? Did Feste make them up? What is Shakespeare telling us about Andrew? What is telling us about Feste?

3. Maria says a "trout" is caught by "tickling" (2.5.19–20). What does she mean? Who is the "trout"? Is she trying to catch someone *besides* Malvolio?

The Man and the Devil, Acts 3–4

Halfway through *Twelfth Night* (3.4), the play turns diabolical. It's a gigantic whirligig of a scene. It begins with Lady Olivia dreaming of Cesario. Malvolio enters, uncharacteristically cheerful, wearing yellow stockings cross-gartered. Olivia concludes it's "very midsummer madness" (3.4.52) and asks Toby—one of the mob who pranked Malvolio—to look after her steward. No sooner does Malvolio depart than Sir Andrew shows up with a challenge for Cesario. Toby has tricked Andrew too, convincing him he needs to show some sauciness to win Olivia's love. Toby and Fabian egg on both Andrew and Cesario until they draw swords and begin the clash of the cowards.

These confusions are born of deception and disguise, but they come crashing back to reality when Antonio intervenes to defend Cesario, whom he mistakes for Sebastian. Antonio is left fuming in bewildered anger when Viola doesn't recognize him. Antonio's appearance foreshadows the more decisive reappearance of Sebastian. In both cases, importantly, the appearance of a *man* in the soft kingdom of Orsino begins to untie the knots of disguise. When a man begins to act like a man, sanity steps onto the stage and begins to break through the madness. Eventually, the women will return to the bias of their natures as well.

For Viola, Antonio's appearance is a breakthrough moment. Antonio names her brother, and for the first time she hopes Sebastian survived the wreck. She speaks some of the loveliest lines of the play, *any* play:

> Methinks his words do from such passion fly,
> That he believes himself; so do not I.
> Prove true, imagination, O, prove true,
> That I, dear brother, be now ta'en for you! . . .
> He named Sebastian. I my brother know
> Yet living in my glass. Even such and so
> In favor was my brother, and he went
> Still in this fashion, color, ornament,
> For him I imitate. O, if it prove,
> Tempests are kind, and salt waves fresh in love!
> (3.4.358–69)

Above, we noted above the importance of "chance" in the captain's effort to comfort Viola. Now Viola takes real comfort because she thinks it's a real possibility: "Perchance" has moved closer to "proof."

Sebastian's name doesn't merely give her hope. It gives her wisdom, a deeper insight into the comic nature of reality. Tempests throw ships against rocks and drown passengers. But what if beneath their fury "tempests are kind"? What if the briny grave of Sebastian and the briny tears of Olivia can turn fresh in love? If those imagined hopes prove true, then the hopeless mourning of Olivia and the hopeless moping of Orsino are unnatural and foolish. If tempests are kind, the life of hope follows the grain of the universe. Mad as it may appear, hope is true sanity. When Viola hears Sebastian's name, she knows time has been picking at the knot. But not merely time. What makes tempests kind is grace, the grace of restored life, the grace of resurrection, the grace that rules tempests.

In this swirl, things turn diabolical. The word *devil* appears seven times in the scene (3.4.80, 92, 95, 226, 262, 279, 355), along with three references to the "fiend" (3.4.86, 105, 208) and a couple to "hell" (3.4.80, 208). Toby alludes to the "Legion" of demons in the Gadarene demoniac (3.4.80), and both Toby and Maria say Malvolio is "possessed." When he comes to Olivia smiling, wearing yellow stockings, and cross-gartered, Maria announces him by saying "He is, sure, possessed, madam" (3.4.8). Toby rushes in, acting as if Malvolio is the Gadarene demoniac from the Gospels: "If all the devils of hell be drawn in little and Legion himself possessed him, yet I'll speak to him" (3.4.80–81). When Malvolio tells Toby and Maria to "go off," Maria responds: "Lo, how hollow the fiend speaks within him" (3.4.84–86). Sir Toby rejoins with "How do you, Malvolio? How is't with you? What, man! Defy the devil. Consider, he's an enemy to mankind" (3.4.91–93), and Maria adds "'an you speak ill of the devil, how he takes it at heart! Pray God he be not bewitched" (3.4.95–96). Toby tries once more, warning Malvolio not to "play at cherry-pit with Satan. Hang him, foul collier!" (3.4.111–12); meaning, a grave man shouldn't sip soup from the devil's spoon.

For the most part, the devilry is fake, a product of Toby's trickery. Not content with shaming Malvolio in front of Olivia, Toby speaks to the steward as if he were demon-possessed. Toby works the devil into his other prank, on Sir Andrew. To frighten Viola, he tells her Sir Andrew is "a devil in private brawl" (3.4.226–27). On the other hand, he frightens Andrew by telling him Cesario is "a very devil" (3.4.262). With each assured of fighting a devil, each enters the fray with dormouse valor.

In a later scene, Feste, disguised as the cleric Sir Topas, comes to Malvolio's dark room to counsel with the wretched steward and to conduct a mock exorcism:

> MALVOLIO
> Sir Topas, Sir Topas, good Sir Topas, go to
> my lady.
> CLOWN
> Out, hyperbolical fiend! How vexest thou
> this man! Talkest thou of nothing but of ladies? ...
> MALVOLIO
> Sir Topas, never was man thus wronged. Good Sir
> Topas, do not think I am mad. They have laid me
> here in hideous darkness.
> CLOWN
> Fie, thou dishonest Satan! I call thee by the most
> modest terms, for I am one of those gentle ones
> that will use the devil himself with courtesy. Sayst
> thou that house is dark?
> MALVOLIO
> As hell, Sir Topas. (4.2.23–39)

There's one *serious* reference to the devil, from Antonio. Antonio is outraged at what he sees as Cesario's ingratitude:

> But, O, how vile an idol proves this god!
> Thou hast, Sebastian, done good feature shame.
> In nature there's no blemish but the mind;
> None can be called deformed but the unkind.
> Virtue is beauty; but the beauteous evil
> Are empty trunks, o'erflourished by the devil. (3.4.350–55)

Antonio lifts the entire scene from farce to philosophy. Toby warns against playing with the devil, but that's what he's actually doing, tainting Malvolio's mind even as he deforms himself with unkindness. And Toby's not alone. True virtue is beauty; beautiful evil is an ornamented chest full of dead men's bones. It's the work of the devil, and Illyria is full of it.

Shakespeare frequently surrounds his villains with satanic imagery. In *Othello*, Iago is described as a satanic figure and uses hellish imagery himself. Over the course of that play, infernal imagery migrates from Iago to Othello, as Othello is slowly poisoned by the lies of the fiend. In *Merchant of Venice*, Shylock is identified as the villain of the story not only by his remorseless pursuit of his bloody bond, but also by frequent use of satanic imagery. In *Twelfth Night*, the fact that Malvolio is called demon-possessed and is associated with the devil over and over again points to his thematic role in the play. Like Satan, he is sick with self-love, falling by the force of his own gravity. Malvolio is a *comic* devil, not nearly so threatening as Iago or Shylock, but he is a devil nonetheless. Malvolio *does* need an exorcism; he's possessed of pride, the devil's sin. But then, Olivia needs an exorcism too, and so do Orsino, and Toby, and Andrew, and Maria, and all the rest of the Illyrians. Fortunately, tempests *are* kind. The storm throws Viola and Sebastian onto Illyria's shores, come to harrow a comedy hell.

Malvolio's devilish pride is manifest in his desire to suppress the gaiety of Olivia's house. *Twelfth Night* is named for the last night of the Christmas season, the final celebration of the incarnation. It is a night for carnival, for suspension of the serious and structured. Malvolio wants to stop the merriment, and his punishment is to be excluded from it. Malvolio is overcome through trickery, practical joking, mirth. Satan digs a pit for the merry, but Satan falls into the very pit of merriment. And it tortures him forever.

Antonio discovers Viola, whom he mistakes for Sebastian, in a duel with Sir Andrew. Olivia finds Sebastian, whom she mistakes for Cesario, in a duel with Sir Toby and whisks him away. Dazed, Sebastian tries to reason out his situation: "Or I am mad, or else this is a dream" (4.1.58). Echoing Malvolio's protests to Feste, he reasons that he cannot be mad: "This is the air; that is the glorious sun; / This pearl she gave me, I do feel't and see't; / And though 'tis wonder that enwraps me thus, / Yet 'tis not madness" (4.3.1–4). Olivia, he concludes, cannot be mad either, since a mad woman couldn't "sway her house, command her followers, / Take and give back affairs and their dispatch / With such a smooth, discreet, and stable bearing" (4.3.17–19). When she proposes marriage, he agrees. "Come, I prithee," she says, "Would thou'dst be ruled by me!" (4.1.61). He makes himself Olivia's servant, and so comes to rule the house.

Malvolio is a lord of joyless misrule, as Sir Toby is a lord of raucous misrule. Both are of the devil's party, however differently. Olivia's house needs more than an exorcism. She needs a man. For much of the play, Olivia believes she has found that man: "I am the man," Viola says. But Viola rejects Olivia's love as decisively as Olivia rejects Orsino's. Olivia and her house need a man more manly than Viola. She needs a man who overcomes death, and so has power to expel the devil. She needs Sebastian, and through all the mistakes and misperceptions, she finds him.

Review Questions

1. Discuss the "diabolical" imagery of *Twelfth Night*. How is it linked with Malvolio?
2. What happens when Antonio encounters the other characters?
3. What does Viola mean by saying "tempests are kind"?
4. What effect does Sebastian's appearance have on the direction of the play?

Thought Questions

1. What do Viola and Feste talk about in 3.1.1–67? Compare this to Sebastian's conversation with Feste (4.1.1–29). How are the two scenes similar? How different?
2. Why do Sebastian and Antonio separate (2.3)? Where do they plan to meet up? Is that significant?
3. Disguised as Sir Topas, Feste quizzes Malvolio about the opinion of Pythagoras about birds (4.2.49–59). What *is* Pythagoras's opinion? How that exchange fit with the rest of the play?
4. What does Feste sing as he leaves Malvolio (4.2.119–30)? How is this connected with the themes of the play?

Resurrection, Act 5

The last Act of *Twelfth Night* is a single long scene. It's one of Shakespeare's masterpieces. He brings all the characters on stage, unties the knots of deception and disguise one by one, and closes with the promise of a double wedding to add to the o'er-hasty wedding of Olivia and Sebastian in Act 4.

"Disguise, thou art a wickedness," Viola says early in the play (2.2.27). Act 5 begins with mounting evidence of the danger of disguise. One after another, characters enter, each with a complaint against Viola:

1. Antonio, still mistaking Viola for Sebastian, accuses Viola of ingratitude and stealing the money he lent to Sebastian.

2. Olivia, now married to Sebastian, mistakes Viola for her husband and charges him with breaking his vows.
3. Andrew Aguecheek, then Sir Toby Belch, accuse Viola of breaking their heads across.

Viola protests her innocence. Hearing Antonio's story, she's as mystified as everyone: "How can this be?" (5.1.89). To Andrew, she insists, "I never hurt you. / You drew your sword upon me without cause" (5.1.182–83). She's right. In every case, the charges arise from mistaken identity. Antonio, Olivia, Andrew, and Toby all think Viola is Sebastian. It's a comic snarl, but for Viola it holds real danger, as Orsino, ever the drama queen, threatens to kill Viola to take revenge on the "marble-breasted tyrant," Olivia:

> Why should I not, had I the heart to do it,
> Like to th' Egyptian thief at point of death,
> Kill what I love? (A savage jealousy
> That sometimes savors nobly.) But hear me this:
> Since you to nonregardance cast my faith,
> And that I partly know the instrument
> That screws me from my true place in your favor,
> Live you the marble-breasted tyrant still.
> But this your minion, whom I know you love,
> And whom, by heaven I swear, I tender dearly,
> Him will I tear out of that cruel eye,
> Where he sits crowned in his master's spite.
> Come, boy, with me. My thoughts are ripe in mischief.
> I'll sacrifice the lamb that I do love
> To spite a raven's heart within a dove. (5.1.114–28)

Orsino is willing to kill his faithful servant to spite Olivia, just to avenge himself because of Olivia's rejection. Everyone is stopped in his tracks when Olivia appeals to Cesario, whom she believes she has married: "Whither, my lord? Cesario, husband, stay" (5.1.140). The priest confirms the marriage, and Orsino dismisses Viola as a "dissembling cub" and orders him to "direct thy feet / Where thou and I, henceforth, may never meet" (5.1.161–66). Viola is on the verge of losing her position in Orsino's house, her love, her life, all at once.

Cracks already appear in the stories before Sebastian enters the scene full of cheerful ignorance. Antonio claims Viola has been with him for three months, but Orsino knows "three months this youth hath tended upon me" (5.1.96). Andrew accuses Cesario of breaking his head and giving Sir Toby a bloody coxcomb, but the duke knows it cannot be true, since Cesario has been with him the whole time.

Sebastian's appearance initially complicates things further. "How have you made division of yourself?" Antonio wonders (5.1.217). Sebastian quickly dissolves the charges against Viola, in reverse order:

> A. Antonio: Viola is ungrateful
>   B. Olivia: Viola has forgotten her vows
>   C. Andrew and Toby: Viola hurt us
>   C'. Sebastian: "I am sorry, madam,
>   I have hurt your kinsman" (5.1.204)
>   B'. Sebastian: "Pardon me, sweet one, even for the vows we made" (5.1.209–10)
> A'. Sebastian: "Antonio, O my dear Antonio!" (5.1.213)

Olivia reacts with stunned awe: "Most wonderful" (5.1.220). Her words are more accurate than she realizes. A "wonder" is a miracle, and Sebastian's survival and appearance are truly miraculous, for he has risen from a watery tomb. "Most wonderful" indeed.

Once Sebastian appears in person, everything works out: Olivia's love for Cesario is (happily enough) transferred to a man, Sebastian, and Cesario is undisguised as a woman, who can openly declare her love for Orsino. At the heart of the closing scene, though, is a deeply moving recognition whose emotional power cannot be captured on the page. It is more than a recognition scene; it is a resurrection scene:

> SEBASTIAN
>   Do I stand there? I never had a brother;
>   Nor can there be that deity in my nature
>   Of here and everywhere. I had a sister,
>   Whom the blind waves and surges have devoured.
>   Of charity, what kin are you to me?
>   What countryman? What name? What parentage?
> VIOLA
>   Of Messaline; Sebastian was my father;
>   Such a Sebastian was my brother too;
>   So went he suited to his watery tomb.
>   If spirits can assume both form and suit,
>   You come to fright us.

SEBASTIAN
>A spirit I am indeed,
But am in that dimension grossly clad
Which from the womb I did participate.
Were you a woman, as the rest goes even,
I should my tears let fall upon your cheek
And say, "Thrice welcome, drowned Viola." (5.1.221–36)

Past tenses ("I had a sister" and "Sebastian was my brother") become presents. Blind waves and surges have coughed up their prey, and the watery tomb has opened to let Sebastian go free. All is redeemed. Every tear is wiped away, every loss restored, every wound healed. Tempests indeed are kind.

Several years ago, I watched Shakespeare's *Pericles* at the Wannamaker Theater in London. It climaxes with a lengthy recognition scene between Pericles and his daughter. It's corny, clichéd, predictable—and *unutterably* moving. The recognition scene between Sebastian and Viola in *Twelfth Night* hits all the same classical tropes of recognition (physical markings, coordination of dates and names). Like the scene in *Pericles*, it is beyond beautiful. I've watched film and stage versions of *Twelfth Night* dozens of times, but I tear up every time I watch it again.

It's an ending, radiant with *the* ending, with *eschatology*. It captures the final joy we yearn for, the joy of having our dreams and imaginations prove true, the joy of seeing the kindness of tempests, the joy, as Orsino says, of discovering life's worst wracks are "most happy." It's the joy of recovery and resurrection and glimpses the day of bliss when our Lord will tell his servants that, for service done him, "you shall from this time be / Your master's mistress" (5.1.315–20).

The story of Viola illustrates the comic trajectory toward resurrection and new beginnings. Viola's ultimate theme is, as she says, that "tempests are kind." Malvolio, humorless and oppressive, is the "devil" of the play and illustrates another side of comedy, the exclusion of the mirthless from final happiness and the power of jollity to defeat Satan. Malvolio storms out of the final scene, a Satan who, in the end, is overcome with nothing more than "cakes and ale."

Review Questions

1. Who brings complaints against Viola in Act 5? What are their complaints?
2. How is Viola in danger?
3. Explain how Sebastian's appearance answers all the charges against Viola.
4. How do Sebastian and Viola recognize each other?
5. How does the end of *Twelfth Night* anticipate the end of all things?

Thought Questions

1. What does Orsino accuse Antonio of? How does Antonio defend himself (5.1.47–89)?
2. What does Malvolio write in his letter to Olivia (5.1.296–305)? What does Malvolio say to her (5.1.324–38)?
3. What is Feste's final song about (5.1.382–401)? How does it relate to the rest of the play?

6

Mercy Seasons Justice

The Merchant of Venice

EVERYTHING IN *THE MERCHANT of Venice* comes in threes. There are three primary settings, three romances, three plots.[1] Each triad overlaps with the others.

The three primary settings are Venice, Portia's home of Belmont, and the house of Shylock, the Jewish moneylender. Venice is a place of daylight, dominated by men, characterized by competitive commerce and law. Venice is a civic order but lacks the softer delights of civilization, especially music. Belmont is a place of night, ruled by a young woman, a place of romance, love, nature, harmony, grace. There is nearly always music playing at Belmont. Within Venice, Shylock's house is a dungeon, an earthly hell in need of harrowing, an Egypt from which Shylock's daughter Jessica longs to be delivered.

Though Venice and Belmont are starkly opposed at many levels, the play complicates the opposition between them. The rough world of Venice runs aground without influence from Belmont, and Belmont is a fairy tale without a connection with Venice. Portia needs a husband in Belmont, and she and her maidservant become the saviors of Venice. Shakespeare's imagination is never completely daylight nor completely night, never merely sun or moon, male or female. Shakespeare aims at

---

1. I borrow this structure from Goddard, *Meaning of Shakespeare*, 1:81–116.

a marriage of day and night, Venice and Belmont, where commerce and music become one flesh.

The plot most closely associated with Belmont is, fittingly, the romantic or "casket" plot. Portia's father is dead. He left her very wealthy, and to protect her and her estate from unscrupulous suitors, he set up a test for potential husbands. As Portia's maid Nerissa explains it:

> Your father was ever virtuous, and holy men at their death have good inspirations. Therefore the lottery that he hath devised in these three chests of gold, silver, and lead—whereof who chooses his meaning chooses you—will no doubt never be chosen by any rightly but one who you shall rightly love. (1.2.26–31)

Each treasure box—called a "casket" in the play—is inscribed with a clue. The gold chest promises "Who chooseth me shall gain what many men desire," the silver "Who chooseth me shall get as much as he deserves," and the lead "Who chooseth me must give and hazard all he hath" (2.7.4–10). We are invited to read these as three perspectives on love: Love as desire, love as desert, love as a demand for self-sacrifice.

The most famous plot of the play, the "bond" plot, is directly linked to the casket plot. Bassanio, a young nobleman of Venice, has heard of Portia's wealth, beauty, and wisdom, and wants to court her. Unfortunately, noble though he is, he doesn't have much money, so he asks his kinsman, Antonio, for a loan. Antonio is the "merchant" of the title. He is wealthy, but his money is invested in various trading ventures. To fund Bassanio's courtship, Antonio seeks a loan from one of Venice's moneylenders, Shylock, a Jew. Like any banker, Shylock wants Antonio to put up collateral, something of value to ensure Shylock won't suffer a total loss if Antonio cannot repay the loan. Antonio's wealth is *future* wealth, wealth he hopes to receive from his trading ventures. Future wealth is uncertain, and Shylock is looking for certainty. Perhaps as a joke, Shylock asks for a pound of Antonio's flesh (1.3.141–49). Shylock and Antonio agree on the terms and sign a contract: Shylock lends Antonio three thousand ducats, which Antonio passes on to Bassanio. If Antonio cannot pay, Shylock will receive a pound of flesh in return.

Bassanio uses the money to buy new clothes and to gather an impressive entourage to visit Belmont. Portia has met him before and already wants to marry him. Happily, Bassanio chooses the correct casket to win her hand. Meanwhile, Nerissa has fallen in love with Bassanio's man-servant, Gratiano. The casket plot is resolved comically, with a double wedding.

This double wedding occurs in Act 3, scene 2, when we still have two Acts to go. We know something will complicate or threaten the marriages. Things darken immediately, as the bond plot casts a shadow over the happy ending of the casket plot. Bassanio and Portia are no sooner engaged than they receive news that all Antonio's trading vessels have sunk. He cannot repay Shylock and will have to give up his pound of flesh. Bassanio rushes from Belmont to Venice to rescue Antonio. Now that he has Portia's money, he offers to repay Antonio's loan, and more. Shylock refuses. He insists on having his pound of flesh.

Shylock's irrational fixity on the pound of flesh is motivated in part by his daughter's flight. Jessica has fallen in love with a Christian man, Lorenzo, who takes her from Shylock's house during a night of public revelry. Jessica takes "two sealed bags" of ducats with her. Shylock already hates the Christians of Venice. Antonio has insulted him as a "dog" and spit on him. But Jessica's departure deepens Shylock's hostility. He demands a pound of Antonio's flesh to take revenge on Christian Venice as much as on Antonio himself.

Bassanio cannot deter Shylock, but Portia saves the day. Disguised as a male lawyer, with Nerissa disguised as her assistant, Portia argues Antonio's case before the duke of Venice. She lures Shylock into a trap, and he is forced to give up his plot against Antonio, donate half of his fortune to Jessica and Lorenzo, and convert to Christianity. The casket plot is resolved when a man goes from Venice to Belmont. The bond plot is resolved when a woman, disguised as a man, goes from Belmont to Venice. A fully comic ending depends on the harmony of the two, the mutual dependence of male Venice and female Belmont.

A third plot is introduced late in the play: the ring plot. At their engagement, Bassanio receives a ring from Portia and Gratiano receives one from Nerissa. Both men promise never to part with their rings. After Portia and Nerissa deliver Antonio from Shylock, the women, still disguised as lawyers, demand that Bassanio and Gratiano give them the rings and, after some hesitation, the men agree. When everyone returns to Belmont, Portia and Nerissa ask their husbands for the rings, and the men are forced to admit they gave them away. The marriages are confirmed when the women reveal that they were the lawyers and that their husbands had unwittingly returned the rings to their own wives.

The three plots are woven together in a complex way:

Act	Casket	Bond	Ring
1.2	Initiated		
1.3		Initiated	
3.2	Resolved		
3.2		Complicated	
3.2			Initiated
4.1		Resolved	
4.2			Complicated
5.1			Resolved

The plots are resolved in order, but each new plot is introduced before the previous one is resolved. The play is a Celtic braid of beginnings and endings.

As this structure indicates, romantic and commercial concerns are linked. The play begins with a romantic plot taken from a fairy tale; it ends with confirmation of the lovers' commitment. But the money-focused bond plot ties the two comic romances together. Commercial Venice unites the love stories of Belmont. Without the love story of Belmont, Antonio would have been slaughtered like a lamb, with the approval of Venetian law. Law and love need each other. More deeply: Principles of commerce and the principles of love do not occupy separate realms, but are identical. Love and commerce are both hazardous adventures that demand self-sacrifice.

From another angle, *Merchant* is a triple story of liberation or resurrection. Lorenzo delivers Jessica from her father's house. She leaves behind her old Jewish home for the new world of Christian Venice. She leaves the darkness of Egypt for the promised land of the "beautiful mount," Bel-mont. Portia too begins the play in a state of death, "contained," as she herself puts it, in the "casket" her father selected (2.9.4–5). Bassanio raises her from her tomb so they can live as man and wife, Adam and Eve, on a magical mountain. Portia's liberation, though, endangers Antonio, and so Antonio has to be rescued from the force of Venetian law.

The two forms of comic plot we examined in chapter 4 are both present in this play. When we follow Jessica, *Merchant* is a comedy of flight or exodus. Yet her liberation depends on Lorenzo's invasion of Shylock's house. When we follow the fortunes of Antonio and Bassanio, the play is a drama of incarnation, as Portia disguises herself as a law clerk and invades the Venetian court. Wearing a masculine/political disguise, she brings the grace of Belmont into the city. But the original plot shows that Belmont also needs to be freed. Bassanio invades Belmont to break the impasse imposed by Portia's father. Liberated from her casket, Portia/Belmont invades Venice and rescues Antonio from Shylock. Allegorically, Portia is the church, saved to become a savior, rescued so she can rescue the friend of the bridegroom. There is a double incarnation, the incarnation of the bridegroom preceding and making possible the incarnation of the bride.

Each of the rescued characters is threatened by an oppressor and a law. We can chart these liberations as follows:

Person rescued	Oppressor	Law
Jessica	Shylock	Father's rules, Jewish law
Portia	Father	Father's will
Antonio	Shylock	Law of Venice

The emphasis on law elevates the play into the realm of theology, as it raises questions about the relationship between Judaism and Christianity and issues about grace and merit that were central to the Reformation struggle between Protestants and Roman Catholics.

One of the crucial issues in the play is the character of Shylock. Over the centuries, he has been treated as a stereotypical villain, often played with exaggerated Jewish features. Since the terrible suffering of the Jews in the Holocaust, productions of *Merchant* have carefully avoided Jewish caricatures and have often made Shylock the hero of the play, or at least a victim of Christian anti-Semitism. His forced conversion to Christianity is treated as an injustice, and his famous speech in Act 3 is presented as a liberal manifesto against prejudice, a statement of our common humanity:

> I am a Jew. Hath not a Jew eyes? Hath not a Jew hands, organs, dimensions, senses, affections, passions?—fed with the same food, hurt with the same weapons, subject to the same diseases, healed by the same means, warmed and cooled by the same winter and summer as a Christian is? If you prick us, do we not bleed? If you tickle us, do we not laugh? If you poison us, do we not die? (3.1.54–61)

It is a magnificent statement of the dignity of all.

But it's crucial to read the speech in context. The whole point of his speech is to justify Jewish revenge against Christians:

> And if you wrong us, shall we not revenge? If we are like you in the rest, we will resemble you in that. If a Jew wrong a Christian, what is his humility? Revenge. If a Christian wrong a Jew, what should his sufferance be by Christian example? Why, revenge! The villany you teach me I will execute, and it shall go hard but I will better the instruction. (3.1.61–67)

"Better the instruction" Shylock certainly does, as he pursues a vengeance that surpasses the vindictive harshness of Christians who have been his teachers.

While treating Shylock with sympathy, Shakespeare makes it impossible to view him as hero or entirely as victim. As in many plays, the imagery tells the story. In *Othello*, infernal imagery clusters around Iago, the manipulative tempter. In *Merchant*, the imagery associates Shylock with the devil, hell, and demons. He is called "devil" many times in the play (1.3.95; 2.2.20–27; 3.1.19–20; 4.1.215, 285), and his house is described as "hell" (2.3.2). The Christians of Venice are partly responsible for making him devilish, but devilish he is.

Shakespeare's contemporaries, moreover, wouldn't have been offended by Shylock's forced conversion. Many Elizabethans believed Paul predicted a future conversion of the Jews in Romans 9–11. A revival among Jews would mark the beginning of a period of glory for the church. As the Westminster Larger Catechism put it (question 191), the phrase "thy kingdom come" in the Lord's Prayer includes the prayer "that the kingdom of sin and Satan may be destroyed, the gospel propagated throughout the world, the Jews called, the fullness of the gentiles brought in." A Jew converting to Christianity was good news. It was a sign of good things to come, of the last day, the resurrection, and life everlasting on a beautiful, heavenly mount.

Review Questions

1. Discuss the triadic structure of *Merchant of Venice*. How are the three plots intertwined?
2. How are Belmont and Venice different? How are they similar?
3. What is the test for Portia's suitors? Who decided on this test?
4. What is the "bond" plot?

5. How are Venice and Belmont related in the resolution of the "bond" and "casket" plots?
6. Is *Merchant* an exodus comedy or an incarnation comedy?
7. How is *Merchant* a play about liberation?
8. Is Shylock a victim or a villain?

Thought Questions

1. Watch a recent film version of *The Merchant of Venice*. Does the film present Shylock as a villain or a victim? Explain how the film does this.
2. What sources did Shakespeare use to write the story of *Merchant*?
3. Find some old pictures of actors playing Shylock. How did the actors make themselves look more "Jewish"?

Venice and Belmont, Act 1

"In sooth I know not why I am so sad," Antonio says in the opening line of Act 1. His friends, Salanio and Salarino, react as friends do, by trying to identify the cause of his sadness. He's worried about his trading ventures, they suggest. His mind tosses on the ocean like his ships. No, says Antonio. He's not worried for his business because he hasn't put all his investment eggs in one basket. Perhaps, Salarino offers, he's in love. No, not in love neither. Antonio has no explanation, except that he's destined for a sad role in life: "I hold the world but as the world, Gratiano: / A stage where every man must play a part, / And mine a sad one" (1.1.77–79).

Scene 2 takes us to Belmont, where we break into a conversation between Lady Portia and her maid, Nerissa. Portia begins with nearly the same phrase as Antonio: "By my troth." Like Antonio, her mood is melancholy: "my little body is aweary of this great world" (1.2.1–2). She chafes against her dead father's arrangements for her future marriage. In order to protect her from scoundrels, he set up a test that only a shrewd and virtuous man could pass, the test of the caskets. This, Portia says, is no way to choose a husband: "I may neither choose who I would nor refuse who I dislike." What a trial, that "the will of a living daughter [is] curbed by the will of a dead father" (1.2.22–24).

In Shakespeare's English, "sad" could mean "satiated" or "sated."[2] This is the meaning that Nerissa fastens on. She has read Aristotle and thinks her lady is world-weary because of the abundance of good fortune. "For aught I see," she advises, "they are as sick that surfeit with too much as they that starve with nothing." Aristotle saw virtue as a middle-point between extremes. Too much is an "excess," and too little a "defect." Too much spirit is folly, too little is cowardice, and courage is the "mean." Too much wealth is excess, too little a defect. Best, Nerissa says, to be in the middle: "It is no mean happiness . . . to be seated in the mean" (1.2.3–9).

Nerissa's diagnosis applies as much to Antonio as to Portia. Both are wealthy. They have all they could ask for, and yet their fulness isn't fulfilling. As both Antonio and Portia will discover, happiness doesn't come through unchanging fulness, but through the self-giving risk of love.

As noted above, Venice and Belmont are contrasting settings. Yet the contrast between the two settings isn't nearly as stark as the contrast between the city and the forest in *Midsummer Night's Dream*. The play begins by highlighting their similarities. Venice has become too rich by its commercial success. Belmont's wealth is excessive by virtue of Portia's inheritance. Each needs its own form of redemption. Each needs an invader to break through.

That invasion is already in the making. Midway through scene 1, Bassanio and Gratiano interrupt Antonio's conversation with Salanio and Salarino. Bassanio wants a favor. He admits his wealth is "disabled" because of the "too prodigal" life he's led (1.1.123, 129). He has wasted *Antonio's* money, but he comes with a plan "to get clear of all the debts I owe" (1.1.134). Not surprisingly, Bassanio's plan requires another loan from Antonio. He has learned of a "lady richly left," Portia of Belmont, who has enough money to pay off all Bassanio's debts. She is "fair, and fairer than that word, / Of wondrous virtues" (1.1.161–63). Bassanio is sincere in wanting a fair and virtuous wife, but he wouldn't look twice at Portia if she were not rich. He's convinced he could "hold a rival place" among Portia's suitors, "had I but the means" (1.1.173–74). Hence his approach to Antonio: Bassanio looks for one last loan to end all loans, a loan to help him reach a fortune to cancel all debt.

---

2. Garber, *Shakespeare After All*, 286.

It's significant the first conversation between Antonio and Bassanio is about loans, debt, repayments. From the first, their relationship is embedded in monetary transactions, as it will be throughout the play. Antonio's response to Bassanio's request—which he gives even before hearing Bassanio's plans—also anticipates the direction of the play: "be assured / My purse, my person, my extremest means / Lie all unlocked to your occasions" (1.1.137–39). Antonio will be forced to take on the extremest risk, to lay down his life for his friend.

Antonio, however, is unable to make the loan directly, since "all my fortunes are at sea" (1.1.177). His ventures will return a profit, and he is confident he can qualify for a loan large enough to satisfy Bassanio's needs. So Bassanio and Antonio negotiate the terms of a loan with Shylock, the Jewish moneylender. Fittingly, Shylock's first words are "Three thousand ducats" (1.3.1), the amount of money Bassanio wishes to borrow. The word "ducats" is in Shylock's mouth throughout the scene and throughout the play. Other characters speak of money, but none as frequently or as passionately as Shylock. He is a money man, who evaluates other men as "good" or "bad" depending on the "sufficiency" of their bank account (1.3.12–17).

Shakespeare was deploying Elizabethan stereotypes of Jews in making Shylock so obsessed with cash. The association of Jews with money was partly due to legal and churchly rules that went back to the Middle Ages. According to church doctrine, Christians were prohibited from taking interest or "usury" on loans. Christians couldn't loan $100 and receive $105 in return.

Thomas Aquinas explains the reasons.[3] Some things can be used without being used up. You can use a shovel again and again to dig different holes over many years. If you rent a shovel from your neighbor, you pay for the *use* of it. But some things are used up by using them. When you eat food or drink wine, they're gone. If you eat at a restaurant, you pay for the *eating* or use of food and the wine. Imagine a restaurant where you pay for the food and *then* pay again to *eat* it. The waiter brings your steak and says, "Oh. You plan to *eat* that? That'll be another $25." That would be extremely odd. Thomas says it more severely: It would be unjust, a double payment for the same thing.

Money, Thomas continues, is more like food than like a shovel. It is consumed by the use. We pay our bills and the money is gone. We

---

3. Aquinas, *Summa theologiae*, II-II, q. 1, art. 78.

pay for the steak, and the credit card company charges us at the end of the month. We can't use the same money over and over to buy different things—not legally, at least. By Thomas's reasoning, usury is unjust because it involves a double payment. Someone loans you $100, and you pay it back a month later. In the meantime, you've used the money to buy groceries or to pay part of your rent. The money you received as a loan is long gone and, Thomas thinks, you can't be charged for using something that gets used up. Interest is like paying once for wine and then paying a second time for drinking it.

Jews weren't under the same restrictions as Christians, so for centuries they were the leading moneylenders in Christian Europe. As *Merchant* shows, usury intensifies religious and racial animosities between Christians and Jews. When Antonio appears in scene 3, Shylock recounts the reasons for his hatred for Antonio in particular:

> How like a fawning publican he looks.
> I hate him for he is a Christian;
> But more, for that in low simplicity
> He lends out money gratis and brings down
> The rate of usance here with us in Venice.
> If I can catch him once upon the hip,
> I will feed fat the ancient grudge I bear him.
> He hates our sacred nation, and he rails,
> Even there where merchants most do congregate,
> On me, my bargains and my well-won thrift,
> Which he calls interest. Cursed be my tribe,
> If I forgive him! (1.3.38–49)

Shylock hates Antonio as a Christian, but his hatred is compounded by Antonio's willingness to loan money without interest. Because Antonio doesn't charge interest, the interest rate stays low and Shylock's profits are lower than they would be. Antonio, on the other hand, hates Shylock for making money from what should be charity.

Merchant seems to draw a simply contrast: Jews are greedy and harsh, while Christians freely give. But the contrast is complicated through the course of the play. Though Shylock is the villain, his harsh business dealings throw light on the harsh dealings of Christian Venetians, who are more devoted to Mammon than they admit. Though Shylock is an outcast, the city depends on him and his fellow Jews. Without Jewish credit, the city could not continue or extend its commercial dominance. The city leaders know they cannot afford to cross Shylock. Shylock represents the spirit of commercial Venice. He is what Venice would be without the gracious interventions of Belmont.

Shylock offers an intriguing biblical defense of usury. Laban promised Jacob the striped and "pied" sheep, and Jacob used a form of trickery or magic to ensure the healthy ewes would produce lambs with the proper markings (Gen 27). Shylock admits Jacob did not take interest "directly," but still cites the episode in support of his money-lending:

> Mark what Jacob did:
> When Laban and himself were compromised
> That all the eanlings which were streaked and pied
> Should fall as Jacob's hire, the ewes being rank
> In the end of autumn turned to the rams;
> And when the work of generation was
> Between these woolly breeders in the act,
> The skillful shepherd peeled me certain wands,
> And in the doing of the deed of kind
> He stuck them up before the fulsome ewes,
> Who then conceiving, did in eaning time
> Fall parti-colored lambs, and those were Jacob's.
> This was a way to thrive, and he was blessed;
> And thrift is blessing if men steal it not. (1.3.73–87)

Antonio asks the obvious question, "is your gold and silver ewes and lambs?" (1.3.92). Shylock points to the analogy with his reply: "I cannot tell; I make it breed as fast" (1.3.93). Aristotle again lurks in the background. He famously rejects interest because money is sterile. It does *not* breed. Shylock claims the opposite. He makes ducats give birth to little baby ducats.

Beyond the specifics of the argument, Shylock identifies himself with Jacob, the man who gave his name "Israel" to Shylock's people. This is only the first of the play's multiple allusions to Jacob.[4] Shylock's servant Lancelot disguises himself before his father Old Gobbo, as Jacob extracted a blessing from his blind father Isaac (2.2.30–105). Shylock swears by Jacob's staff, a reminder of Jacob's departure from his father's house with only a staff in his hand (2.5.36). Shylock also thinks of himself as Abraham. He refers to Lancelot as "Hagar's offspring," a son of Ishmael, son of Abraham and Hagar (2.5.43). "Hagar's offspring" appear in Jacob's story too, since Jacob's brother Esau marries Hagar's granddaughter. Shylock thinks his position in Venice is similar to Jacob's in the house of Laban. In

---

4. Mahood, "Shakespeare's Use of the Bible," 197–98.

his own mind, Shylock isn't a villain but a victim. Like Jacob, he shrewdly turns a profit despite the Venetians' cruel prejudice and hatred.[5]

Whatever the force of Shylock's argument, it doesn't convince Antonio. To him, it only proves "The devil can cite Scripture for his purpose" (1.3.95). Shylock is a "villain" who has "a smiling cheek" but is "a goodly rotten apple at the heart" (1.3.97-99). It's the first time Shylock is called a devil, but it won't be the last.

Antonio refers to Jacob's sheep-breeding as a "venture" rather than usury (1.3.88). Unlike interest, a "venture" is hazardous. A moneylender is assured of his profit. Whatever happens to the borrower, the lender gets his money back. If the borrower cannot repay, the lender can take him to court for satisfaction (as Shylock does with Antonio). Antonio's ships, though, are vulnerable to seas and storms. In Antonio's view, Jacob was an adventurer rather than a usurer, and his venture was "A thing not in his power to bring to pass, / But swayed and fashioned by the hand of heaven" (1.3.89-90). As a Christian merchant, he lives by expectation rather than the certainty of money-lending (1.3.156-57). For Antonio, this is godly commerce, since it is business by faith, not sight.

Shylock and Antonio represent different models of commercial life. Instead of hoarding, Antonio has put his talents out in the wide world, risking loss in order to gain. He assists Bassanio, even when his own funds are tied up, obeying Jesus' command to "give to him that asks of you" (Matt 5:42). Antonio is willing to "risk and venture" all he has—his credit, even his life—for his friend. Love and commerce operate by the same principles.

For Shylock, by contrast, business is all about thrift, savings, hoarding. He considers commerce wasteful, a squandering of resources (1.3.20-21). He despises Antonio's practice of lending money *gratis*, despises the festivities of the Christian Venetians as much for their waste as for their prurience, cries "my daughter, my ducats" when Jessica plunders his house. Selfless love, if Shylock experiences it at all, exists in a realm completely separate from commerce.

As they conclude their deal, Shylock plays the role of the Christian, suffering wrong without revenge. He agrees to loan *without* usury: "I would be friends with you and have your love, / Forget the shames that you have stained me with, / Supply your present wants, and take no doit / Of usance for my moneys" (1.3.135-38). In "merry sport," he proposes a different sort of interest:

---

5. See Lewalski, "Biblical Allusion," 327-43.

> If you repay me not on such a day,
> In such a place, such sum or sums as are
> Expressed in the condition, let the forfeit
> Be nominated for an equal pound
> Of your fair flesh, to be cut off and taken
> In what part of your body pleaseth me. (1.3.144–49)

Shylock's motives for this arrangement are murky. Perhaps he does, as he says, intend the proposal playfully. Perhaps the contract expresses ironic humor about Christian objections to usury. Usury was often seen as a "bite" taken from the borrower; moneylenders were seen as predators preying on the weak. Shylock makes the "bite" literal. Perhaps he secretly hopes Antonio will default, and Shylock will be able to kill his enemy legally. Later Jessica reports she heard her father tell "his countrymen / That he would rather have Antonio's flesh / Than twenty times the value of the sum / That he did owe him" (3.2.285–88).

Whatever his intention, his suggestion is symbolically powerful. Unlike Jews, Christians do not circumcise for religious reasons, since Christians believe the Spirit gives a "circumcised heart." Shylock proposes to circumcise Antonio's heart quite literally. Shylock also sets up a situation where Antonio is forced to follow the Christian demand of self-sacrifice, where he must indeed lay down his life for his friend.

As they conclude their bond, Antonio calls Shylock "kind" and "gentle" (1.3.175–76): "The Hebrew will turn Christian" (1.3.176). When he says it, Antonio is wrong. He's forgotten his earlier warning that falsehood can hide itself in a "goodly outside" (1.3.98–99). Shylock is not ready to turn Christian, though his daughter Jessica is. In the long run, though, Antonio is not wrong. In the end, the Jew becomes another "kind" of man. The Hebrew will indeed "turn Christian."

Review Questions

1. Why is Antonio sad? Why is Portia weary of the world?
2. What kind of life has Bassanio led? Why does he want a loan from Antonio?
3. Describe the relationship between Antonio and Shylock.
4. Why does Antonio need a loan from Shylock to help Bassanio?
5. What is "usury"? Why did Thomas Aquinas think it was wrong?

6. What is Shylock's defense of usury? How does he identify with Jacob?

7. Explain how "risk" and "venture" fit into the casket and bond plots.

Thought Questions

1. How does Bassanio describe his school days (1.1.140–52)? How does this fit with the play's emphasis on ventures, hazards, and risk?

2. Shylock calls Antonio a "fawning publican" (1.3.38). What is a publican? Why would Shylock describe Antonio this way? What, if anything, does this have to do with Luke 18:9–14?

3. After Shylock recounts the story of Jacob and his sheep, Antonio tells Bassanio, "O what a goodly outside falsehood hath!" (1.2.99). How does this comment fit with the play's other references to appearance and reality? Why is it significant that Antonio accuses Shylock of hypocrisy?

Portia in a Casket, Acts 2–3

Portia's little body is aweary of the world (1.2.1), so she and Nerissa amuse themselves by mocking the suitors who visit Belmont. The Neopolitan prince is a "colt" who can talk of nothing but his horse. The count of the Palatine is humorless, and Portia fears he will become a "weeping philosopher" as he ages. The French visitor, Monsieur Le Bon, is a chameleon: "he is every man in no man," and if Portia marries him she'll marry "twenty husbands." The English baron from Falconbridge doesn't know Latin, French, or Italian, and his clothing is a mishmash of fashions from all over Europe. The German duke of Saxony is vile when sober and vile when drunk, which he is every afternoon (1.2.37–86).

There's more than mockery in the scene. Nerissa already knows the current suitors are leaving (1.2.95–100), and as the two women complete their catalogue of dolts, a servant enters to confirm, "The four strangers seek for you, madam, to take their leave" (1.2.118–19). The test is too hard for them. Portia is persuaded her father was "ever virtuous" and his test was an "inspiration" (1.2.26–27). She bows to her father's will, vowing to "die as chaste as Diana unless I be obtained by the manner of my father's will" (1.2.101–3).

We get our first glimpse of the selection process when the Prince of Morocco arrives. Portia tells him the stringent terms of this game of love. If he chooses the wrong casket, he may never "speak to lady afterward / In way of marriage" (2.1.40–42). It's an all-or-nothing choice, Portia or lifelong singleness.

Morocco's race highlights the importance of appearance and reality. He asks Portia not to pay attention to his dark "complexion" (2.1.1). Skin isn't as important as what's inside, and Morocco claims to have the reddest blood and the fieriest temperament. As proof, he swears the "best-regarded virgins" of his home country appreciate his sexual prowess (2.1.2–12). Tip to young lovers: Don't try to impress a girl by recounting how many virgins you've deflowered.

Standing in front of the caskets, Morocco forgets his own caution. He dismisses the lead chest: "Is't like that lead contains her? 'Twere damnation / to think so base a though; it were too gross / To rib her cerecloth in the obscure grave" (2.7.49–51). Besides, he's frightened by the lead casket's inscription, "Who chooseth me must give and hazard all his hath." "Hazard for lead?" he asks. Men hazard when they have "hope of fair advantages," when they believe their risk will pay off with gold. A "golden mind" like Morocco's won't "stoop" for lead. The silver casket tempts him, with its talk of desert: "I do in birth deserve her, and in fortunes, / In graces, and in qualities of breeding," but most of all "in love I do deserve." Finally, though, he chooses the gold casket, concluding that *Portia* is "what many men desire" (2.7.13–60). Notice: Morocco doesn't choose what *he* desires, but what *others* desire. Winning Portia will, he thinks, make him an object of envy to other men. He's less interested in Portia than in proving his superiority to his rivals.

The contrast of appearance and reality is a common motif of drama, but Shakespeare knows that seeing past the appearance isn't our only problem. Like Morocco, we're also plagued by forgetfulness. As Portia says, we rarely practice what we know: "I can easier teach twenty what were good to be done than to be one of the twenty to follow mine own teaching." If doing were as easy as knowing, "chapels had been churches, and poor men's cottages princes' palaces" (1.2.12–19).

Morocco's obsession with appearances connects with the larger contrast between Jews and Christians. In his treatise *On Christian Teaching*, Augustine linked the contrast of appearance and reality with that between

Jew and Christian. Jews under the Old Testament system were subjected to signs, albeit useful signs designed by God himself. But the Jews didn't recognize the "thing" to which the sign pointed, that is, Christ (3.22). They became spiritual slaves because they treated "signs as things" and were "incapable of raising the mind's eye above the physical creation so as to absorb the eternal light" (3.21). Obsessed with circumcision, food laws, purity, and all the other shadows, they couldn't see the reality when it was right in front of them. Whether or not Shakespeare knew Augustine's book, he too links "appearance" to Jews and "reality" to Christians.

Morocco's forgetful obsession with appearances costs him. Inside the gold casket he finds a skull and a further inscription:

> All that glisters is not gold;
> Often have you heard that told.
> Many a man his life hath sold
> But my outside to behold.
> Gilded tombs do worms infold.
> Had you been as wise as bold,
> Young in limbs, in judgment old,
> Your answer had not been inscrolled.
> Fare you well; your suit is cold. (2.7.65–73)

The next contestant, Aragon, refuses gold because *everyone* likes gold. He stands above the mass of men and believes the world functions best when honors are given to the most deserving. He bets on merit rather than desire, and chooses the silver casket.

> Who shall go about
> To cozen fortune, and be honorable
> Without the stamp of merit? Let none presume
> To wear an undeserved dignity.
> O that estates, degrees, and offices
> Were not derived corruptly, and that clear honor
> Were purchased by the merit of the wearer!
> How many then should cover that stand bare,
> How many be commanded that command;
> How much low peasantry would then be gleaned
> From the true seed of honor, and how much honor
> Picked from the chaff and ruin of the times
> To be new varnished! Well, but to my choice.
> "Who chooseth me shall get as much as he deserves."
> I will assume desert. (2.9.36–50)

Aragon applies principles of social order to the realm of love. The relevance of merit in social life is questionable. In love, merit is completely out of place. Fittingly, Aragon discovers a fool's head inside the silver casket. As he leaves, he speaks with mournful self-awareness: "With one fool's head I came to woo, / But I go away with two" (3.1.74–75).

There's a theological dimension to Aragon's choice. "Merit" plays a significant role in Reformation debates about salvation. According to Catholic teaching, by God's grace sinners can do good to become worthy of salvation. Luther and the other Reformers insisted that salvation was based completely on the merit of Jesus. Aragon thinks like a Roman Catholic; love is something you can earn. The winner will have to think like a Protestant. The theological issue raised here will return in the trial scene in Act 4.

Portia has already chosen Bassanio before he ever sees the caskets (cf. 1.2.107–11), and she does all she can within the limits of her father's will to guide him to the right treasure chest. While he examines the caskets, she arranges for a song that repeats words rhyming with "lead" (bred, head, nourish-ed, fed; 3.2.63–72) and that also reminds Bassanio about the dangers of appearance: fancy is bred "in the eye, / with gazing fed" (3.2.67–68).

Bassanio is a man moved by music. That's important, since he's vying for the lady of Belmont, a house of music. Bassanio knows "the outward shows [may] be least themselves," and recognizes the world is "deceived with ornament." Corrupt legal arguments and decisions are "seasoned with a gracious voice," every vice dresses itself up in virtue, and beauties end in the grave like everyone else. Even in religion, a "damned error" is blessed and approved by "hiding the grossness with fair ornament" (3.2.73–80).

"All that glisters is not gold," the gold casket told Morocco, and Bassanio knows it. "Gaudy gold" is a trap, silver a "pale and common drudge / 'Tween man and man" (3.2.101–4). Lead it is, and in the lead box he finds "fair Portia's counterfeit" (3.2.115). "I am locked in one of them," Portia had said (3.2.40). By choosing rightly, Bassanio gives her new life, unlocks her grave, and raises her from her "casket." Bassanio even receives back double for his venture: As he wins Portia, Gratiano has been wooing Nerissa (3.2.196–98).

Bassanio pushes the lesson of the casket to another level, one that opens up the central themes of the play. Beautiful as the portrait of Portia is, it is nothing to Portia herself: "look, how far / The substance of my praise doth wrong this shadow / in overprizing it, so far this shadow / Doth limp behind the substance" (3.2.126–29). Bassanio's praise is inadequate to the portrait, and the portrait a mere "shadow" in relation to the "substance."

The terminology may come from Plato. Plato taught that there are two worlds, the sensible world we live in and a word of forms or ideas. "Ideas" don't exist only in our minds. They are real; in fact, they are *more* real than the things we can see and touch and hear, because they are the models for the things we sense. We never encounter goodness in its full reality in the world of experience. Ice cream is good, but only a faint hint of the Form of the Good. The good things we sense are only "shadows" of the "substance" that exists in the world of ideas. For some in Shakespeare's audience, Bassanio's contrast of shadow and substance might have reminded them of Plato's theory.

For others, it would have echoed with something they heard in church: The law, Paul says, "was a mere shadow of what is to come, but the substance belongs to Christ" (Col 2:17; cf. Heb 8:5; 10:1). In the Bible, appearance and reality are not "ontological" but "historical" categories. Shadow and substance don't name two "worlds" but two *time* periods, the period before Christ versus the period after Christ. The old covenant is a covenant of signs and shadows that give a foretaste of the substance of the new. When the Sun of God rises, Jewish shadows give way to Christian substance.

"I crave the law," Shylock shrieks in the open court (4.1.204), scoffing at Portia's claim that "mercy seasons justice" (4.1.195). Shylock stands for law because he stands for Torah, the law of Moses that, Christians say, has now given way to the grace and truth of Jesus. Antonio, by contrast, and Portia too, stand for mercy, for the law of Christ, the law of self-sacrificing love that rewards the one who "give[s] and hazard[s] all he hath" (2.7.9).

Review Questions

1. What does Portia think of her suitors?
2. Which casket does the Prince of Morocco choose? Why? What does his choice imply about his understanding of love?
3. What lesson does Morocco learn from the casket?

4. What did Augustine says about the Jewish understanding of signs?
5. What casket does Aragon choose? Why? What does his choice imply about his view of love?
6. How does Bassanio know which casket to choose?
7. Discuss the significance of Bassanio's reference to "shadow."

Thought Questions

1. In the 1973 film production of *Merchant*, Aragon finds a mirror in the silver casket. What's the joke?
2. Portia describes her marriage as a "conversion" (3.2.167). How does this anticipate Shylock's later "conversion" to Christianity?
3. What has Jessica done with Shylock's ring (3.1.109–14)? Why does Shylock react as he does? How is this related to the later ring plot?
4. "I stand for sacrifice," Portia says (3.2.57). Look at the surrounding lines and explain what she means.

In Shylock's House, Acts 2–3

The first Act of *Merchant* alternates between Venice and Belmont: Venice (scene 1), Belmont (scene 2), and Venice (scene 3). Act 2 begins in the same alternating fashion but soon breaks from it to introduce a third setting, Shylock's house. Act 2 is a series of short, rapid-fire scenes, and the first seven are bracketed by scenes of the Prince of Morocco at Belmont:

> Belmont: Morocco arrives, 2.1
>   Shylock's house: Lancelot and Old Gobbo, his father, 2.2
>   Shylock's house: Jessica and Lancelot, 2.3
>   Venice: Lorenzo plotting to steal Jessica, 2.4
>   Shylock's house: Jessica and Shylock, 2.5
>   Shylock's house: Lorenzo takes Jessica, 2.6
> Belmont: Morocco makes his selection, 2.7

Act 2 closes with two additional scenes. In 2.8, Salarino and Salanio discuss Shylock's reaction to Jessica's departure, and in the final scene we are again back at Belmont, where the prince of Aragon selects the silver casket and fails to win Portia's hand.

Shylock's devilish character becomes more pronounced in Act 2. Shylock thinks of his house as the household of Abraham. That's not how Jessica and Shylock's servant, Lancelot, see things. Lancelot carries on an internal debate about whether or not to leave his master. The "fiend" encourages him to run, but his conscience reminds him of his obligations as a servant. Shylock is also a fiend, "a kind of devil" and "the very devil incarnation." Whether Lancelot leaves or goes, he follows a fiend. In the end, he decides to opt for the devil he doesn't know rather than the devil he knows (2.2.1–29).

In the long run, Lancelot doesn't make the decision. Shylock sells him to Bassanio (2.2.131–38), and so Lancelot becomes part of the entourage that goes with Bassanio to court Portia. Lancelot doesn't simply escape from Egypt into the bewilderingness of Venice. He escapes from hell to find a place in the heavenly city of Belmont. The fact that his escape is legally secured foreshadows the climax of the play, when Antonio will be rescued from Shylock not by ignoring the law but by enforcing it. Throughout the play, the law is upheld. Miracles don't cancel law. Miracles happen when upholding law opens a crack for the entry of grace.

In Act 2, scene 5, Shylock is preparing to go out for dinner and talking about Lancelot leaving his service for Bassanio's. But his train of thought is interrupted by repeated calls to Jessica. He searches for his daughter, but all the while he thinks about his servant changing masters. The biblical allusion in 2.5.43 adds another dimension to the plot. Lancelot is delivering a message to Jessica from Lorenzo, but to keep Shylock from overhearing he murmurs under his breath. Shylock sees him talking to Jessica and asks his daughter, "What says that fool of Hagar's offspring? Ha?" Shylock implies that Lancelot is like one of Hagar's children. He has been living in "Abraham's tents"—Shylock's house—but is now preparing to leave. But the syntax is unusual: Does "fool of Hagar's offspring" mean a "fool from Hagar's tribe"? Or does it mean "what does that fool say *about* Hagar's offspring?" The ambiguous syntax hints at Jessica's departure. If the question is taken as "What is that fool saying about Hagar's child?" Jessica's answer is revealing. She implies the fool is saying goodbye to Hagar's child, which means she herself is Hagar/Ishmael leaving Abraham's house. She's about to become a "Gentile," marrying a Christian.

Like Lancelot, Jessica regards her father's house as a devil's house: "Our house is hell" (2.3.2). Her escape is her salvation, and Lorenzo is her savior. Jessica recognizes this in a later conversation with Lancelot: "I shall be saved by my husband. He hath made me a Christian" (3.5.17–18).

Portia welcomes her to Belmont as a refugee, saying she purchased "the semblance of my soul / From out the state of hellish cruelty" (3.4.20–21). Jessica's deliverance is like Jesus' rescue of spirits in prison. Jessica, in short, hasn't merely exchanged one human master (her father) for another (her husband). She has moved from old to new, from Judaism to Christianity, from law to grace, from the devil's clutches into the loving hands of her savior. The fact that she takes Shylock's money with her fits the theological dimension of her action. Long before, Shylock's Jewish forefathers plundered Egypt, and before that Jacob plundered Laban. Tables are turned, and the plunderer gets plundered, by his own daughter. Shylock misidentified himself. He's not Jacob, but Laban.

Jessica's experience foreshadows Portia's in a number of ways. She's the first woman to get married, though unlike Portia she defies her father's will. She escapes Shylock's house with a "casket" (2.6.33), reminiscent of the "caskets" in Portia's house. Lorenzo regards Jessica as a "lead casket," an apparently unpromising Jewish exterior that contains something beautiful. He chooses from the "leaden" Jews, but finds a true Christian underneath. Jessica disguises herself with male clothes, foreshadowing Portia's later disguise. Both women deprive Shylock of property. Jessica leaves with gold and jewels, while Portia keeps Shylock from getting his pound of flesh and eventually deprives him of all his wealth. Jessica all but ruins Shylock. She takes "two bags of ducats" with "two stones, two rich and precious stones," an unwitting reference to Shylock's sexual organs (2.8.18–22). Jessica takes away his child (herself) and his future descendants, the "family jewels." Shylock's grandchildren will be Christians, not Jews. Even before Portia impoverishes Shylock, Jessica has unmanned him. Since "she hath the stones upon her," she's now the man of Shylock's house (2.8.22).

Jessica escapes from her father's house during a festival. Lorenzo uses the disguises and activity of the masque to cover up his actions, but the party atmosphere has a more than practical significance in the play. In separating himself from Christians, Shylock deliberately separates himself from Christian *festivity*. As he leaves for dinner, he gives Jessica strict instructions to close herself in the house:

> What, are there masques? Hear you me, Jessica:
> Lock up my doors; and when you hear the drum
> And the vile squealing of the wry-necked fife,
> Clamber not you up to the casements then,
> Nor thrust your head into the public street

> To gaze on Christian fools with varnished faces;
> But stop my house's ears—I mean my casements;
> Let not the sound of shallow foppery enter
> My sober house. By Jacob's staff I swear
> I have no mind of feasting forth to-night;
> But I will go. (2.5.28–38)

For Shylock, the man of commerce and law, festivity is foolish, "shallow foppery." Jessica wants the joy of Venice at night and ultimately the joy of Belmont. Despite himself, Shylock will eventually end up joining the revelers.

In Act 3, Shylock's house is less prominent, but the results of Jessica's flight ripple out to the other settings. Act 3, scene 1 shows Shylock engaged with Christian and Jewish characters. He is mourning his daughter, treating her departure as her death: "I would my daughter were dead at my foot, and the jewels in her ear!" (3.1.81–82). Death is better than conversion and marriage to a Christian. In the same scene, Tubal gives him the news that Antonio's ships have sunk coming from Tripolis. The juxtaposition of the two themes is significant. Shylock already hated Antonio, but after Jessica departs he ferociously hungers for revenge. Jessica has been stolen from him, along with his ducats. *Christians* stole his daughter and his money, and *Christians* will have to pay him back. Antonio's pound of flesh is compensation for his loss.

For Shylock, the symmetry of crime and punishment is even more exact. Jessica is his flesh and blood (3.1.34), and she has been stolen. So Shylock exacts his revenge by taking *Antonio's* flesh (3.1.43–46). In Shylock's view, Jessica is truly dead. All his actions for the rest of the play rest on this conviction (3.1.77–83). Shylock doesn't think her death is a metaphor; the Christians killed her. He doesn't care that he would kill Antonio by taking a pound of flesh. That's the whole point. Antonio will pay with his life, as a substitute for all Christians, for the murder of Jessica. Shylock stands for law, eye for eye, tooth for tooth, life for life.

Like Act 2, Act 3 ends in Belmont:

> Venice: Shylock demands pound of flesh, 3.1
>   Belmont: Bassanio selects the right casket, 3.2
> Venice: Shylock and Antonio, the latter a prisoner, 3.3
>   Belmont: Lorenzo and Jessica welcomed to Belmont, 3.4
>   Belmont: Lancelot, Jessica, and Lorenzo at Belmont, 3.5

In the middle of Act 3, just after Bassanio chooses the lead casket, Belmont receives the news that Antonio is in trouble. He has lost his ships, and Shylock is demanding payment of his bond. Bassanio rushes to Venice with Gratiano, leaving Portia and Nerissa plotting to help Antonio. The next time we see them, they, like the revelers who stole Jessica away, will be disguised for a rescue operation.

Review Questions

1. Discuss the structure of Act 2.
2. Who is Lancelot? How does he escape from Shylock's house?
3. Who is Jessica? How does she escape her home?
4. How does Shylock react to Jessica's departure? What does his reaction say about his character? How does Jessica's escape affect Shylock's actions in the rest of the play?
5. Discuss the structure of Act 3.

Thought Questions

1. The 1973 production of *Merchant* starring Lawrence Olivier as Shylock (available on YouTube) skips nearly all the scenes with Lancelot and his father Gobbo, as well as the scene of Jessica's escape from Shylock's house. Why would the writer or director decide to leave those scenes out?
2. Shylock warns Jessica to shut the "ears" of the house and explains that he's talking about the windows (2.5.28–36). Why doesn't he want his house to "hear" what's going on outside? How is his hostility to Venice's nighttime activities related to his understanding of business?
3. The word *prodigal* is used several times in *Merchant* (2.5.15; 2.6.14; 3.1.41). What does the word mean? How might these uses be related to Jesus' parable of the "prodigal son" (Luke 15:11–32)?
4. Why does Shylock agree to go to dinner with Christians? (2.5.11–18). Discuss this in connection with what Shylock says in 1.3.30–35.

5. Why is Shylock happy to get rid of Lancelot? What does he hope Lancelot will do to Bassanio? How does this fit with other things we know about Shylock?

Mercy Seasons Justice, Act 4

The trial scene in *Merchant* (4.1) is one of Shakespeare's best-known scenes and is justly celebrated. It is highly dramatic, teetering on the edge of tragedy, and gives Shylock some of the most forceful lines in any of Shakespeare's plays. Just as it seems there will be blood, with Portia's understated "Tarry a little, there is something else" (4.1.303), the scene, and the audience, breathe a sigh of relief. In the flicker of an eye, the world goes right side up. Antonio is rescued and Shylock undone. I know what's going to happen, yet I'm moved every time I see it. Shakespeare strums some strings deep in the heart.

Merchant is packed with comedies of exodus. Portia is rescued from her "casket" by Bassanio's visitation to Belmont. Jessica escapes from the devil's house, with great plunder. Antonio is eventually rescued from Shylock and ends the play with the rest of the characters in Belmont. But the hinge of the play, the turning point that ensures a comic outcome, is an "incarnation," as Portia disguises herself as a lawyer to invade the Venetian court and untie the knots in which Venetian law has tangled itself.

At one level, the legal conflict is between Shylock and Antonio. They freely agree on a contract. Shylock loans Antonio three thousand ducats for three months, and Antonio, freely if foolishly, agrees to put up a pound of his own fair flesh as collateral. Antonio can't repay, and Shylock demands repayment. The court of Venice, the duke of Venice presiding, must decide between them.

Even at a personal level, the conflict opens up larger themes. As a Jew, Shylock represents the dominion of law. Bassanio offers to pay, to pay double, the repayment that Torah requires for theft. Shylock refuses. The legal contract is binding: He wants flesh, not money, just as the law demands.

As we have seen, Antonio and Shylock also represent contrasting ways of life and ways of business. Antonio represents Christian generosity, lending his money without interest. Shylock demands interest. He loans to make his money breed. As the play has developed, though, the contrast between the two men has become more complicated. When he stands before the caskets (3.2), Bassanio admits even Christian Venice is obsessed with ornamentation and externals. Augustine to the contrary, that is not merely a fault of Jews. Venice's Christians are close to *becoming* Jews.

Besides, Antonio the Christian doesn't treat his enemy Shylock with the love Jesus demands of his followers. Even before their legal dispute, Antonio despises Shylock. When Portia arrives at the court, disguised as a lawyer, she asks Antonio and Shylock to stand forward and asks, "Which is the merchant here and which the Jew?" (4.1.172). The difference should be immediately clear. Jews wore distinctive clothing, and most stage productions have exaggerated Shylock's Jewish features. But the question points to a central problem of the play: As different as Jew and Christian seem, are they kin beneath the skin? We recall Shylock's "Hath not a Jew eyes?" speech. It's a defense of the humanity of Jews; is it also an indictment of the "Jewishness" of Christians? In Venice at least, where gaudy appearance distracts from leaden reality, Jew and Christian might become indistinguishable. Shylock's trial puts Venice on trial. Venice needs to be rescued because, like Jessica, it threatens to become a hell. And it will be rescued only when Belmont descends from the heavens.

The trial is a constitutional crisis for the city. As Antonio recognizes when he is arrested, Venice depends on the stability and reliability of its laws:

> The duke cannot deny the course of law;
> For the commodity that strangers have
> With us in Venice, if it be denied,
> Will much impeach the justice of the state,
> Since that the trade and profit of the city
> Consisteth of all nations. Therefore go.
> These griefs and losses have so bated me
> That I shall hardly spare a pound of flesh
> Tomorrow to my bloody creditor. (3.3.26–34)

If the duke doesn't support the contract between Shylock and Antonio, no one will trust Venetian law. Other cities will be reluctant to trade, because they won't be sure their contracts will be honored. Of course, if the duke enforces *this* contract, Venice will gain a reputation a vicious city, one that literally lets citizens get away with murder. Shylock has the duke and the city over a barrel and he knows it:

> The pound of flesh which I demand of him,
> Is dearly bought, 'tis mine, and I will have it.
> If you deny me, fie upon your law!
> There is no force in the decrees of Venice.
> I stand for judgment. Answer: shall I have it? (4.1.99–103)

The legal and constitutional dimensions of the trial raise the stakes for Antonio. He wants to save his life, but he doesn't want to save his life at the cost of destroying Venice. Early in Act 4, he tells the Duke he is resigned to his fate:

> I have heard
> Your grace hath ta'en great pains to qualify
> His rigorous course; but since he stands obdurate,
> And that no lawful means can carry me
> Out of his envy's reach, I do oppose
> My patience to his fury, and am armed
> To suffer with a quietness of spirit
> The very tyranny and rage of his. (4.1.6–13)

Some readers think Antonio is still melancholy, as he was at the outset of the play, perhaps even suicidal. More likely, he is being a stoic, who strives to retain a calm spirit even in the most stressful circumstances. Given the setting, it seems best to read this speech in a more Christian vein. He's ready to die because his death will save Venice. He's ready to die for his friend, and he is ready to die for his people. Antonio's resignation to death raises the trial scene to another level: Shylock stands for the Jews who demand the death of Jesus, while Antonio plays the role of Christ the sacrificial Lamb.

Portia appears in the middle of the scene, disguised as Balthasar, a "young doctor of Rome" (4.1.152–53), and immediately takes charge of the trial. She's not a mere consultant, or Antonio's defense attorney. She assumes the role of judge, though the duke renders the official verdict. Like Antonio, Portia understands the contract cannot be set aside. Bassanio asks his disguised wife to make an extra-legal decision: "Wrest once the law to your authority: / To do a great right, do a little wrong, / And curb this cruel devil of his will" (4.1.213–15). It seems a reasonable appeal: Overrule the contract to protect Antonio. Portia refuses: "It must not be. . . . It cannot be" (4.1.216, 220). Once a law is set in Venice it cannot be overturned. Making an exception here, where a "little wrong" seems to be the way of justice, will corrupt Venetian justice. "It must not be."

Portia seems to have her plan set from the beginning. She makes three offers to Shylock: She asks him to relent and show mercy; she offers him three times his loan to give up his case; and she offers him a combination solution, in which he would relent and also take his money. Later, she asks if Shylock has provided for a surgeon to be present to stop the bleeding (4.1.255–56). Shylock dismisses the request. If it's not in the contract, he's not bound to do it. He stands for law, the strict letter of the law and nothing but the law. Shylock wants the law enforced regardless of human feeling, compassion, mercy, or even common sense. Shylock and the audience are unaware of it, but Portia is cornering him.

Portia's first request is for Shylock to show mercy: "Then must the Jew be merciful." Shylock bristles. He cannot be required to show mercy (4.1.181–82). Portia agrees. Mercy cannot be coerced:

> The quality of mercy is not strained;
> It droppeth as the gentle rain from heaven
> Upon the place beneath. It is twice blessed;
> It blesseth him that gives and him that takes.
> 'Tis mightiest in the mightiest; it becomes
> The thronèd monarch better than his crown.
> His scepter shows the force of temporal power,
> The attribute to awe and majesty,
> Wherein doth sit the dread and fear of kings;
> But mercy is above this sceptered sway.
> It is enthroned in the hearts of kings,
> It is an attribute to God himself,
> And earthly power doth then show likest God's
> When mercy seasons justice. Therefore, Jew,
> Though justice be thy plea, consider this:
> That in the course of justice none of us
> Should see salvation. We do pray for mercy,
> And that same prayer doth teach us all to render
> The deeds of mercy. I have spoke thus much
> To mitigate the justice of thy plea,
> Which if thou follow, this strict court of Venice
> Must needs give sentence 'gainst the merchant there.
> (4.1.182–203)

Mercy, Portia says, is a gift of heaven, an attribute of God. Earthly cities need laws, contracts, courts, penalties, jails, but if earth is to be livable, it must be seasoned by heaven. The justice of the earthly city must be infused with the mercy of heaven. Portia refers to the Lord's Prayer ("we do pray for mercy"). In context, it's a subtle reminder of Shylock's Jewishness. He stands outside Christian revelry, doesn't share Christian meals, and he never kneels among Christians at prayer. He doesn't pray the prayer for mercy, and, by implication, his prayers do not impel him to "render the deeds of mercy." Shylock cannot be compelled to show mercy, but Portia calls him to a higher way of life. If he wants to be Godlike, if he wants to mimic the "throned monarch," if he wants to live the life of heaven on earth, he will be merciful. Lovely and wise as Portia's speech is, it falls on deaf ears. Shylock will have nothing to do with compassion. He stands for law. He clings to the shadowy appearances, instead of the substance, God-like mercy.

Portia's speech seems to justify Bassanio's suggestion. If "mercy seasons justice," why not "do a little wrong" to do a great right? That's not Portia's approach. She never budges from her insistence on law. She traps Shylock by being even more strict about the letter of the law than *he* is. Just as Shylock is ready to cut his pound of flesh from Antonio's bosom, Portia interrupts him with an observation about the contract: "This bond doth give thee here no jot of blood" (4.1.304). Shylock is free to take Antonio's flesh, but he has no right to Antonio's blood, since there's no blood in the contract.

"Jot" is deliberate. It means "a small amount," a "drop," but Elizabethan audiences would hear an echo of Jesus' Sermon on the Mount, where he teaches that "not one jot or one tittle" of the law will pass away (Matt 5:18, Geneva). Like Jesus, Portia insists on the enduring significance of the law. She doesn't set it aside, even on the tiniest point or for the most plausible reasons. Like Shylock, *more* than Shylock, Portia "stands for law."

Aeschylus's *Oresteian Trilogy* ends with Athena's intervention to stop a cycle of blood vengeance. She overrules the rules and establishes a modernized system of courts. Athena brings the bloodshed to an end, but it seems arbitrary. She's literally a *dea ex machina*, popping in at the last minute to save Orestes.

Portia's triumph over Shylock is more satisfying, and more in tune with the biblical categories the play employs. According to the apostle Paul, we cannot be saved by the Torah. We're saved by Jesus, by grace through faith. But the grace of Jesus doesn't nullify the law. Rather, Paul says, it establishes the law (Rom 3:31). Jesus establishes the law because the law foreshadows him. Besides, God doesn't simply cancel his punishments for sin. The curse is enforced, but enforced on *Jesus* rather than on

Israel as a whole. Portia's resolution of the legal conflict echoes Pauline theology: She outdoes Shylock at his own game. She doesn't nullify the contract, but fulfills it, in all its jots and tittles.

It gets worse for Shylock. Portia cites Venetian law: "in the cutting it if thou dost shed / One drop of Christian blood, thy lands and goods / Are by the laws of Venice confiscate / Unto the state of Venice" (4.1.307–10). Besides, he can take only *one pound* of flesh, no more or less. If he takes more, if the scales "turn / But in the estimation of a hair" (4.1.328–29), Shylock is subject to the death penalty.

Shylock scrambles for a solution. He asks for the money Portia offered earlier. He asks to have his principal returned to him. Portia is firm. His money won't be returned because "he hath refused it in the open court" (4.1.336). He will have nothing but what the law allows—a pound of flesh, no more or less, and no blood with it. He cannot even defend himself by saying he never touched Antonio. *Conspiracy* to murder is as much a crime as murder itself: If an alien "by direct or indirect attempts / . . . seek the life of any citizen," then the victim receives half of his property and the rest is delivered to the state (4.1.345–52). The duke can also impose the death penalty (4.1.352–53).

Portia's false name, Balthasar, reminds us of the prophet Daniel's Persian name, Belteshazzar (Dan 1:7). When Portia insists that the duke cannot overturn the law, Shylock hails her as a "Daniel come to judgment" (4.1.221). The story he has in mind isn't from the Bible but from the Apocryphal books *Bel and the Dragon* and *Susanna*, where the prophet Daniel turns detective to solve mysteries. In both stories, he devises tricks to trap people in their lies. Shylock thinks Portia a Daniel because she seems to support his lawsuit. By the end of the courtroom scene, the tables have turned. Portia springs a trap on Shylock, and Gratiano is the one hailing Portia as a "Daniel" (4.1.331–32).

The final decision is just to *everyone*. Shylock's fate lies in the hands of Antonio, a neat inversion of the original situation, where Antonio was at Shylock's mercy. Instead of insisting on Shylock's death, Antonio lets him live and gives him new life by requiring him to become a Christian. For most modern people, including many modern Christians, the idea of an enforced conversion is wicked. Religion is a matter of choice and can never be imposed on anyone without their consent. Christians who baptize babies think differently, since we (I am among them) are willing to impose a Christian identity on our infants. In Shakespeare's world, Shylock's forced conversion would have been seen as an act of mercy. By insisting Shylock become a Christian, Antonio accepts him as a brother and gives him the greatest gift he could give, the gift of salvation.

Instead of taking half of Shylock's wealth for himself, moreover, Antonio requires Shylock to give "all he dies possessed / Unto his son Lorenzo and his daughter" (4.1.387–88). Giving Lorenzo an inheritance forces Shylock to acknowledge Lorenzo as his son. He must acknowledge his daughter—who has been dead to him—as a daughter, and as alive. Bassanio raised Portia from her casket. Now, in disguise as a lawyer's lawyer, Portia raises Jessica from the dead.

Antonio operates within the law, but he fulfills the vision of Portia's speech. He has found mercy, and so does deeds of mercy. Mercy seasons Antonio's justice.

Review Questions

1. What is the court case in Act 4 about?
2. Why is the court case so important to Venice?
3. What is Portia's disguise?
4. Explain Portia's "The quality of mercy" speech.
5. How does Portia trap Shylock? How does she spring the trap?
6. Why is the prophet Daniel brought up in the court scene?
7. How is justice reached in the duke's decision?
8. What are Antonio's demands on Shylock? What does Antonio's action say about him, and about Venice?

Thought Questions

1. Before she disguises herself for court, Portia speaks of "purchasing the semblance of my soul / From out the state of hellish cruelty" (3.4.20–21). In context, what is she referring to? How do these lines strengthen the parallels between Jessica and Portia?
2. According to Antonio, what is the "commodity" of Venice (3.3.26–36).

3. Where do Portia and Nerissa say they're going while Bassanio goes to Venice to rescue Antonio (3.4.26–35)? Why?

4. Shylock seems obsessed with "rats" (1.3.21–26; 4.1.44–46). How is the reference to rats an answer to the duke's question? Why does Shylock keep talking about rats?

Mark the Music, Act 5

Tragedies end with everyone dead on the stage. Comedies end with everyone married. *Merchant* flirts with the edges of comedy. It has a comic ending, but we come very close to seeing Antonio murdered. Besides, the marriages (Bassanio and Portia, Gratian and Nerissa, Lorenzo and Jessica) take place in the *middle* rather than at the end. The events of the final two Acts don't test lovers' love on the way to marriage. Antonio's crisis tests marriages that have already started, and in Act 5 Portia and Nerissa subject their husbands to another test, the test of the rings.

After the bright light of the Venetian courtroom, Act 5 takes us to moonlight and music. Some commentators see this as a drastic change of tone—from the somewhat tragic events of the court to the calm comedy of Belmont. As we've seen, the outcome at court isn't tragic. Shylock gets his comeuppance and is shown mercy, Jessica gets her inheritance, Antonio is delivered from the threat of death, and all the while the letter of Venetian law is upheld. Belmont's mercy has seasoned Venice's justice, and now the characters enter into rest.

Act 5 opens with a playful dialogue between Lorenzo and Jessica. Each uses the refrain "in such a night as this" (5.1.1, 6, 9, 12, 14, 17, 20), as they recount stories of love. Most are stories of tragic love—Troilus on the walls of Troy sighing for his Greek love, Cressid; Pyramus killing himself in the mistaken belief that his lover, Thisby, has been killed by a lion; Dido going mad for love of Aeneas as he departs for Italy. The storytelling comes to a climax with the love of Lorenzo and Jessica:

LORENZO
    In such a night
 Did Jessica steal from the wealthy Jew
 And with an unthrift love did run from Venice
 As far as Belmont.

JESSICA
>In such a night
>Did young Lorenzo swear he loved her well,
>Stealing her soul with many vows of faith,
>And ne'er a true one.

LORENZO
>In such a night
>Did pretty Jessica, like a little shrew,
>Slander her love, and he forgave it her. (5.1.14–22)

Their love is another of the great romances of the ages, though theirs has a comic ending that makes the pathos of the other romances more notable.

Jessica and Lorenzo speak of love and music. Earlier, before Bassanio chooses the lead casket, Portia explains how different types of music accompany different outcomes for love. If Bassanio chooses the wrong casket, "he makes a swanlike end, / Fading in music." If he wins, "music is / Even as the flourish when true subjects bow / To a new-crowned monarch." If he brings Portia from her casket, the music will be like "those dulcet sounds in break of day / That creep into the dreaming bridegroom's ear / And summon him to marriage" (3.2.40–53).

Music and love naturally go together. Music harmonizes different notes into melodies and chords, as love harmonizes the very different orientations and strengths of a man and a woman into one life-song. Lorenzo offers one of Shakespeare's most memorable meditations on music. Jessica comments that she cannot be merry when she hears "sweet music" (5.1.69). Lorenzo earlier musings on music explain why. Music orders the heavens: "There's not the smallest orb which thou behold'st / But in his motion like an angel sings." The music of the spheres echoes as a "harmony . . . in immortal souls" with sounds too refined for bodily ears to hear (5.1.60–63). Music saddens us because it gives us a taste—but *only* a taste—of the harmony of the sky.

Music has unique power because it connects heaven and earth, the cosmos and the soul:

>The reason is, your spirits are attentive.
>For do but note a wild and wanton herd
>Or race of youthful and unhandled colts
>Fetching mad bounds, bellowing and neighing loud,
>Which is the hot condition of their blood;
>If they but hear perchance a trumpet sound,

> Or any air of music touch their ears,
> You shall perceive them make a mutual stand,
> Their savage eyes turned to a modest gaze
> By the sweet power of music. Therefore the poet
> Did feign that Orpheus drew trees, stones, and floods;
> Since nought so stockish, hard, and full of rage
> But music for the time doth change his nature.
> The man that hath no music in himself,
> Nor is not moved with concord of sweet sounds,
> Is fit for treasons, stratagems, and spoils;
> The motions of his spirit are dull as night
> And his affections dark as Erebus.
> Let no such man be trusted. Mark the music. (5.1.70–88)

A trumpet blast can stop a stampeding herd, and the music of Orpheus gave life to trees, stones, and floods. No matter how stolid the hearer, music "for the time doth change his nature." When we hear music, our chaotic souls are tuned.

Some are impervious to music, and Lorenzo warns Jessica to beware of such men, who are fit for "treasons, stratagems, and spoils." Jessica doesn't need to be warned. She grew up with a man who "had no music in himself." In *Merchant*, music is linked with beauty, art, the moonlit world of grace. Shylock has no Belmont in his soul, and so "the motions of his spirit are dull as night." He's not to be trusted. Here's the key to judging men: "Mark the music." Mark whether, and how, men listen to it.

The casket plot has been resolved: Bassanio has come to Belmont and chosen the right casket, proving he has music in himself. The bond plot has been resolved: Because Portia has brought Belmont into Venice, she has rescued Antonio and Shylock has been stymied and converted. One last plot remains to be resolved, the ring plot.

It begins in Act 3. After Bassanio wins Portia, she gives him a ring that represents the conversion of herself and all her property to Bassanio:

> Myself and what is mine to you and yours
> Is now converted. But now I was the lord
> Of this fair mansion, master of my servants,
> Queen o'er myself; and even now, but now,
> This house, these servants and this same myself
> Are yours, my lord's. I give them with this ring,
> Which when you part from, lose, or give away,
> Let it presage the ruin of your love
> And be my vantage to exclaim on you. (3.2.166–74)

Portia knows love is a risky venture. She "converts" to the married state, giving and hazarding all she has. Since the ring represents Portia herself, Bassanio must never part with it. If he loses it, it will "presage the ruin of your love." Nerissa gives Gratiano a ring and exacts a similar promise.

After the trial scene, Portia and Nerissa, disguised as lawyers, ask Bassanio and Gratiano to give them the rings. It's a love test, and it's no wonder the women want it. During the trial, Bassanio got carried away with expressions of love for Antonio. His wife, he says, "is as dear to me as life itself," but he would happily give it all up—"life itself, my wife, and all the world"—to rescue Antonio from "this devil" (4.1.280-85). It's an understandable sentiment. Antonio risks his life for Bassanio; Bassanio reciprocates with a love willing to "give and hazard all." Gratiano one-ups Bassanio, wishing his wife Nerissa were dead and in heaven "so she could / Entreat some power to change this currish Jew" (4.1.289-90). Bassanio and Gratiano don't know their wives are listening. Hearing their husbands are willing to sacrifice them for Antonio, the women decide they need to confirm their husbands' love.

At first, Bassanio and Gratiano refuse to hand over the rings to the "lawyers." Portia shames Bassanio by saying he is "liberal in offers" but not generous in action (4.1.436). He promises much, but delivers little. Antonio finally convinces Bassanio to give the ring: "My Lord Bassanio, let him have the ring. / Let his deservings, and my love withal, / Be valued 'gainst your wife's commandment" (4.1.447-49). With that, Antonio forces Bassanio to put his love in the balance, weighing his love for Antonio over against his love for Portia. In the moment, he chooses Antonio. Bassanio sends Gratiano to take the ring to Portia and Nerissa: "My Lord Bassanio upon more advice / Hath sent you here this ring" (4.2.6-7).

With all the principal characters regathered in Belmont, Portia asks Bassanio for the ring. He's forced to admit he doesn't have it, and Gratiano is forced to admit the same to Nerissa. The women playfully torture their husbands, pretending to believe they have been unfaithful: "I'll die for't but some woman had the ring," Portia accuses (5.1.208). She threatens to avoid Bassanio's bed until he can produce the ring, and says she won't sleep with anyone except the lawyer who has her ring: "I will become as liberal as you; / I'll not deny him anything I have, / No, not my body nor my husband's bed" (5.1.226-28). Even after she produces the ring, she continues the playful test: "I had it of him. Pardon me, Bassanio, / For by this ring the doctor did lie with me" (5.1.258-59). Nerissa confesses "that same scrubbed boy, the doctor's clerk, / In lieu of this last night did lie with me" (5.1.261–62). They are literally correct: The lawyer and his clerk are Portia and Nerissa, and they *did* sleep with themselves. Disguises create a double truth, a situation where things both are and are not, where "nothing that is so, is so" (*Twelfth Night*).

Playful though it is, the ring test has a serious undertone. Antonio is present in the final scene and guarantees Bassanio will remain faithful. As he once lent "my body for his wealth," so he now promises "your lord / Will never more break faith advisedly" (5.1.249–53). Antonio's friendship with Bassanio is folded into the household of Belmont and becomes a facet of the married love between Bassanio and Portia. It has to be. Portia knows she takes on all Bassanio's obligations and friendships: "this Antonio, / Being the bosom lover of my lord, / Must needs be like my lord" (3.4.16–18). *Merchant* doesn't play friendship and romance off against each other, as some of Shakespeare's plays do. Rather, the grace of Belmont harmonizes all loves. Friendship is knit into the married love of the lord and lady of Belmont.

The ring plot also reveals the depth of the romantic plot. Portia wants to give the ring the first time, but she also *has* to, bound as she was by her father's will. When she gives the ring a second time, she gives herself freely. Her love is no longer forced by a dead father's will, but is the free choice of a living daughter. For his part, Bassanio wrongs Portia, but in the magical graced realm of Belmont all is forgiven, "the whole crisis dissolved in laughter and amazement." Bassanio is "tried" by Portia and found to be a sinner. But, as in the courtroom, mercy triumphs over justice.[6]

Portia's ring represents herself, her conversion to Bassanio's lordship as her husband. It may seem Portia has lost all by submitting to Bassanio as her "lord." By giving up the ring, Bassanio (unwittingly) gives Portia back to herself. The ring represents Portia and her wealth, and in giving it Bassanio replicates the love of Antonio. He gives all he has. But then Portia gives herself *back* to Bassanio. In the end, Portia and Bassanio each give a ring to the other. Their wedding is, as it were, stretched out over three Acts. Portia becomes fully herself in giving herself to Bassanio and receiving herself back from him. Bassanio becomes fully Bassanio because he receives Portia, returns her, and receives her again. Here is

---

6. Lewalski, "Biblical Allusion."

Merchant's model of married love: Portia and Bassanio give *themselves* to one another. Giving all is, in the end, gaining all. Losing life, each finds life.

But soft, no haste. Tarry a little. There is something else. Act 5 should be triumphant. Antonio lives. Shylock is undone. At least for one night, justice and mercy reign *together* in Venice. But Bassanio enters the scene at Belmont with his love in ruins. In fact, his state is worse than that. When Bassanio first receives the ring, he says loss of the ring will be his death: "when this ring / Parts from this finger, then parts life from hence; / O then be bold to say Bassanio's dead!" (3.2.183–85). He doesn't realize it yet, but because he gave the ring away, he's dead. He needs to be raised to life. And so he is, when Portia returns herself, her life, all that is hers, to her husband.

Merchant is a comedy of resurrections. Portia has risen from her casket, Jessica has escaped the house of the dead, Antonio has been saved from Shylock's knife. Back at Belmont, Portia lavishly distributes new life: She informs Jessica of her inheritance, brings news that Antonio's ships are safe, tells the story of her escapade at the Venetian court. The ring plot is her final wonder. Risen from her casket, ascended back to her beautiful mount, Portia performs one last miracle, one final resurrection.

Review Questions

1. What are Lorenzo and Jessica talking about in the opening speech of Act 5?
2. How do love and music go together?
3. What is the "ring" plot? How is it resolved?
4. Why is Antonio present in the final scene?
5. What vision of marriage does the last scene of *Merchant* depict?

Thought Questions

1. In many modern productions of *Merchant*, Jessica is melancholy in the final Act, regretful of her decision to leave her father to marry Lorenzo. Is there any support for this in the text of the play?

2. In the last line of Act 4, scene 1, Bassanio urges Antonio to "Fly toward Belmont" (4.1.455). Why "fly"? What does that tell us about Belmont?

3. Portia tells Nerissa that "nothing is good . . . without respect" (5.1.99). What does she mean? How does this apply to the music she hears?

4. Write a brief summary of the myth of Orpheus, which Lorenzo alludes to.

Bibliography

Aristotle. *Poetics*. Translated by S. H. Butcher. http://classics.mit.edu/Aristotle/poetics.1.1.html.
Augustine. *On Christian Teaching*. Translated by R. P. H. Green. Oxford: Oxford University Press, 1997.
Badiou, Alain. *Plato's Republic*. London: John Wiley, 2013.
Bethell, S. L. "Shakespeare's Imagery: The Diabolical Images in *Othello*." In *Aspects of Othello*, edited by Kenneth Muir and Philip Edwards, 29–47. Cambridge: Cambridge University Press, 1977.
Bevington, David, ed. *Four Tragedies*. New York: Bantam, 1988.
Bradley, A. C. *Shakespearean Tragedy*. London: Macmillan, 1919.
Brooke, Nicholas. *Shakespeare: King Lear*. Studies in English Literature. London: Edward Arnold, 1963.
Cantor, Paul. *Shakespeare's Roman Trilogy: Twilight of the Ancient World*. Chicago: University of Chicago Press, 2017.
Costain, Thomas B. *The Last Plantagenets*. New York: Doubleday, 1962.
Craig, Harold. *Of Philosophers and Kings: Political Philosophy in Shakespeare's Macbeth and King Lear*. Toronto: University of Toronto Press, 2001.
Downer, Alan S. "Feste's Exposure of Orsino." In *Twentieth Century Interpretations of Twelfth Night: A Collection of Critical Essays*, edited by Walter N. King, 100–101. Englewood Cliffs, NJ: Prentice-Hall, 1968.
Dunn, E. Catharine. *The Concept of Ingratitude in Renaissance English Moral Philosophy*. 1946. Reprint, Whitefish, MT: Kessinger, 2010.
Eagleton, Terry. *Shakespeare and Society: Critical Studies in Shakespearean Drama*. New York: Random House, 1975.
Elyot, Thomas. *The Boke Named the Governour*. http://www.luminarium.org/renascence-editions/gov/gov1.htm.
Freud, Sigmund. "Some Character-Types Met with in Psycho-Analytic Work." In *Writings on Art and Literature*, 151–75. Stanford, CA: Stanford University Press, 1997.
Frye, Northrop. *On Shakespeare*. New Haven, CT: Yale University Press, 1988.
Garber, Marjorie. *Shakespeare After All*. New York: Anchor, 2005.
Ghose, Indira. *Shakespeare and Laughter: A Cultural History*. Manchester: Manchester University Press, 2008.
Girard, Rene. *A Theater of Envy: William Shakespeare*. Herefordshire: Gracewing, 2000.

Goddard, Harold. *The Meaning of Shakespeare*. 2 vols. Chicago: University of Chicago Press, 1951.

Gress, David. *From Plato to NATO: The Idea of the West and Its Opponents*. New York: Free, 1998.

Hart, David Bentley. *The Beauty of the Infinite: The Aesthetics of Christian Truth*. Grand Rapids: Eerdmans, 2004.

Hollander, John. "*Twelfth Night* and the Morality of Indulgence." In *Twentieth Century Interpretations of Twelfth Night: A Collection of Critical Essays*, edited by Walter N. King, 75–89. Englewood Cliffs, NJ: Prentice-Hall, 1968.

Jagendorf, Zvi. "*Coriolanus*: Body Politic and Private Parts." *Shakespeare Quarterly* 41.4 (1990) 455–69.

Johnson, Samuel. "Preface to Shakespeare." In *Miscellaneous*, 1–54. Works of Samuel Johnson 12. Troy, NY: Pafraets, 1903.

Knapp, Jeffrey. *Shakespeare's Tribe: Church, Nation, and Theater in Renaissance England*. Chicago: University of Chicago Press, 2002.

Leggatt, Alexander. *Shakespeare's Political Drama: The History Plays and the Roman Plays*. London: Routledge, 2016.

Leithart, Peter J. "City of In-Gratia: Roman Ingratitude in Shakespeare's *Coriolanus*." *Literature & Theology* 20.4 (2006) 341–60.

———. *Deep Comedy: Trinity, Tragedy, and Hope in Western Literature*. Moscow, ID: Canon, 2006.

———. *Gratitude: An Intellectual History*. Waco, TX: Baylor University Press, 2014.

Lewalski, Barbara K. "Biblical Allusion and Allegory in *The Merchant of Venice*." *Shakespeare Quarterly* 13.3 (1962) 327–43.

Mahood, M. M. "Shakespeare's Use of the Bible in *The Merchant of Venice*." In *The Merchant of Venice*, by William Shakespeare, edited by M. M. Mahood, 196–200. New Cambridge Shakespeare. 2nd ed. Cambridge: Cambridge University Press, 2003.

Moulton, Richard. "1893—From *Shakespeare as a Dramatic Artist*." In *Richard III*, edited by Harold Bloom and Jaynce Marson, 161–86. Bloom's Shakespeare Through the Ages. New York: Infobase, 2010.

Patterson, Annabel. *Shakespeare and the Popular Voice*. Oxford: Blackwell, 1989.

Pepys, Samuel. *The Diary of Samuel Pepys*. https://www.pepysdiary.com/diary/1662/09/29/.

Plutarch. "Life of Coriolanus." In *Lives*, translated by John Dryden, 2:53–103. 5 vols. Boston: Little Brown, 1906.

Saccio, Peter. *Shakespeare: The Word and the Action*. N.p.: The Great Courses, 2013.

———. *Shakespeare's English Kings: History, Chronicle, and Drama*. Oxford: Oxford University Press, 2000.

Salingar, Leo. *Shakespeare and the Traditions of Comedy*. Cambridge: Cambridge University Press, 1974.

Seneca. *De Beneficiis*. Translated by Aubrey Stewart. London: George Bell, 1887.

Shakespeare. *The Complete Pelican Shakespeare*. Edited by Stephen Orgel and A. R. Braunmuller. New York: Penguin, 2002.

Shuger, Debora K. "Subversive Fathers and Suffering Subjects: Shakespeare and Christianity." In *Religion, Literature, and Politics in Post-Reformation England, 1540–1688*, edited by Donna B. Hamilton and Richard Strier, 46–69. Cambridge: Cambridge University Press, 1996.

Stampfer, Judah. "The Catharsis of *King Lear*." *Shakespeare Survey* 13 (1960) 1–10.
Thomas Aquinas. *Summa Theologiae*. 5 vols. Translated by the Fathers of the English Dominican Province. Notre Dame, IN: Christian Classics, 1948.
Tillyard, E. M. W. *The Elizabethan World Picture: A Study of the Idea of Order in the Age of Shakespeare, Donne and Milton*. New York: Vintage, 1959.